After Chancellorsville

Letters from the Heart

D1280221

Jarvis U.S. Ge[neral]
10. P.M. Frid[ay]

My Dear Friend

Yours has [come]
and I hasten to reply. [My]
first experience in nursing
soldiers. I have improved [much]
since I left home and as [the wounded]
have been coming in [fast]
for a few days past, I vol[unteered to]
do what I could to relieve [the]
sufferers and my services [were accepted]
as nurse. I have scarcely [had time]
to eat, since morning but [most]
of the patients are now snoreing
right smart gate I thought

After Chancellorsville

Letters from the Heart

*The Civil War Letters
of Private Walter G. Dunn
& Emma Randolph*

Edited by

Judith A. Bailey & Robert I. Cottom

MARYLAND HISTORICAL SOCIETY

Baltimore, Maryland

MARYLAND HISTORICAL SOCIETY
201 West Monument Street
Baltimore, Maryland 21201
Founded 1844

First Edition
Manufactured in the United States of America
ISBN 0-938420-62-3

LIBRARY OF CONGRESS CATALOGING-IN-PUBLICATION DATA
Dunn, Walter G., d. 1866
    After Chancellorsville : the Civil War letters of Private Walter G. Dunn
and Emma Randolph / edited by Robert I. Cottom and Judith A. Bailey.
        p.   cm.
    Includes index.
    ISBN 0-938420-62-3 (alk. paper)
    1. Dunn, Waler G., d. 1866—Correspondence. 2. Soldiers—United
States—Correspondence. 3. United States—History—Civil War, 1861–
1865—Personal narratives. 4. Randolph, Emma, d. 1866—Correspondence. 5. Baltimore (Md.)—History—Civil War, 1861–1865—Personal
narratives. 6. New Jersey—History—Civil War, 1861–1865—Personal
narratives. 7. United States. Army. Veteran Reserve Corps. Battalion,
2nd. Company, 72nd (1863–1865) 8. Plainfield (N.J.)—Biography. I.
Randolph, Emma, d. 1866. II. Cottom, Robert I. III. Bailey, Judith A.,
1952–
    E601.D89   1998
973.7'81'0922—dc21   98-35805
[B]   CIP
∞ The paper used in this publication meets the minimum requirements of the
American National Standard for Information Sciences — Permanence of
Paper for Printed Library Materials, ANSI Z39.48-1984.

COVER: Ambulances from the 57th New York Volunteer Infantry in the field.
Undated Matthew Brady Studio photograph. (Maryland Historical Society.)

For Ruth Washburn Bailey

Contents

List of Illustrations

Preface

It is an understatement to say that interest in the American Civil War has never been greater. Battles and generalship have been studied and restudied. Scholarly works appear regularly on virtually every facet of the war, and reënactors by the tens of thousands have taken the field in search of the Civil War experience. For various reasons, large numbers of Americans in the last months of the twentieth century long to know what their forbears faced and endured, what they thought and felt, how they lived, and why they died. We want to know what kind of men and women fought the war, at home and at the front, how they differed from us (for surely they must have been different to endure so much so stoically) and in what ways can we perhaps identify qualities we still share. Their lives generally astonish, leaving us stunned at contemplation of their bravery and sacrifice. Revived interest has spawned renewed efforts to preserve papers and artifacts once so casually tossed away. As caches of letters surface from attics, basements, and ancient roll-top desks, we gain clear glimpses of Civil War lives. In some cases, they lead us to places far into the past. In other cases we are given cause to wonder if we are so far removed from them after all.

The letters Walter G. Dunn and Mary Emma Randolph wrote to one another are just such a discovery. Walter was seventeen when the war broke out, Emma sixteen. If they cared about sectional politics, beyond a firm conviction that the Union must be preserved, it remained unwritten. Walter enlisted in August 1862, a time when volunteers came to the flag knowing that the war was no longer a lark. Added to his patriotism was a sense of family history; his grandfather had served in the Revolution and had returned to a household that had been ransacked by British troops. Walter carried with him a portfolio by which he correspondended regularly with a dozen friends from home. One of them was Emma, a distant cousin who at seventeen was so attractive she entertained five different suitors.

Surviving letters begin in July 1863, two months after Walter was severely wounded at Chancellorsville and reassigned to a hospital in Baltimore. With a Confederate minié ball still in his shoulder he assisted surgeons as the wounded from Gettysburg poured into the already crowded wards. Though his arm was weak, his eye was clear, and he presented his cousin with a firsthand look at Baltimore in wartime. Emma wrote back with growing interest in the young man, though we will never know how much. The following summer, when Confederates again marched through Maryland, Walter burned her letters, leaving to posterity a correspondence that is lamentably one-sided.

When Emma's letters finally appear in mid-1864 they are a revelation and a joy. Rich in the details of everyday life at home in Plainfield, New Jersey, they have left us a nearly complete portrait of a young woman. Emma lived for her large, extended family and for her church, the New Market Seventh Day Baptist congregation. She wrote of buggy rides and strawberry festivals, ice cream and trips to the beach. She was at once nurse, washerwoman, cook, and clerk in the family business, and a stalwart in church activities. A mysterious illness nearly killed her, and chronic headaches tried her strength, but she wrote to Walter with indomitable humor, energy, and good cheer, and increasingly with love. When Walter underwent an operation to remove the ball in his shoulder and his letters ceased coming, Emma wrote with a degree of fear and pain and finally relief that no reader will soon forget. Neither will they dislodge the image of Emma, sitting in her bedroom window—the "cool window"—after putting her younger sisters to bed, to think of Walter and quietly take up her pen.

In the end theirs is a love story that is at once charmingly distant from our time and still utterly recognizable. Every man who has donned a uniform and served at some distant post will recognize a little of Walter in his experience; every woman who has written to such a man will share a moment with Emma. The letters are timeless, moving, and tragic. It is history, theirs—and ours.

J.A.B.
R.I.C.
August 1998

Acknowledgements

In the long process of bringing the story of Walter Dunn and Emma Randolph into print we shamelessly taxed the tolerance, abilities, and cheerful nature of friends, relatives, and accomplished professionals. In New Jersey we would like to thank the members and staff of the Plainfield Historical Society for their help with our research with a special nod to the ever kind and hospitable Jean Mattson. We also thank Jenneatte Fitz Randolph Durea for her generous hospitality and for permission to use her family photographs. Bernice Paglia, a reporter for the *Courier-News* contributed to the research, and Jeri Cross and Ed Pagliarini, also of that newspaper, arranged photographs for our use. Thanks, too, to Ron Becker and the Special Collections Research Staff at the Alexander Library of Rutgers University for photographs and assistance, and to the research librarians at the Plainfield Public Library, especially Ellen Kastel.

Reverend Don Sanford of the Seventh Day Baptist Historical Society in Janesville, Wisconsin, helped us search that church's history and provided critical photographs. Laurie McFadden, of the Herrick Library, performed a similar service on behalf of Alfred University.

From Maryland, we thank Rob Schoeberlein of the Prints and Photographs Department in the Library of Maryland History at the Maryland Historical Society. His enthusiastic support of the project and masterful knowledge of the society's extensive collections produced the images of Walter Dunn's wartime Baltimore. We extend our gratitude, in this case humble, to Donna Blair Shear and Patricia Dockman Anderson, editors in the society's publications division, whose knowledge and keen eyes for detail saved us from the usual assortment of typographical errors and editorial blunders.

Special thanks are due to Diana and Jacquie Bailey, who helped transcribe the letters and who offered encouragement every step of this long path.

The turning point in the life of every manuscript comes when an experienced editor or publisher turns his kindly eye upon it. In our case, that point occurred three years ago and the eye belonged to Ernest L. Scott, the publisher at the MHS. We thank him heartily for recognizing the jewels that lay in those manuscript pages.

We reserve our deepest thanks for Ruth Washburn Bailey, who gave us the letters. Without her generosity, encouragement, and support, the story of Walt and Emma would have remained in a stack of time-worn envelopes, as do the stories of the countless other men and women whose lives and sacrifices in that war have been misplaced or forgotten.

A Note on Editorial Method

In presenting these letters we have tried to remain faithful to the past and to the correspondents. Spelling, capitalization, and punctuation have been left as they are in the originals in so far as we have been able to determine clearly what was written. Where a word is indecipherable or a meaning unclear, we have provided what we believe was meant in brackets.

We have made two stylistic alterations. Walter and Emma both placed words in quotation marks with uncommon frequency, possibly for emphasis, but so many words were thus emphasized that distinction became virtually meaningless. Except where they were actually quoting someone else or using the marks in other usual and accepted ways, we did not reproduce them. Further, Emma's handwriting was so tiny that it was often impossible to determine whether she used a comma or a period, and her capitalization was inconsistent. In many cases we opted for the comma and lengthened sentences. The result is the elegant, sometimes lyric style we believe she intended.

Prologue

Early on the morning of May 3, 1863, in thick woods a few hundred yards west of the Chancellor House, in a part of Virginia known as the Wilderness, a regiment consisting largely of eighteen- and nineteen-year-old young men struggled to control their fear as a Confederate battle line bore down upon them in the smoke-filled dawn.

The 11th New Jersey Volunteers had been recruited in the summer of 1862, at a time when ardent young men still rushed to the colors. Colonel Robert McAllister, a no-nonsense, abstemious Pennsylvania Presbyterian, who made up in stern paternalism what he lacked in military imagination, had trained his men hard and well. After embarking on trains from Camp Perrine amid waving families, wives, and girlfriends, and laden with basket lunches and fresh fruit, the regiment had gone to Camp Ellsworth outside Alexandria and begun the life of attrition that afflicted every Civil War outfit. Mud, cold, fevers, and measles took an abnormally high toll in the regiment before it ever heard a Confederate rifle. At Fredericksburg in December the 11th did not take part in the fatal assaults that decimated the Army of the Potomac on the slopes before Marye's Heights, but a badly executed maneuver in January, appropriately called the "Mud March," and a wet spring of various illnesses, continued to deplete the regiment. By the time they arrived at Chancellorsville on the evening of May 2, only about five hundred could answer as present and fit for duty.[1]

Like the rest of the army, they were in high spirits, for they had a .

---

[1]Robert McAllister's letters have been collected and edited. See James I. Robertson, ed., *The Civil War Letters of General Robert McAllister* (New Brunswick: Published for the New Jersey Civil War Centennial Commission by Rutgers University Press, 1965). The 11th New Jersey's regimental history was written by one of its sergeants and has a down-to-earth quality. See Thomas B. Marbaker, *History of the Eleventh New Jersey Volunteers* (Trenton, 1898; repr. Hightstown, N.J.: Longstreet House, 1990).

daring new commander, Joseph "Fighting Joe" Hooker. It looked as though the Army of the Potomac had at last found someone who could outsmart and outmaneuver Robert E. Lee. Leaving a portion of his army in the Fredericksburg lines, where they had been since December, Hooker had taken the bulk of his force around Lee's right and into the Wilderness to a crossroads named after a large brick structure there, the Chancellor House. All day on May 2 the fighting raged along the roads and in clearings. Matters looked to be in hand as the 11th New Jersey marched down the road from Ely's Ford late in the afternoon. Within sight of the Chancellor House itself they left the road and moved off into the woods to bivouac.

They had hardly taken off their knapsacks when a change in the firing told them something was wrong. Anxiously they looked into the setting sun, toward their right flank, and listened to the sounds of trouble: organized volleys moving nearer, met by quickening blasts from the artillery; in the distance the faint echo of the "rebel yell"— closer at hand the shouts of angry, fearful men. Veterans knew all too well what it meant, for they had heard it at Bull Run, Second Manassas, and Antietam. Somehow, instead of outflanking Lee, they had been flanked themselves. The Rebels were rolling down their line, inflicting the most disastrous blow an army could suffer.

The 11th moved out at the double-quick and formed in line west of the Chancellor House. Their left flank rested on the Orange Turnpike, down which the Confederates were driving, and the line extended northward into the thick woods. Panicked fugitives stampeded through them but the boys took heart from McAllister and from the grim-faced gunners forming a line of artillery across the road. The battle line surged toward them as darkness fell then, blessedly, paused for the night. Sporadic outbursts of firing lit the blackened woods from time to time. Nervous men and boys wondered when it would start up again.

The night passed fitfully. The 11th was in the second line of battle, about one hundred and fifty yards behind the first. In Walter Dunn's company were a number of friends and townsmen from New Market and nearby Plainfield. They would have talked softly until nervousness caused voices to rise before falling again to a hurried murmur. Their first test was coming in the morning and they knew it, so the talk would have touched upon the things that mattered most to them—

whether they might live or die, of course, but just as important, would they face death bravely. Friends and family all expected them to meet the foe squarely—to fall, if they must, with their faces to the enemy. To run, to hide or take the coward's way—that was a cause of real fear, even for a nineteen-year-old boy. With bayonets they scraped out a shallow trench and settled into it for the night, nursing the water in their canteens. There was little water to be had in the Wilderness.

The battle resumed at first light with the booming of artillery and a rattle of musketry that soon grew into a roar. The 11th might have fired their rifles into the air to clear them of charges loaded hours before and to relieve nervousness once the fighting began. Then they waited as the woods filled with smoke, listening intently for sounds of the enemy's advance. It was impossible to see a hundred yards, then fifty, then thirty. All too quickly the line in front of them gave way, first on the left, then on the right. Its survivors clawed their way back through the brush or drifted farther north into the woods. Minié balls ripped the trees overhead, accompanied by the fierce shriek of that infernal Rebel yell. In the growing confusion, McAllister ordered a half wheel to the left to meet the oncoming assault. The 11th obeyed and fired. Then, as the Rebels poured through the woods behind them, they wheeled full to the right. "The storm of lead was terrific," one of them wrote later, ". . . and the pattering of bullets as they struck the trees was not unlike the clatter of hail stones upon a roof."[2]

The end came with impossible, hellish fury. The first men began to fall before they could see who was shooting them down. After a volley, or perhaps two, they fought on their own, loading and firing as fast as they could. Officers screamed at them over the din to aim low, but in their fear they probably too often fired high, as most soldiers did. They would not have realized until too late that the regiments on their right had given way and withdrawn, leaving them unprotected. Rebels moved in and took them in a crossfire. The 11th fell back to the

---

[2]Two fine studies of the Battle of Chancellorsville have recently appeared. See Ernest B. Furguson, *Chancellorsville 1863: The Souls of the Brave* (New York: Alfred A. Knopf, 1993) and Stephen W. Sears, *Chancellorsville* (Boston and New York: Houghton Mifflin Company, 1996).

Additionally, the National Park Service office at Chancellorsville can provide detailed maps of the battle, making it possible to follow the footsteps of each regiment involved.

clearing near the Chancellor House, leaving its wounded in the woods. In the clearing they rallied around McAllister and the colors and gallantly charged back into the woods to carry their wounded out.

One of those who fell in the woods, or perhaps in the counterattack, was Walter G. Dunn of New Market. He had been shot in the neck. A minié ball had entered at the base of his throat and passed slightly downward, through his lung until it stopped behind his right shoulder blade. Stunned and helpless, he might have been conscious as his friends dragged or carried him over the rough ground to the clearing near the Chancellor House. That is where he would have been placed on the ground to await an ambulance, or possibly he was taken into the house itself. Where or how long he waited is impossible to know. Perhaps no ambulance had room for him that morning, and he was carried hurriedly north on a litter, back up the road he had marched down the day before. Behind him, Confederate artillery smashed into the Chancellor House and set it ablaze.

By day's end, the Confederates had swept through the field, past the burning buildings. One of them picked up Walter's knapsack, looking for anything useful. He would have found Walter's portfolio and in it a number of letters from home. Among the more prized were those from an attractive cousin of his father's, Mary Emma Randolph, of Plainfield. She was his own age and besieged by suitors but she wrote him cheerful letters on a regular basis. At some time on the painful journey that began in a springless ambulance bouncing along the rutted roads of Virginia and ended at Jarvis U.S. Hospital in Baltimore, he doubtless thought of her, though he had many other things to think about. It was too soon to be certain, but it seemed that God had chosen to spare him. Moreover, Walter Dunn was no coward.

---

[3]The 11th New Jersey Infantry suffered among the highest casualties of any Federal regiment at Chancellorsville, 18 killed, 146 wounded, and 5 missing, out of about five hundred engaged. William F. Fox, *Regimental Losses in the American Civil War, 1861–1865* (repr. Press of Morningside Bookshop, 1974), 250.

After Chancellorsville

Letters from the Heart

Part I: Jarvis U.S. Hospital, Baltimore

Walter Dunn's whereabouts immediately after the battle at Chancellorsville is a matter of conjecture. In all probability he was taken to a field hospital for examination, where a surgeon determined that it would be more dangerous to attempt to extract the bullet than to leave it undisturbed. That is not to say Walter's chances of recovery were any better, although if the examination was minimally invasive, his risk of infection was lower. He then would have been sent to a larger hospital in Washington or Baltimore for the next critical weeks.

Walter left no record of where he was sent except that after a time he received a medical furlough to return to his home in New Jersey. How long he remained there is uncertain. The first letter to his friend, Emma Randolph, is dated from Jarvis U.S. Military Hospital in Baltimore a few days after the battle of Gettysburg. Wounded from the battle poured into Baltimore by ambulance, wagon, and train, and hospital operating tables were awash in blood.

For the first year of the correspondence we have only Walter's letters to Emma. She answered him and he kept her letters as he had the others until a Confederate raid into Maryland the following July prompted him to burn them lest they again fall into Rebel hands. Though one-sided in nature, the letters give a glimpse of wartime life in Baltimore. We can follow as the war turns brutal in 1864 with the massacre of black troops at Fort Pillow in April and the opening of the savage Wilderness Campaign in May. Confederate sympathizers sometimes suffered rough treatment at the hands of the Union army in Baltimore, but a young man in Federal blue could find numerous diversions—walks in the park, the theater, and, of course, young women. So many were Baltimore's charms that in May Walter failed to notice his correspondent had fallen desperately and critically ill and was in danger of losing her life.

My Dear

Friend

Jarvis US General Hospital[1]
10 P.M. Friday, July 10th 1863

My Dear Friend

Yours has just arrived and I hasten to reply. Today is my first experience in nursing wounded soldiers. I have improved quite rapid since I left home and as the wounded have been coming in by the hundreds for a few days past.[2] I volunteered to do what I could to relieve the poor sufferers and my services were accepted as a nurse. I have scarcely found time to eat since morning but as the most of the patients are now snoring away at a right smart gaile I thought that I would improve this opportunity, not knowing how busy I may be in days to come. In this ward there are several very bad wounds but we are all getting allong well. Nothing suits me better than to relieve sufferers. One patient who is suffering from a wound in his right hand, seems to talk a considerable in his sleep, if he continues to interrupt me much longer, I'll take down some notes.

How cheering the news have been for a few days past—almost every day brings with it news of some new success of our troops.

---

[1]Located on the confiscated estate of Confederate General George Hume Steuart in Baltimore.

[2]The wounded were from the Gettysburg campaign and may well have included men from the 11th New Jersey, which took heavy casualties on July 2 as part of General Daniel Sickles's Third Corps.

Meade's victory in Maryland,[3] surrender of Vicksburg, the expected fall of Ft. Hudson and the chase after Bragg,[4] what glorious news. I think that Rebeldom is soon to cave in.

You spoke of the proceedings of evening previous the one you wrote the letter was it for the capture of Richmond? You said, you imagined that I would be half sitting under one of those beautiful shade trees when I received your letter, allow me to inquire where you would imagine the other half to be.

I presume from what you said that the fourth passed off very pleasantly in Plainfield. How is your ice cream in a fun parlor?

There it goes again, the poor cripples are continually thinking and talking fight. Yes, the loyalty of Baltimore has been rather dubious during this war but this last raid of Lees has much changed the tide of sentiment. When Baltimore was threatened, many who were thought to be disloyal, volunteered for its defence. A great many of its streets have been blockeadeded with large hogsheads[5] filled with dirt and stone to prevent a rapid progress of cavalry. I like to sit in the front door of the hospital which opens into the street and whistle at the secesh girls, as they promenade up and down the street, to tease them. A disloyal man has to be very carefull what he says now or down he goes. A few days ago while some prisoners were passing through on their way to Ft. McHenry, a citizen sung out three cheers for Jef. Davis, and the surgeon in charge of this hospital who was standing by knocked him down, a cavalryman saw him fall, run up and commenced cutting him over the head with his sabre and would have killed him

---

[3]As the Army of Northern Virginia withdrew from Gettysburg across Maryland to the Potomac, its rear guard fought off Union cavalry in a series of minor actions. Skirmishes, sometimes sharp, broke out in Hagerstown, Boonsborough, and Williamsport (July 6), and Downsville and Funkstown (July 7), but the Army of the Potomac under the command of George Gordon Meade undertook no vigorous pursuit and no pitched battle occurred.

[4]The Confederate garrison at Vicksburg surrendered to General Ulysses S. Grant's Union forces on July 4, 1863. On July 8, Port Hudson, Louisiana, also surrendered, opening the Mississippi River and splitting the Confederacy in two. Confederate General Braxton Bragg had concentrated his army around Chattanooga, after losing most of Tennessee to the Federal Army of the Cumberland under the command of General William S. Rosecrans.

[5]Large wooden barrels.

Jarvis U.S. General Hospital, Baltimore, Maryland. (Maryland Historical Society.)

had not some one drug him out. Served him right; such a mans head should be severed from his body. Some parts of this City are very pleasant and nice while others are not fit to live in.

I saw your cousin Lewis Dunn[6] when I was out to the front—but he did not see me I do not think.

I should judge by the way that you answered a certain question, that I asked you just before I left you last, that you thought that I was rather forward or ahead of myself. I have no doubt but what I was and if such was the case I feel very sorry that I did it and hope that you will overlook it?

How are Dave and Sallie[7] getting along since the Fourth? Well I

---

[6]Emma had two cousins named Lewis ("Lew") Dunn, one of whom was Walter's brother. Walter is here probably referring to the other.

[7]Probably David L. Randolph of Brooklyn, New Jersey, and Sallie Johnson, frequently mentioned in the letters. No further identification found.

see that I have my sheet nearly filled but with what I cannot say for I have been called up to dress wounds I don't know how many times but you must consider my circumstances when you read it. I have come near the jumping off place and in the words of my inspired correspondent—I must close and so it goes.

—Ever Yours, W. G. Dunn

The request for a speedy reply is supposed to be understood.

W. G. Dunn

Brick House, Jarvis Genl. Hospital
July 30th 1863

Dear Friend

I feel sorry to say that I have been obliged to allow your letter, which I received the 20th, to remain so long without an answer. Since I received your letter I have been very sick and obliged to keep my bed, but now I am much better. I am patient now instead of nurse. I think that I will never enjoy good health as long as I stay in the hospital and I am going to improve the first opportunity to get away. Ike has also been quite sick but is now recovering. My shoulder is nearly well. I have found the ball and am waiting on the Surgeons motion to have it extracted. He says that it is in a very critical place and it would not be safe to cut it out now but thinks that in course of time it will work nearer the surface. It is behind my shoulder.

I heard a few days ago from N[ew] Market that they supposed that James Beatie[8] was killed. If such is the case, I feel almost as though I had lost a brother. Have you heard anything concerning him?

I see in the papers that they have quieted the mob in New York[9] but I believe that the draft has been suspended has it not? How is the draft progressing in Plainfield?

----

[8]Probably Pvt. James Beatty, Walter Dunn's age and a member of Company D, 11th New Jersey Volunteers, who had enlisted on the same day that Walter did. Beatty was listed as missing in action at Gettysburg on July 2, 1863. The War Department later listed him as having died on that date.

[9]On July 13, 1863, opposition to the draft in New York City erupted into a riot that lasted three days and was completely quelled with the arrival of Union troops rushed from the Gettysburg campaign. The riots were savage and severe, and contemporary newspaper accounts greatly exaggerated the extent of the destruction.

A detail from the print of Jarvis U.S. Hospital on page 7, showing the operating room. Its octagonal design was probably to facilitate better lighting for surgery.

Did the threatened rioters make out much? If anything of the kind happened in Plainfield I would like to have a hand in it. I would like to have a scratch with some of those Jersey Copperheads, I would show them no quarters. In my opinion they are worse than the rebes themselves.[10]

[10]The term "Copperheads" refers to Democrats who were outspoken in their opposition to the war effort. Democrats were particularly strong in New Jersey, and Republicans in New Jersey regiments were unusually defensive about the loyalty of their state—one reason for Walter's vehemence. For a full account of New Jersey politics in the Civil War era, see William Gillette, *Jersey Blue: Civil War Politics in New Jersey, 1854–1865* (New Brunswick: Rutgers University Press, 1995).

I expect that one of the patients in this ward will have his foot amputated either today or tomorrow. The Surgeon told him that he would either loose his life or his foot. They have taken up two arteries in his foot and tied them to keep him from bleeding to death. I think that if you had seen me when the doctors were performing the opperation, you would have thought that I was a butcher, I was so covered with blood.

A few days ago one of our patients died and about an hour afterward his wife came to see him. I never saw a woman so struck with disappointment as she was when I told her that he had just died. She was out of employment in the city where she lived and the Surgeon in charge gave her employment here as a nurse.

I suppose that you are thinking of going to Florida[11] as it is about time. I have had an invitation to a dancing party in the city next week and I think that that will have to do for my Florida this year. If you go to Florida this year I hope that you will get home before 9 o-clock next morning. With the hope of an early reply, I will close and remain ever your Friend, W G. Dunn

P.S. When you read this consider that it was written by a patient.

W G Dunn

Jarvis General Hospital
August 17, 1863

My Dear Friend

In consequence of a delay in the mail, I did not receive yours of the 3rd untill the 14th. I began to think that you had not received mine or meant to retaliate—as I did not answer your previous one very promptly. I am glad to know that that was not the case.

This morning is quite cool and agreeable to what the wheather has been for a week past. Quite a large number of people have been sunstrucke within the last week. The warm weather is very much against the sick and wounded soldiers and they are dying off very fast.

Friday evening one died in an adjoining ward from the effects of a wound and sore throat. It is an every day occurance to see a funeral procession pass through this part of the City.

---

[11]Florida beach was a bathing area frequented by Emma Randolph and her friends a short distance from Plainfield.

A few days ago some of our cripples were furnished with crutches and last night a nurse and myself took them to the Parks for a walk. The Parks were crowded and we had a very pleasant time. I enjoyed the fresh air very much after being confined to the house so long. My health is much better and I think that I can spend very many evenings in the parks and other places of resort—if I am not taken sick again. During my sickness I lost nearly all my strength and am now very nervous which you have probably noticed in my writing before this.

I have not seen an Official report from our Regiment of its loss in the last battle—and did not know that Andrew Webster[12] was wounded until I read your letter. Yesterday I saw a man of Company I and he said that Henry Moleson[13] who married one of Levi Clausons daughters had one of his feet blown off with a shell.

Have you heard from Will Smith[14] since the battle?

I received a letter from Tom Titsworth a short time ago, stating that Jimmie was missing and had not been heard from.[15] I feel very sorry for him, he was such a fine and obliging young man.

I am glad that you had such a pleasant time at Florida and hope that you will enjoy yourself if you go again. If you see fit I would like to hear the details of the trip. Before I was taken sick I spent a couple of evenings with some Baltimore ladies very pleasantly. Card playing is considered the most fashionable entertainment for young folks in the City. I do not consider this letter worthy of the name of an answer to yours but it is according to my feelings and I hope that I will be better

---

[12]Andrew Webster of Company B was eighteen at the time of his enlistment in July 1862. He was wounded at Gettysburg.

[13]Henry L. Mollison was also wounded at Gettysburg. The 11th New Jersey was positioned about a hundred yards north of the Peach Orchard on July 2, 1863, when it was attacked and severely mauled in the charge of Barksdale's Mississippi brigade. One of the stories surrounding Barksdale's charge is that an entire Federal company was given the responsibility for shooting down Barksdale, a striking figure with flowing white hair mounted on a white horse. That company was from the 11th New Jersey, and they succeeded. Barksdale would die later that day from five bullet wounds.

[14]Pvt. William H. Smith of Plainfield, eighteen when he enlisted, was severely wounded at Gettysburg. He later died, becoming the only soldier from the Plainfield Seventh Day Baptist Church not to return from the war.

[15]Tom Titsworth, also from New Market and two years older than Walter, was a member of Company D, 11th New Jersey. The "Jimmie" referred to here is probably James Beatty (see note 8).

prepared to answer your next. Please excuse my many mistakes and accept from your

Invalid Friend
W G Dunn

P.S. Answer promptly

Jarvis Genl. Hospt.
Sept. 2nd 1863

Dear Friend

Yours of Aug. the 28th arrived on sunday. I am very sorry to learn that you have been so ill and hope that ere this reaches you, you will have entirely recovered. The extreem warm weather that we have had this summer is allmost enough to make any person sick, I know that it has been very hard on me. The weather here for a few days past has been quite agreeably cool. I have enjoyed much better health and the majority of the patients have improved rapidly since the warm weather left us.

I received a letter from Mary a few days previous to yours, inform-ing me of the sudden and rather unexpected marriage of Jersey and Eugene.[16] I expected to hear of it over one year ago. I thought that things indicated it while I was calling at your house previous to my enlisting. I admired the sense that they persued by waiting, for now they are both old enough to take care of themselves. I wish them all the joy imaginable.

I should judge from what you said that you are on more sociable terms with Lew.[17] I do not know what cause you had for thinking that Lew and I were at enmity with each other. I never thought of such a thing.

When I came from Alfred[18] I was not aware that you and Lew were

---

[16]Emma's sister, Jersey Ann Randolph, was born in 1840. On August 6, 1863, she married Eugene Runyon, and on December 19, 1864, they had a son, Walter Grant Runyon. Eugene ran a grocery business in New Market, New Jersey, with William Shotwell and Alexander Dunham under the name, "Shotwell & Co." Jersey died on April 23, 1897.

[17]Possibly Emma's cousin Lew, but more likely Lewis Dunn, Walter's brother.

[18]Alfred University, a Seventh Day Baptist school, opened in 1836 and was incorporated as a university in 1857. Tuition and other costs amounted to

so intimate; had I known it; I would not have done as I did, but regardless of all that passed, I do not remember that one word of hard feelings passed between us. I have always corresponded with Lew on the most familiar terms and as far as I am concerned always will.

The current news of to-day are that Lee has crossed the Rapenhannack and is trying to flank Meade or cut off his retreat. The paper this morning stated that Lee would meet a rather hot reception if he attacks the thined ranks of the Army of the Potomac.[19] I am glad that Andrew[20] has the privaleg of coming home to see his friend. How is Will Smith getting allong? Does he talk of coming back again soon?

We are going to have a concert in the dining room this evening. I will extend an invitation to you. The last one that we had passed off very pleasantly and everyone present enjoyed themselves. Dr. Dickson takes an active part; he is an exelent singer and does a great deal towards making it interesting. Yes, the ladies of Baltimore are goodlooking and agreeable company but as for telling you the names of my favorites, I have none. I feel sorry that I do not feel in a mood for writing to-day and as I cannot write anything that would interest you I must close, promising to do better next time.

Truly Yours, W. G. Dunn

P.S. Please reply soon.

P.S. Please write Brick house on the left lower corner of the envelope of the next letter.

I have often thought of that important question that is under consideration and would like to see it settled. I expect to visit the Park tomorrow evening and would like to take a pleasant stroll in your company. I have often thought of the pleasant hours spent in your society and desire many more.

Walter

---

about fifty dollars a term. It offered preparatory courses for teachers of public schools and four-year programs in Ancient and Modern Languages, Scientific and Literary Subjects, and a three-year course in Theology. In 1861 thirteen young men and a professor enlisted in the army. Walter had attended briefly before enlisting himself.

[19]The reports of Lee's crossing the Rappahannock were erroneous, and were probably precipitated by a series of light cavalry skirmishes in Virginia the previous day.

[20]Andrew Webster.

SPECIAL ORDERS !

NO. 46.

I.   No smoking of pipes or cigars will be permitted under any circumstances in or near the Hospital buildings, either by patients or attendants.

II.   Nurses and others must be careful in the use of fire and matches about the Hospital wards and buildings.   They are reminded that a conflagration of these barrack wards and out-houses would in all probability be attended with loss of life.

III.   The Night Watchman and Guards must be strictly vigilant in guarding against the danger of fire and must report any offender of these rules for immediate punishment.

IV.   Hospital Steward C. C. Robbins, U. S. A., and the Ward Masters, will make frequent and nightly inspections of the wards, kitchens, etc., to see that these rules are enforced, and will confine in the Guard House any attendant or patient who may thus wilfully expose the lives of others.

DEWITT C. PETERS, Asst. Surg'n, U. S. A.,
SURGEON IN CHARGE.

JARVIS U. S. A. GENERAL HOSPITAL,
BALTIMORE, MD., JUNE 13TH, 1864.

A copy of Special Orders No. 46 issued by the ranking medical officer at Jarvis Hospital, Dewitt C. Peters. (Maryland Historical Society.)

Jarvis General Hospt.
Baltimore Sept. 22nd/63

My Dear Friend

I received yours of the 17th inst. last Sabbath[21] eve. It was a very pleasant evening and I almost wished myself home where I could enjoy a buggy ride. After I read your letter I accepted an invitation to go to the Park to spend the evening. The Park was crowded with visitors who were promenading in the beautiful gravel walks. I saw there a great deal of which Baltimore can boast, vis. female beauty.

I presume that you had a gay time at Uncle Barzilia's[22] while they

[21]For Seventh Day Baptists, the Sabbath is Saturday.

[22]Barzillia J. Randolph, Emma's father (and Walter's cousin), was born in Piscataway, New Jersey, in 1817 and married Mary R. Dunn on February 11, 1840. He was a tailor by trade, and died on May 9, 1883, in Piscataway.

were at Flemington. I always enjoy visiting there because Dave is so full of his fun and mischief. I would have liked to have stepped in and seen what sort of times you were having. Nan has been living there some time has she not? I told Dave that I would venture to bet that there would be an addition to their family before I returned home again. Does Harry still make occasional calls there?

A few days ago there was a man killed in the next block. He was digging under a bank and it fell upon him causing his death in a few minutes. His wife who reached the spot just as his breathing ceased, took it very hard. She was left with one son about 10 years old. He told his mother that there was no use of crying for it would not help it at all and tried to console her by telling her that he was large enough to take care of her. I think I never saw a child of his age take it cooler at the loss of a parrent than he did.

Our concerts are still kept up weekly. We are going to have one tonight. They are very interesting and quite a passtime to the soldiers. There is a great deal of dancing but as yet I have never been engaged in it. I like to see dancing but I am very backward in taking a part. Last Friday evening I attended a party down in the City. I enjoyed it very much considering they were mostly strangers.

I presume that the Johnny Rebe's still hold your picture. It was in my knapsack which I left on the battlefield.[23] If the one that has my Portfolio will give me his address I will send him the key, I think that it would be of some benefit to him. I cannot write anything interesting and the less the better so I will close. Answer soon.

Very Truly Yours

W. G. Dunn

You said that you had come to a conclusion of that question, please tell me what your conclusion is. What night a[t] 10 oclock did you refer to? I received the paper that you sent me. I was very glad you sent it. The soldiers letter was very good indeed.

Walter

---

[23]At Chancellorsville. The 11th New Jersey had left its knapsacks under guard in the woods north of the Chancellor house before moving west into line on the evening of May 2, 1863. The entire area was overrun by Confederates in their sweeping victory the following day.

Jarvis General Hospital
Baltimore, Md. Oct. 23rd/63

Dear Friend

I received your tardy letter on the 14th. I was wondering what was the cause of your delay and finaly came to the conclusion that you wished to drop the correspondence, which would probbably be a good thing as we have kept up correspondence for over one year and I have no doubt but my letters have long since ceased to interest you, if such is the case, I concur.

The reports regarding my being transfered to Newark are false. All that I have said about it was that since I have received a wound which makes me unable for field duty and as I will probbably have to remain in the hospital the remainder of my time, I might as well be transfered to some hospital near home which would make it much pleasanter for me. I do not expect to go to Newark, as we will soon be mustered in the Invalid Corps[24] to do light duty in this hospital. To-day we had our Invalid Jackets given us. They are made similar to a Zuave[25] jacket—sky blue color.

As soon as I am mustered in the I.C. [Invalid Corps], I have nothing more to do with the 11th Regiment of NJ or that with me, my name is then crossed off of all the company books. The seccond class to which I belong is to be armed with sabres and revolvers.

My shoulder is quite lame this afternoon which causes the un-steadiness of my hand and I will therefore have to close.

Please accept, from Walter

Jarvis General Hospital
Baltimore, Md, Nov. 5th 1863

My Dear Friend

Yours of Oct. 27th was received and I regret that I have not had time to answer it before. Since I received yours we have been mustered into the I.C. [Invalid Corps] received our arms and my time has been

---

[24]A military organization for those who were wounded too severely to return to their regiments but capable of performing lighter duties such as those of hospital orderlies, clerks, etc.

[25]Walter referred to a Zouave jacket. Some volunteer regiments from New York and Pennsylvania wore uniforms modeled after the dashing French Zoauve units—a short blue jacket, baggy red pantaloons, and a fez.

Unidentified park in Baltimore during the 1860s. (Maryland Historical Society.)

completely confined going from here to our Company headquarters. I belong to the 12th Comp[any] 2nd Battalion Invalid Corps. We are armed with swords and revolvers, very savage weapons for Hospital use.

I am quite sorry that you mistook the meaning of my last letter. I wrote what I thought before I received your letter, but had no such idea after I read your letter. It is not my desire for any means to cease corresponding with you, the reading of your letters is a source of great pleasure, I only wished to give you to understand that if it was your desire, that I would not be burdensome. Instead of your letters being without interest as you said you supposed they were, they have been right the reverse and I should feel it a great loss to loose such a correspondence as you have been for over one year. And again, I suppose that the length and manner in which I wrote my last probably lead you to think that it mattered not to me whether I ever heard from you or not but I sincerely say that I did not mean it as such, the reason why I did not write more was as I stated, that my arm was very nervous and I was suffering from my shoulder. I should feel very sorry to cease the correspondence for I have not only received yours but have answered them with pleasure when I thought that I could interest you.

Taking your word for it my letters have been more interesting to you than I supposed and believe me, when I say that yours have triple paid me for writing. I hope that I may never hear you doubt about the interest of your letters.

If all that has been written can be blotted out and forgotten I sincerly ask for a continuance of the correspondence and hope that it may meet your approval, which will assure me by an answer at your earliest convenience.

Please excuse this tardy, offhand letter and believe me to be candid in all that I have said.

Please accept from

Your unworthy Friend Walt

Jarvis General Hospital
Baltimore, Md, Nov. 15th/63

My Dear Friend

Yours of the 10th was received and read with pleasure. It is my desire that hereafter our correspondence may run smoothly and that nothing may happen to cause dissatisfaction between us.

Today is what Virginians call a "right-smart-rainy day." Thus far this Fall the weather has been very pleasant, but very few days we have been obliged to build a fire for comfort. I never knew so much pleasant weather for this season of the year, not even in Virginia.

One year ago this morning at 2 o'clock we broke camp near Fort

Ellsworth[26] and opened our Winter Campaign, a very unsuccessfull one as it has since been proved.

I should judge by the number of sick ones in your family, that you are running quite a hospital but I presume that your patients get better care and more attention paid them than the patients in the hospitals that contain hundreds and your patients have maternal care which many a soldier has died for the want of. This hospital will then be capable of holding over one thousand patients.

According to the Official report there are at present fourty thousand, one hundred and ninety-five patients in the USA General Hospital.

They would make quite an army if they were all effective men. There are not less than twenty thousand in the Invalid Corps. This will give you a limited idea of the number who have been made invalids during this war, besides the great number who have been discharged.

It is reported that the 2nd Battln. I.C. is going to Columbus, Ohio to guard rebes. Our Commanding Officer is there and it looks quite probbable that we may go, the sooner, the better.

Last Thursday evening we had a very interesting concert. It was composed of vocal and pianno music, accompanied by the Brass Band of Ft. McHenry which made it very entertaining.

I must close. Reply as early as convenient.

As ever Walter G. Dunn

(Excuse the blots.)

---

[26]Ft. Ellsworth—a Union stronghold on the top of Shuters Hill near Alexandria, Virginia. It was named after Col. Elmer Ellsworth, a one-time student in Abraham Lincoln's law office who commanded a Zouave regiment recruited from the New York fire department. In May 1861 the regiment moved across the Potomac into Alexandria after the Confederates fell back. Seeing the Stars and Bars still flying from the Alexandria Hotel, Ellsworth recklessly raced upstairs and tore it down. As he descended, the innkeeper appeared in the dark passageway and shot him point-blank with a shotgun. Ellsworth was given a funeral at the White House, and a grief-stricken Lincoln wept openly.

The newly recruited 11th New Jersey was stationed at Fort Ellsworth to drill and learn military life before joining the Army of the Potomac.

Jarvis General Hospital
Baltimore, Md. Nov. 28th 1863

My Dear Friend

Your welcomed letter of the 21st inst. has arrived and I will attempt to improve this opportunity in answering it, being the first that I have had since I received it.

I hope that ere this instead of your being discouraged with the news of a defeat that your hopes are brightened with the news of a Glorious victory of our army of the S.W.

Official reports from Maj. Genls. Grant and Thomas to Maj. Genl. Halleck state that they have driven Bragg from his position with heavy loss both in prisoners and firearms.[27]

The number of prisoners is not less than 5,000,[28] 60 peices of Artilery and a large number of small arms.

Maj. Gen. Hooker has had a prominent part in the late victory. He is daily gaining his once lost reputation, I hear some say, but I say that it has never been lost, as corps commander he cannot be exceled in the US.[29] The battle of Gettysburg was fought by the carrying out of his plans and I believe that if he had had command at that time that our army would have been as successfull, if not more than they were, but it is not ours to say what might have been done, only what has been.

The Army of the Potomac is again on the move. It has crossed the Rapidan river in three columns and ere long we may expect to hear something from that quarter.[30]

I hope soon to hear of the army of the Potomac as well as the army of the Southwest being crowned with a glorious victory, the fall of

---

[27]The battle of Chattanooga, Tennessee, November 23–25, was fought when Union forces trapped in Chattanooga after the defeat at Chickamauga broke out and assaulted Lookout Mountain and Missionary Ridge, on which the Confederates had created strongly fortified positions. Though the fighting was at times desperate, casualties were relatively light for a major engagement. Confederate general Braxton Bragg was compelled to retreat.

[28]The actual number was closer to 4,000.

[29]Hooker led three divisions in the successful assault on Lookout Mountain. He had been under something of cloud after Chancellorsville.

[30]Responding to calls from Washington that he assume the offensive, General Meade crossed the Rapidan in an attempt to force Lee's right flank and compel him to fall back on Richmond. Lee instead gave battle and blocked the Federal offensive at Mine Run.

Richmond and the annihilation of Lees army with an equal sucess of our arms at Charleston which will bring this cruel war to a close. But it is no time to be discouraged now, nor even when our cause meets defeat after defeat for the more reverses we have the more energy we should use to accomplish our object in such a case as this.

Thanksgiving day passed off very pleasantly. The Ladies of the Union Relief in this City gave the soldiers in this Hospital an excelent dinner. Yesterday morning, one of the City Police, an acquaintance of mine gave me an invitation to dine with him, which I very willingly did and a better dinner I could not ask for. The draft is going on in this City and it is the subject of conversation of all parties.

I have a couple of pictures left and I will send you one but will not warrant it to be a very good one.[31]

Hoping this will find you in perfect health. I will close.

As Ever, Walter

Jarvis Genl. Hospital
Baltimore, Md. Dec. 7th 1863

My Dear Friend

Yours of the 1st has been received and read with more than usual interest. I hope that ere this you have been relieved of the Headache you was complaining of when you wrote me. I feel quite thankfull that the blessing of good health is still extended out to me when I so little deserve it. I never enjoyed better health than I do at the present.

The death of Aunt Susan was quite unexpected to me and I feel that I, as well as many others have met with quite a loss. She was an example of patience in suffering and a true Christian.

Although we feel it a great loss we would not call her back again to this world of sorrow and suffering but bid her a gladsome adieu, trusting that she is with the Angels of God in Heaven where she will recive her reward for her patience and faithfullness.

On Friday last I received a letter from Eld. Rogers.[32] He spoke of

---

[31]Regrettably, no pictures of Walter Dunn have been found.

[32]Elder Lester Courtland Rogers (1829–1900), pastor of the New Market Seventh Day Baptist Church from 1858 to 1868 and highly regarded by its members. In September 1862 he enlisted in a New Jersey regiment as a private, claiming that he "wished to share the privations of the common soldier, to partake of their fare, to endure their hardships, to carry the

the mercifullness of God in sparing the lives of so many of us who left his flock and gave me very good advise. In speaking of the necesity of many more who would have to go to war, he said that he was ready to bear his part. I think that he has already done his part— and hope that he will not leave our Church to waste his life away by sickness in the camp.

Yesterday I attended chapel and heard an excellent discourse delivered by the Rev. Mr. Brauns, our Chaplin from 2nd Timothy 2nd Chapter and 3 verse.[33] The subject was quite appropriate and the Chapel was crowded.

I see that long service has worn off some of Jonts[34] patriotism and I don't blame him in the least for not seeing the point of reenlisting.

It is reported that the 2nd Battalion I.C. [Invalid Corps] is to be broken up. All who belong to it are to be examined and those fit for it are to be put in the 1st Battalion, those unfit to be discharged, either my regiment or a discharge, no 1st Battalion I.C. for me, no, no.

I am quite tired of this inactive life. I prefer one of action and am soon going to do what I can to be transfered back to the Bloody 11th and share with my comrads the fate of war.

Em, we have been corresponding as you will admit for a considerable over one year and now I want you to tell me frankly if you had any other object in view in wishing our correspondence to continue, more than merely a correspondence of friendship.

What did you mean when you wrote that there would be a battle in earnest between the A. Centurions and the Baltimorians?

Please accept and reply at your earliest convenience.

Your Friend

W. G. Dunn

---

musket side by side with them, that he might be enabled fully to sympathize with them." He was promoted to sergeant and became a chaplain, though his frequent appearance later in the correspondence is evidence that he found reason to return to New Market. He later pastored churches in New York and Wisconsin. See the [Seventh Day Baptist] *Sabbath Recorder,* September 18, 1862.

[33]"Take your share of suffering as a good soldier of Christ Jesus."

[34]Possibly Jonathan Drake (1833–1911), who married Emma's cousin, Mary Jane Randolph, on December 27, 1863.

Jarvis Genl. Hospital

Baltimore Md. Dec. 23rd 1863

My Dear Friend

Yours of the 17th was received the next day after date and now I will attempt to answer it although I feel but little in the humor of writing.

Everything is so dull, and the same thing over and over every day that it is with difficulty that I find anything to write about—so you need expect as little as usual this time.

The weather which has been so warm and pleasant this season is now growing quite cold. I have scarcely been out of the house to day, it has been so cold and the Sentinel in front of the house has to walk his beat quite rapid in order to keep himself warm.

Since I wrote you last, I have attended church once and a Theatre once, one concert and one party. I enjoyed myself at each place but for reasons that I will not now mention, I did not remember the text.

Prepparations are being made for a grand dinner on Christmas to be given by the ladies of the Union Relief of this City. They gave us a large dinner on Thanksgiving day and are going to do the same on both Christmas and Newyears.

Many thanks are due the Patriotic ladies of this City for what they have done for the comfort of the sick and wounded soldiers who have been in the Hospitals in this City. I know of one very patriotic lady whose husband is an Officer on Folley Island, near Charleston, and she told me that she had lately received a letter from him, requesting her permission to resign, she wrote back, never, never resign as long as there is an armed rebel in the Country. The same woman told me that sometimes she had almost wished herself a man so that she could enlist and fight for her Country, what an illustration of patriotism. Have you ever felt such a degree of patriotism? I know that you are very patriotic but I never heard you express yourself that way, but I have not doubt that you have that within you. I suppose that the difference in the furlough of Mart[35] and Lewis is their being in different places. Mart is in a Convalescent Camp and Lewis is in the field. At Washington they give furloughs for 30 days and here for 15 days. You

---

[35]Possibly Martin D. Titsworth, who enlisted in the 11th New Jersey Infantry in July 1862, became a corporal, and was discharged from Augur U.S. Army General Hospital in Alexandria, Virginia.

asked me when I was coming home, how could you ask me to come North this cold weather. It is cold enough for me here, I do not know what I would do nearer the North Pole. I cannot say when I will come home but I will let you know before I come. I may possibly get a furlough sometime between now and Spring. Keep mum.

If you think two sheets will spoil me, write three and try that. Please accept this with my love and reply as early as convenient.

Your absent though true friend W. Dunn

Brick House Jan. 4th 1864

Dear Friend, Emma —

Your last and most interesting letter has been received. I feel quite sorry that I have to write this letter under so late a date, but as you know that none, but causes of the greatest importance prevent me from writing to you, I will make no apology but ask you to forgive, and accept this tardy letter.

I read the details of your Christmas occupation and am assured that you had a very pleasant time indeed, much pleasanter than your unworthy correspondent: I intended on going out on Christmas Eve but my shoulder was very painfull and I was compelled to remain at home. Christmas was dull and New Years day was duller, which is no name for it — it was so dull.

I am very glad to hear that you are having so much skating, for it is certainly a very pleasant amusement. I would like to be at home a few days while the skating is good, I think that I could enjoy myself. I have not skated any in four years but I do not think that I have entirely forgotten how. The skating would have been quite good here had it not commenced snowing yesterday morning. It fell to the depth of three inches and now the rain has commenced falling and where will the snow be tomorrow, I think that it will be minus.

I hope that those ties of affection which bound Harrie and Nan,[36] have not been severed. I have thought for a long time that the matrimonial bond would soon link them together, have you not had similar thoughts?

---

[36]No further identification.

I have heard that Jonathan Drake[37] and Mary Jane Randolph[38] have been married at last. I am quite sure that they were old enough and courted long enough to make a permanent match, what think you of long courtships? Why when I was but a little chub I heard of his visiting her.

Old regiments that have enlisted in the Veteran Corp[s] are daily passing through the City on their way home for thirty-days furlough. A great many of the old soldiers in this Hospital have reenlisted.[39]

Large numbers of conscripts arrive here daily on their way to the front and the majority of them look downhearted.

This afternoon I have been assisting the Surgeons in performing an opperation on a young mans limb and I have not yet got entirely over the influence of the Aether so you must excuse this for I feel rather stupid and drowsy.

Please accept this and answer as early as possible.

Ever Yours, W. G. Dunn

Baltimore, Md.
Jan. 17th 1864

My Dear Friend

As is usual your letter of the 10th reached here the next day after being mailed. I suppose that you will ask what apology I have to make for this delay, which apology I will make in the following lines. I have been waiting that I might right more to a certainty, when I shall start for home on a furlough. I have had the promise of one about the 20th and may be home between that time and the 25th but I cannot say positive.

---

[37]Jonathan Drake, son of Andrew and Hannah (Dunham) Drake, was born on December 24, 1833, in Dunellen, New Jersey. He married Emma's cousin, Mary Jane Randolph, on December 27, 1863. In 1867 they moved to Wisconsin. Jonathan died on July 2, 1911, in Walworth, Wisconsin.

[38]Emma's cousin, Mary Jane Randolph, daughter of Reuben and Sarah Fitz Randolph, was born on April 4, 1837. She was a member of the New Market Seventh Day Baptist Church. Her brother-in-law, Jeremiah Dunham, a member of Walter's Company D in the 11th New Jersey, had been killed a few months earlier, on November 27, 1863, at Locust Grove, Virginia.

[39]The terms of enlistment of many Union regiments were due to expire in the spring of 1864. To keep these men in the field, the government appealed to their patriotism and offered them a thirty-day furlough if they would reënlist. Many accepted the offer.

A contemporary photograph of the Holliday Street Theater in Baltimore. (Maryland Historical Society.)

Owing to the short distance that I have to travel to reach my home, compared with men of Wisconsin and other remote states, I can only get a furlough for (10) ten days. I expect to send in my application in a day or two and if nothing prevents, I think that I may be in N.J. about the 25th or there abouts. Please keep mum as you promised me.

Last evening I attended a lecture by Prof. Le R. Baugher, a resident in Gettysburg and an eyewitness of the battle on the battle of Gettysburg. He stated very many facts and with the aid of a large map of the battlefield gave all who have any knowledge of military terms quite an idea of the position of the two great Armies.

As he spoke in praise of each Corp[s], the boys belonging to that Corp[s] would give three loud cheers. Each Corp[s] in the Army of the Potomac was well represented and with a large number of citizens made a large audience.

I attended Chapel this afternoon and heard an excelent sermon preached by the Rev. Mr. Brauns from Phillipians 3 v. 3.

You asked if I thought of reenlisting, I think that I should if I was in the field and provided I had served long enough to enlist in the V.C. but I would not enlist in the I.C. by any means, it is too dull, not enough excitement for me. I hope to be out of it soon. Veterans are daily passing through this City on their way home on thirty days furlough.

Hoping that I may soon see you face to face, which is better than writing, I will draw to a close and untill then, farewell.

Yours, W. G. Dunn

Baltimore Md.
Jan. 29th 1864

Dear Friend

You are doubtless thinking me at or on my way home, according to my last letter. I will endeavor to undeceive you by writing a few lines.

Oweing to a lack of promptness, to return at the expiration of their furloughs, of some few who are now absent, mine has been delayed.

Five are allowed to be absent at one time, out of a company and no others are granted furloughs until their return.

Last night, one man returned after an absence of two weeks on a five (5) day furlough.

Overstaying a leave of absence is quite wrong, for it not only leaves the person liable to be punished for desertion but prevents others who are waiting to get their furloughs.

When I wrote you last I thought that I should be home the 25th or thereabouts but now I do not think that I will reach there untill the latter part of next week, and doubtfull, if then.

I am in no fear because having it will be good when it comes.

I presume that I shall experience quite a change in the weather in traveling northward for it is now warm and pleasant here, it appears more like May than January weather.

I have had an invitation and expect to attend a Military Ball next Monday evening.

There has been several of them held in this City and they have proved to be the source of enjoyment to the large crowds that attend them.

I am really tired of Hospital life, it is so dull, the same thing over and over all of the time and no excitement to keep a person alive. You have no doubt noticed a dullness in the writing of my letters, well I write just as I feel and I feel just as I write so you can imagine just what sort of a pickle I am in, dull is no name for it.

Has Lewis Dunns furlough expired yet?

I suppose that Jont, Will or Jim Hardy[40] have not reenlisted, have they?

Next Monday I will have just one half of my term of enlistment served. I hope that my term will see the war closed and peace restored. I must close hoping that you will answer immediatly.

Your Friend W.G. Dunn

Baltimore Md.
Feb. 8th 1864

My Dear Friend

I have been waiting for a good opportunity to answer yours of the 2nd and also that I might give you some positive information as to when I shall receive my furlough but I find that after waiting so long, I am as much in the dark as before.

For some reasons, unknown to me, my furlough has not been

---

[40]No information is available on Jim Hardy.

Baltimore in the 1860s. (Maryland Historical Society.)

granted according to promise. On the 20th of Jan Lieut. Gross told me that I would receive it between five and ten days from that time and now it has been about twenty days and nary a furlough yet, nor much of a prospect of one this Winter. I have not the least idea now when I shall receive it. I shall wait and let time inform me. However I shall not give up all hope, but think that it may come some time between now and the 4th of July next, if we should not receive any marching orders.

It was my intention to go to the Washington Depot this morning to meet Walt Smith,[41] but I never thought of it untill after 8 O-clock. I am quite sorry that I missed the chance for I am quite anxious to see him. He gave me a good drink of Whiskey the evening of the same day that I was wounded which did me a considerable good. I presume that you had

[41]Walter G. Smith was a member of the Plainfield Seventh Day Baptist Church. He served in the army but not in the 11th New Jersey.

a very pleasant time both at Lew Dunns and at your house, on the evenings of the 2nd and 4th, had you not? I would liked to have been with you but that was as impossible as to change the direction of the wind.

I hear cannonading from the Fts. in the Bay. I suppose that it is the fireing of salutes over the news of the capture of Mobile, with eight thousand prisoners, one hundred thirty peices of Artilery and a large quantity of cotton. I cannot say as to the truth of this report, but such a report is flying about this city.[42]

Prepparations are being made for a grand time here on the 22nd. Our new Brass Band will appear in public on that occasion for the first time. They are practiceing daily and will be well prepared. There will be a concert in the evening and wind up with a Ball I expect.

If you did not think your letter worthy of an answer, what do you think this worth? I think, not worth notice.

Do not look for me home untill you see me and then you will not be disappointed if I should not come at all. Answer immediatly.

Your friend Walter

Baltimore, Md.
Feb. 17th 1864

My Dear Friend

Yours of the 14th has been received.

Last evening I received a letter from Lew stating that he had been to Newark but said nothing about you and Jennie[43] being with them. You had a pleasant time without doubt. Sayres[44] has at last gone in the Navy, what I have long expected to hear. When I was at home last Spring I saw that his mind was made up in going into some branch of the service of his Country. I am glad that he has made the start and pray that Heavens best blessings may attend him.

---

[42]Union commanders had urged an attack on Mobile, Alabama, throughout the month of January, and Confederates anticipated one, but it did not take place. Months later, on August 5, Admiral David Farragut's fleet passed the outer forts and won control of Mobile Bay, clearing the way for land operations against the city.

[43]Jane Augusta "Jennie" Randolph, Emma's sister, was born in Plainfield on August 10, 1847. On September 26, 1865, she married Vermont "Mont" Fitz Randolph.

[44]Sayres Nicols, Emma's cousin.

I have just read a letter from a discharged soldier who used to be in my ward— He reached home just in time to see a sister die. While traveling home he anticipated a great deal of pleasure, meeting his friends but as he neared home death was about to visit the same spot. He had not heard of her illness and her death was a great shock to him. He was a fine young man and one with whom I have spent very many pleasant hours and his departure was felt almost like a brothers but the best of friends must part here and how joyfull it will be when, if we are worthy, we meet where parting is no more.

I could have had my furlough and been home ere this but I let a young man go in my place who received a letter that his mother was quite sick and as I have had one furlough which he has not, I thought that it would be doing as I would like to be done by, to let him go first. When he returns which will be 30 days from last Monday I will receive mine. I hope that you will give up looking for me untill about the 15th of March. He is from Maine and received a 30 day furlough as it will take him some time to go and come.

You ask my opinion when this war is to be settled. I think that the coming Spring campaign which will be a vigorous one will nearly if not quite close the war. I believe that Meade, Grant, and Gilmour[45] will all strike at one and steake the Southern Confederacy so that it will fall. Jeff. Davis is making a great deal of dissatisfaction and it appears that they are breeding war among themselves. The idea of forcing troops to serve after their terms of enlistment expires is ridiculous and they will not stand it. I hope that the different States will raise their Quotas by volunteering and if not I want to see the draft speedily enforced so that the old regiments which have had their ranks thined out by long service and hard fought battles can be filled up, our Army and Navy strengthened and then I will talk to you about settling the war.[46] I am anxious to go to the field but it is impossible, the Surgeons tell me that my shoulder will not stand active service therefore I must be content

---

[45]General Quincy Adams Gillmore was in overall command of a Federal expedition in Florida which met with some successes. Two days after Walter wrote this letter, the U.S. Senate passed an act reviving the rank of lieutenant general with Ulysses S. Grant in mind for the promotion. In March, Grant would assume command of all the Union armies.

[46]In 1863, to raise more men for the army, the federal government had passed the Conscription Act, the general provisions of which were that each state was to furnish a quota of men by recruitment, and, failing that, by a

and remain where I am. I have been examined by five different Surgeons since I came here and all say that the ball lies in a very critical place in my shoulder and I think what five experienced Surgeons all agree upon must be about so.

The weather is very cold, quite a contrast to the weather last Sunday when it was pleasant as May. I think that to day is the coldest one of the Season. The wind is blowing very hard and it is indeed a very unpleasant day.

You said that you had been expecting a talk with me, was it upon any particular subject, if so, what was it; and by my knowing beforehand I will be better prepared when I come home.

In 30 days more I think that I will get home without doubt. I am well with the exception of a cold. Please accept and reply as early as convenient.

Your Absent Friend W. G. Dunn

Jarvis U.S.A. Genl. Hospital
Baltimore Md. March 9th 1864

My Dear Friend

Your kind letter of more than usual interest was recd. last evening. I need not tell you with what pleasure I read its contents, as I was extremely anxious to hear from you.

Yes I am here and all settled down after my short visit home. It begins to appear almost like a dream to me but still I know that I have realised it for no such pleasure could come from a dream. I left home rather earlier on Thursday morning than I had before expected. After waking from a short nap, I got up and said that I should take no more rest or sleep untill I reached Baltimore. Upon looking at the time

---

draft, with subordinate jurisdictions assigned individual draft quotas. Men could escape conscription for medical reasons (fraud was prevalent), by paying a commutation fee of $300 which excused them from service, or by hiring a substitute. Reluctant to draft their own citizens, counties, cities, and towns enticed men with a variety of bounties. The draft was exceedingly unpopular and politically controversial, and brought relatively few men into the army, men who were generally despised by those who had earlier volunteered out of a sense of duty and patriotism. For an overview, see Eugene C. Murdock, *One Million Men: The Civil War Draft in the North* (Madison: State Historical Society of Wisconsin, 1971).

table, I saw that a train left New Brunswick for this City at 10 A.M. and told Father that I should like to take that train.

As soon as possible after breakfast, I started for New Brunswick but as the train that I wished to take, was due the above named place twenty minutes earlier than advertised, I missed it and had to wait untill 11-20 A.M. The intervening time was very pleasantly spent with Father[47] in the City. A few minutes before the time I went to the Depot, procured a ticket, bade Father farewell and stepped aboard of the cars, which were off in a very short time, reaching Philadelphia at 2-30 P.M. Wilmington, 3-20 P.M., Havre de Grace at 5-45 P.M. and this City at 7-30 P.M. My trip though on a very pleasant day was everything but pleasant to me, as I felt so mean. My head ached a considerable, so that I could hardly bear the slaming of the doors of the cars, togather with a very stupid feeling that I cannot describe, nor never again wish to realise. There was a young man who wished to make himself rather sociable, but as I felt but little like talking, I put him off by merely saying yes and no to his questions, but he kept buzzing me and before we reached Baltimore I wished him in "Hail Columbia" or some other good place. As soon as I reached the Hospital I struck for my bunk and throwing myself upon it— took the one hundreth part of a seccond for reflection and went to sleep, but nary a dream, I was so completely exhausted.

In answer to your question as to where I was on Sunday evening last at 8 oclock, I can say what many cannot and that is, I was to church, at the Fayette St. Methodist. I thought of the Sunday evening spent with you and spoke to my friend on our way home. I told him that I should not seriously object to being where I was one week previous, he said I suppose not.

With the exception of the evening that I reached here, I have scarcely been in one evening. I have been to the Theatre twice, to meeting once—to Ft. Federal Hill[48] one evening and last evening to LaFayette Square. You may think that I am getting to be quite a

---

[47]Joel A. Dunn was born on February 15, 1811, in Piscataway. In 1836 he married Rhoda Fitz Randolph. After her death he married her sister, Joanna (Joan) Fitz Randolph, on June 11, 1842. He was Walter's father and Emma's cousin. He died at his home near New Market on May 23, 1894.

[48]Federal Hill, on the southern rim of Baltimore's inner harbor, was occupied as a fortification in May 1861 by Federal troops under the

Theatre goer but not so. I went one evening to gratify a friend who expected to go to Ohio on the next day and the other for to gratify my own feelings. The peice that was played that evening was titled Woman or love against the World, it was good. The great actress Mrs. D. P. Bowers was the principal character. I do not think that I shall attend again very soon.

While coming up Exeter St. this evening, I met two ladies and after I passed them some two or three doors, I heard my name called by a voice that seemed familiar and upon turning arround, who should I see but the lady nurse that I spoke to you about; it's being the first time that I have seen her since she left which was nearly four months since. I went up to her and reached out my paw and such a shake it has not lately had. I began to wish that my whole arm had been insured. She appeared terrible glad to see me and gave me all kinds of invitations to come and see her. I think that I shall sometime when I feel as though I would like a good square meal for there is just where I can get it.

While reading your letter last evening, where you spoke in refference to the veil, I could not help laughing right out loud. Lew was about as stupid as I was when I spoke to him about it. The first that I discovered of it was near Mr. Wattermans, when it swung out in the moonshine and attracted my attention, it was then too late to turn and take it back and I thought that Lew would fullfill his engagement with you that evening so you would probbably get it as soon as you would want to use it. I expect that I shall hear more about it when Lew writes.

Yes Em— I have had my breakfast— I took a peice of fruit-cake and some water to stop my long breathing. I cannot account for that, if it was not caused with the expansion of the heart, what is your opinion of it?

The war news are not very exciting this evening. Col. Dahlgren who was with Killpatrick on his last raid to Richmond is killed and his command captured with the exception of a very few.[49]

No I do not have the head ache as much as I did at home, nor do I

command of Benjamin F. Butler. Over the next few months the position was greatly strengthened and manned with heavy artillery aimed at various points in the city. At the time of Walter's visit, companies of the 8th New York Heavy Artillery were in garrison there.

[49]On February 28, 1864, Judson Kilpatrick and 3,500 Union cavalrymen crossed the Rapidan intent on penetrating the light defenses of Richmond and freeing Federal prisoners held there. A series of minor skirmishes cost

Many of Baltimore's citizens openly sympathized with the South. Here in an 1861 woodcut Confederate prisoners are transported across the city surrounded by a friendly crowd. (Maryland Historical Society.)

have those gentle hands, which once were a great relief, to bathe it.

Em— will you be so kind as to tell me, what reason you had of feeling as you said you did in my company, rather reserve. Was it my fault? I hope that you will rid yourself of that feeling and write to me as a friend in whom you can trust and I assure you, you will not be deceived. Write as you say you do to Jont anything that comes in your head, I am sure that I will be interested. How is the Lamb?

---

the Federals the element of surprise, and though they came within two miles of Richmond itself they were forced to withdraw. Part of the column commanded by Col. Ulric Dahlgren had split from the major force. This element marched into an ambush on the retreat from Richmond. Dahlgren was killed and more than a hundred of his five hundred men captured. The raid on Richmond ended as a dismal Union failure.

I hope that you have entirely recovered from you headache, and if not, you have my hearts sympathy. The bugle has long since sounded Taps, and I must extinguish my lamp or there will be a fuss in the family, so good night— and pleasant dreams of the past. Please accept from a friend who holds you dear to him and reply when convenient.

Truly W. G. Dunn

Jarvis U.S.A. Genl. Hospital
Baltimore, Md. March 17th 1864

My very Dear Friend

I was made the most happy recipient of your last the evening of the 15th. I need not tell you what pleasure accompanied the reading of it, it was so very interesting. You need never fear of writing in much of just what comes in your head for such letters I love most, when the thoughts of the head and the feelings of the heart are expressed.

I have just returned from the Chief Mustering Office of the 8th Army Corps,[50] where I am on duty as a clerk. I have been temporarily detached from my company at this Hospital and I can assure you that it is quite an agreeable change from the monotonous life of the Hospital. In the Office there are six clerks and we have all the writing that we can do from 9::30 A.M. to 4::30 P.M. day after day. The Office is situated in North St. No. 34 in the midst of the business part of the City and it is quite amusing to see the different characters pass to and fro of all styles and classes. At our Office and the P.M. Genl. Office there are thirteen clerks and orderlies and we are going to mess togather. We have a inman and a contraband[51] that we have confiscated to cooke and keep home for us. We intend to have a gay time when we get in to wholesale housekeeping, then we will be glad to have visitors, and I will extend an invitation to you, be sure and not forget the place, 34 North St.

Mother has sent me a letter that she has lately received from Col. J. C. Rafferty, stating the impossibility of my being discharged. Dr. Peters values my services too highly to discharge me. You know that in order to make machinery work well it is necessary that every ball and screw be in its propper place, and a removal of either would cause an

---

[50]Headquartered in Baltimore.
[51]The term applied to a former slave.

irregularity in the working of the machine, well, I comprise one of these in Uncle Samuels monstrous machine and if I should be discharged it would remove (what might not be easily replaced) which would cause a disorder and then I would like to ask you what would become of this once great and about to be Glorious Union of ours? Do you think it would hold together. Mother told me to be contented, it might be for the best. I am sure that I am contented for I have not been disappointed it has turned out just as I thought it would. I am just as well satisfied as I would have been had I received a discharge. This cruel war will soon be over then all who are left can come home to enjoy the sweet peace that they are now fighting for. I hope that happy day is not distant.

My friend just returned from his furlough. I had just seated myself beside my table to write you last ere when he came in and we got to talking and the evening was spent before I commenced to write. This delay you must lay to him. He gave me an account of his visit from begining to end and said that he enjoyed himself very much indeed and would like to go again. His mother was much better when he left.

Last Sunday evening I attended the 7th Baptist Church on the corner of Pacca and Sarratoga Sts.[52] and for the first time saw baptism performed in a Baptistry. The discourse was an excelent one preached from Revelations 3::12.[53] It was the first Baptist Church that I have attended in the City.

Before I forget it, I must acknowledge the receipt of the Waverly and accept my thanks in return. Em— please take notice should you see our number in the list of advertised correspondents of one addressed Box 599, Baltimore P.O. Do not understand that it is one that I had just put in, but I am only acquainted with the advertiser.[54]

Em, I often think of your illness and would like the chance of doing something to relieve you, if I only know what to do. I should

---

[52]The Baltimore streets are Paca and Saratoga.

[53]"He who conquers, I will make him a pillar in the temple of my God; never shall he go out of it, and I will write on him the name of my God, and the name of the city of my God, the New Jerusalem which comes down from my God out of heaven, and my own new name."

[54]The *Waverly Magazine* was a vehicle by which young women placed personal advertisements seeking "a soldier correspondent." Needless to say it was in great demand among soldiers.

never weary in doing it. Yes Emma Dear I will truthfully promise you that I will not harbor the thought that you are growing cold, it is a thought that I would not wish nor hope I may never harbor. I wish you only knew my feelings at this time, my heart is too full for expression. I say but little and think a great deal I would like to have the chance of batheing your head but would rather you would not have the head ache. I shall ever remember the gentle batheing that my forehead got while at Clarks. I wished those soft hands might bathe my head that night. Often I reached this place. My feelings at that time were better imagined than described but I feel very different now. I think that I would enjoy a seat beside you on the sofa to night but circumstances will not permit and I will imagine myself there. I have thought of those evenings spent with you as the sweetest by far that I spent while at home and you know what I think of my dear parrents and judge from that my feelings toward you. I have a great deal more that I would like to write but my time will not permit so I must close and put out my lamp as the bugle has sounded the signal. Please excuse the writing of this letter as my arm is very tired. I have written nearly all day steady. I wish you sweet rest and the pleasantest kind of dreams and dear Emma do not forget me in your evening prayers and rest assured that you are not forgotten by me. Good night and with it accept a kiss. If anything that I have written is disagreeable please pardon and forget. Please reply as soon as possible.

Your affectionate friend, Walt

Jarvis U.S.A. General Hospital
Baltimore Md. March 24th 1864

My very Dear friend

I have just received and read yours of the 20th. Upon looking in my portfolio, I find that I have five unanswered letters but as you stand No. 1 in the catelogue of my friends, I will answer yours first and if possible meet your request regarding the time that you wished to receive it. Please tell me why you prefer receiving it on the evening mentioned.

For the past week I have been very busy indeed, working at the Muster out Rolls of the parolled prisoners of the 9th Md. Vols.[55] About

---

[55]The 9th Maryland Infantry (U.S.) was a six-month regiment organized

one week since a Telegraph Dispatch was sent to the Office with an order from the War Department to use the quickest-possible means to Muster out the parolled prisoners of the 9th Md. Vols. and it has kept us busy night and day untill yesterday, when they were mustered out. The Mustering Officer told us that after the job was done we should all have a holliday and this afternoon I told him that I should like to be excused as I had some writing that I would like to do at Jarvis and his reply was certainly. I like him first rate and can get allong with him as easy as rolling off a log. Although he is in a place that requires the utmost patience, yet I never hear an angry word from him. He is also uncommon full of fun for a man at his age, which makes the time pass pleasantly by. The rush of business is over for the present and I shall have it easier for a while.

We are getting allong finely with our family matters. This morning we had Buckwheat cakes, no not Buckwheat, but — but — oh — I have it now, Flap Jacks or something like that— there was a Jack in it anyhow. I would like very much to have you step in and dine with us, I assure you that we would give you all the pork that you could eat— as there are but few of us who believe in eating swine, rather Jewish in the pork line. If I had been home when you were visiting there, I think that you could not have got my place at the table as easy as you did, for I am generally on hand when I hear the dishes rattle but I would give you the next chair. If Father intends that you shall have my place during my absence, I wonder if he won't make a place for you when I return. If he does not, I will, if agreeable on your part. You asked my opinion in refference to the Union of H and N. My personal acquaintance with Nan has been so brief, and Harrie has changed so much since I left that I should not do the expression of an opinion on so delicate a subject, justice. You are much better acquainted with them than I am and I shall agree with you. If they are satisfied and can agree I am sure that I will make no opposition.

---

in Baltimore during June and July 1863. After Gettysburg it was assigned to guard the B&O Railroad. On October 18, 1863, five companies were overwhelmed and captured at Charles Town, West Virginia, by General John D. Imboden's Confederate cavalry, which included Harry Gilmor's 2nd Maryland. Many of those captured died in Southern prison camps. Harold R. Manakee, *Maryland in the Civil War* (Baltimore: Maryland Historical Society, 1961), 117.

In refference to the advertisements in the Waverly, I can say that I know nothing of the particulars more than the fact that there was such an advertisement. I shall make some inquires and if I can gain any information, I will transfer it to you. I believe the name of one of the advertisers is Wm. West, at least he is the one that spoke to me about it while I was reading the one you sent me.

Yes indeed I realise a great deal of pleasure in reading your letters. more than I have ever yet expressed. You would think so, if you only knew my feelings when I receive them. You have to take my word for it as I have no other means of proving it, and believe me, Dear, to be candid. You said, one evening while I was at your house, that you could love but one and allow me to ask if I come seccondary in your affections? You wished to know my thoughts while opening your letter. While opening it I was enjoying a hearty laugh over a remark made by the young man who has taken my place in getting the mail since I left. As soon as I entered the room I saw him and asked him if he had any mail for me, he said that he had and a big fleshy one too which he soon forked over.

I was thinking just before I received it that probbably I had said something disagreeable in my last which caused you to delay the answer longer than usual, but you stated nothing of the kind in yours and I hope that such was not the case. If you dreamed as you said you would often writing my letter, please tell me what your dream was. You wished me to tell you what I did to win the affections of my home circle. I do not know that I have done anything more than trying to do what I thought was my duty. I do not know that I am more thought of than the rest of the family. Probbably my absence would cause a natural affection to exist that would not if I was under their immediate care. They do not think more of me than I do of them, that is impossible. Dear Emma you know not the secrets of your parrents hearts. I have reason to believe from what I have seen that you are held by strong ties of affection by your parrents and I can assure you that you are loved by one, though he is absent, still the remembrance of past is sweet indeed sweet to him. I must close. I feel far from felling well at this time and I cannot think that this will interest you.

Yours until death
Walter

P.S. I have thought of burning this, but as I feel unwell, you will probbably overlook it when you read it.

If anything that I have said does not please you, I ask full forgiveness.

Please reply as soon as convenient. Address me as before "untill further orders." Walter

If you should receive this Sabbath eve, imagine me at bed and sleeping soundly at an Early hour, Sunday at Church.

Walter

I had heard that John Hardy was missing. The news were quite sad to me. Those boys have seen so much service without the loss of one of them, that I was in hopes that they might return home without their numbers being lessened, but such is war. The name of the Invalid Corps has been changed to the Veteran Reserve Corps. The Corps numbers are over 25,000 men enough to stop the units of Jeffs army (one at a time). Please accept this and know that my right arm is very tired and weak.

Ever yours W. G. Dunn

Jarvis U.S.A. Genl. Hospital
Baltimore Md April 1 1864

My very Dear Friend

Em, imagine me in a room, all alone, seated beside a table, talking with you by means of the pen. There's a vacant chair beside me that you might occupy if you were here and I dearly wish you were. I think I could express my feelings better and enjoy an interview with you face to face with much more satisfaction, what is your opinion? Since I commenced this the matron has been in the room. I told her that I was taking the advantage of the solitude and hinted to her that I could enjoy myself full as well at present without her company, as with, so on the strength of it, she has [vanished].

Owing to some delay in the mail I did not receive your letter of the 26th until yesterday (31st). I received one also from *Mother* that was written the same day and to day I received one that was written yesterday from Eld. Rogers and a very interesting one — two sheets *chuck* full.

I generally receive your letters the next day after being mailed, but the last one was four days on the road. You may think that I am delaying the answer of yours, but it is my first opportunity since I received it and when you learn that I did not receive it untill a late date you will be convinced that it is not a delay on my part.

I suppose that you are moving or have got moved by this time, I hope so at least, for I know that it is no small job for a family the size of yours to move from one house to another.[56] I know from experience that it is quite a task to change camp even when you only have *kitchen furniture* without any parlor *fixings,* especially when we have to march twenty or thirty miles to make the change. If you are living in your new house, how do you like it? Is it as pleasant as the old one was? Are there any trees in the front yard where a fellow can hide behind and say, "Nothing much"? And what's most important of all, has it a "cool window" to sit by Summer eve's and dream about ___, if it has, the house must be complete, if not, it is deficient, for without a cool window, where would the *"question be considered"* How are you question?

Em, what a good thing it was that I was not at home when you were there, for there would certainly have been some *quarreling,* if you had insisted upon having my place, for I consider what's *mine* is *mine,* and what belongs to me is my *own* and in that light, I look upon my place at Uncle Joels table. Ah, I see now why you do not come to fathers when I am at home.

Yes, Lew told me of having a visit from the past. I am quite glad to hear that Harrie is improving. He is so changed he does not appear like Harrie to me any more. Him and I used to have some gay times togather when we were boys, but those days are past, only to be thought of but never to be realised again. Would that I could once more enjoy my school days. I think that I would improve them better, but there is no need of bawling over spilt milk.

I think that I can lead you in the letter line, I have received twelve since last Friday, but what is worse, I have seven of them to answer yet. I am wrong. I have received fourteen, with yours, making two a day. How would you like to have seven letters to answer at once? I think that you would think as I do, not know which to answer first. What is your oppinion?

Tis Friday evening. How very different my Sabbath eves are spent

---

[56]Emma's family has moved from a house on Second Street to Sixth and New Streets.

The Maryland Institute, site of the Maryland U.S. Sanitary Fair. (Maryland Historical Society.)

here to those spent at my *quiet* and *loved* home. I would like to step in and see how you are spending this eve. I presume you are either at meeting or at home, probably reading your bible, am I correct in thinking so. You may be lying on the sofa with a headache, if so I would like to be with you to *bathe* it for you and apply some cold water, but I hope that such is not the case. You said that you often kissed Maggie[57] for me. I am much obliged to you but I don't enjoy it when you kiss Maggie as well as I would should I be the direct recipient of your sweet kiss. No, I have no one to kiss for you, nor no one that I could kiss for you, *Dearest*, they would lack so much of being what you are, in my estimation.

---

[57]Maggie, Emma's sister, was born on September 6, 1861. She died, unmarried, on September 26, 1888.

You asked my opinion upon that question, I hardly know what to say. My object in asking the question was to find out how I stand in your affections, if at all. I may have asked too much but you were at liberty to answer it [or] not as you deemed proper. You stand primary in my affection, so I would like to stand in yours, but that is not for me to say. You may have some friend that you hold dearer than I, if so, do not allow me to intrude. I have enjoyed very many sweet hours and have enjoyed the reading of your letters and have taken pleasure in writing to you when I could think that my letters were of interest and I hope that it has been a pleasure to you. You say so and I cannot distrust your word, you have proved too true for me to think such a thing. If you understand the object in asking you that question, please answer it according to your pleasure. If there is any thing obsure, please let me know in your next and I will enlighten you if it is in my power. What did you mean when you said that you thought that by sending me your letters, that it would prevent a person from receiving one from me, which person did you refer to? Dear Emma, I must bid you a sweet good night, it is growing quite late and I am quite weary and unwell. I was excused from the office this morning on account of being ill and I feel but little better tonight, I trust that I will feel better after having a good nights sleep. Please accept this and consider the circumstances under which it is written. I will try to answer the remainder of your questions in my next.

I remain your true friend, W. G. Dunn, V.R.C.

Second Edition
Office of Comis. Musters
8th A. Corps, Balto. Md.
April 2 1864

Dear Emma—

As I have not yet had a chance to mail your letter, and as I have a few leisure moments before I commence the business of the day, I will devote them in writing to you.

I felt quite ill when writing your letter last evening, but after a good nights rest, I feel much better, so I thought I would come to the Office and do what I could. It is a very rainy Sabbath morning. How I would like to attend New Market church and hear our much loved

Pastor preach. I received a very good letter from him yesterday, he writes just as he talks.

It looks verry little here like Sabbath-keeping, or at least you would think so, should you see my table, all covered with papers and rolls of different kinds and in my drawer I find several sets of bills, put there for me to endorse and I suppose that I will keep my Sabbath, in this business way as there is no other way that I can keep it in my situation. I suppose that at this time you are preparing for church, what a contrast between your situation and mine.

I shall attend church tomorrow once or twice if the weather will permit. I wish it was so that you could go with me to hear Dr. Fuller, Pastor of the 7th Baptist church of this City. I have not the least doubt but you would like him. I was never in a church that I liked better than that, the church itself is so accommodating and the services are performed with such harmony. Their music is exelent, having a large organ and an exelent choir. Dr. Fuller is a good loyal man and that is one of the many prefferences that I have for him.

I did not know a young man in "B" Company by the name of Buck, but I knew a boy by that name in "K." A portion of the time that I was with the Regiment, Comp. "B" was on the extreem left of the line and our Company being on the right, we were quite strangers. There might have been a dozen men by that name and I not know them. I think that you never before acknowledged to be the originator of that valentine. Have you told Mollie Bogarts what become of it? if not, please do not. I must close, it is near time for the mail to close, and I want this to go in the earliest mail. While I have been writing this I have kept up a continual argument with a young man who came here on business, about the war, he did not agree with me nor I with him, so you can see what an opportunity I have had for writing this. Consider when you read this that I was doing two things at the same time as writing and accept.

As ever your Friend W.

Office of Coms'y. of Musters, 8th Corps
Baltimore, Md. April 8th 1864

Loved Friend

As a few moments [intervene ere] the time to commence the business of the day, I will devote them, in writing you a few lines in

Baltimore's largest and most attractive park, Druid Hill, opened in 1859. (Maryland Historical Society.)

answer to yours which I received last evening. I will not attempt to describe with the pen, the pleasure that accompanied the reading of it, for it was of more than usual interest. Do not understand that your previous ones have not been interesting, for indeed they have been verry interesting and the last one, was more than verry interesting.

I wrote you a short time since that our hurry was over. It was at that time but now we are just coming into the rush of business. At present, we are preparing the Monthly Reports, to send to the War Department and I can assure you that it is no small job to make out a Monthly Report of an Office that does the business this does. We have been busy night and day for several days past and not near through yet. Last evening, shortly after supper, I skedaddled from the Office and went up to Jarvis as I expected your letter, and you may be assured that my expectations were more than realized.

The Sun has shone itself again, after being hidden from our view for nearly a week. It is a lovely morning. The weather is so warm and pleasant that it is comfortable in the Office with the windows open, and how pleasant the fresh breeze feels. It feels verry much like May weather. The window I sit by faces Holliday St. Theatre, not a grave-yard nor a railroad. Although I am so near the Theatre, I have not attended it, since I came to this Office. I do not think that much good comes from such places of amusement, but a great deal of evil.

No, I shall never forget the pleasant hours that we have spent togather, (or the ___) time will never erase them from my memory. I look back upon them as the source of much of my happiness. My thoughts often wander to the past and in my dreams I see your pleasant smilling face, which often times makes me feel sad because, it is not real.

You spoke in refference to your family being broken by Death, that you would wish to go first, and also that we might not meet again in this world. I do not like to hear you say thus, it gives me pain. Please promise me that you will not harbor such thoughts but be reconciled to the will of an all wise Providence who has your days numbered and will, at the expiration of your allotted period, remove you from this world of sin and sorrow to a better world on High. I think it is wrong for us to wish that we might die, and a sin for us to desire that Gods plans should be changed. He does everything for the best and let us be satisfied with his will.

Do not understand me to mean reproof, for I do not. Please promise me that you will not allow such thoughts to linger in your mind, will you? They will have a tendency to dampen your enjoyment here below and be an hindrance to you in acomplishing the great object of your life. Please expell all such thoughts and resign yourself to a Being who cannot err.

I think I understand you Dear, I take you to mean what you say, and doubt not, but what you say, what you mean. Should you prove untrue, could you ask my forgiveness? I think that I could not ask yours, should such be the case, but I trust not. (Should we both live and nothing arrise to cause hard feelings to exist between us, may I not, in some future day recognize you by a title nearer than Friend?)

Answer at your pleasure. The time that I allotted for to write you has expired and I must close as my services are very much needed this morning.

Please accept this letter of few words with much love and believe me true as ever toward you

W. G. Dunn

P.S. You need not fear to write me what you would say if I was present, for I am the only person who reads your letters, and trust, you are the only one who reads mine. I received the last. The young advertiser has gone home on a furlough to attend the funeral of his mother. I hope I may not be called home to do the like. Farewell, Dearest. W. G. Dunn

I hope you may receive this Sabbath eve, if you desire it.

N.B. An early reply will greatly oblige me. Is this too soon to answer yours?

Office of Coms'y. of Musters, 8th Corps
Baltimore, Md. April 18th 1864

Dear Emma

You are probably thinking that I am delaying the answer of your letter, by writing under so late a date, but I trust the knowledge of the facts of the case, will undeceive you. For some unknown reason, yours of the 10th did not reach me until last Friday evening, and this is my first opportunity to reply, as I have been quite busy since. I generally receive your letters, day after being mailed but your last was nearly five days coming. I hope such a delay will not occur again.

This evening, the Maryland State Sanitary Fair[58] opens. It is to be

---

[58] The United States Sanitary Commission organized a number of fairs in cities throughout the North to raise money for hospitals. For a complete account of the Maryland Sanitary Fair, see Robert W. Schoeberlein, "A Fair to Remember: Maryland Women in the Aid of the Union," *Maryland Historical Magazine*, 90 (1995): 467–88.

held in the Maryland Institute, a few blocks from this Office. President Lincoln is expected to be present, at the opening and will probbably make some appropriate remarks.

If business will permit, I think I shall go and hear what the "Rail Splitter" has to say. Large prepparations have been made for the Fair and I doubt not, but it will do honor to the State.

Yesterday I attended the Union Square Methodist Church. Text was Proverbs 20::1[59] and a portion of the 23rd Chapter. The substance of the discourse was Temperance. He illustrated the Drunkards life from the first sip of the "deadly poison" to the Delirium Tremendous and spoke quite reprovingly to the "moderate drinkers" which (I am almost ashamed to confess) struck me quite forcibly. I am verry glad I heard that discourse for it may be the means of my reform. I hope it may, at least. I would like for some of the New Market boys to have heard it. I think it might have done them good.

While speaking of dreams, I dreamed one, one week ago yesterday morning, which I will describe as near as I can with the pen. My first reccollections were, that we (a party of young folks) were standing on the side walk, in front of your Uncle Jims in New Market after having tea and were preparing to disperse, when you come up to me and said "Walt, you did not bring me here but I think you might take me home." I repeated the answer. "I will" and was just assisting you into my buggy, and anticipating a pleasant ride, when one of the boys called me to breakfast, and oh! how I felt when I awoke and found myself at Jarvis with my expectations all blasted. It made me mad like fire whenever I thought of it. I think it is a misterious dream, what think you?

Think not for one moment that I could take offence from your reply. When I ask a question I consider the persons asked at libberty to answer as they see fit. Such was my desire, or I should not have proposed to you, but if complying gives you pain or in any way displeasure, I could not ask it. It is a question of vast importance and should not be answered without carefull meditation and I wish you to consult your feelings and answer accordingly, regardless of offending me, which you need not fear. I do not know but I have asked too much of you, if I

---

[59]"Wine is a mocker, strong drink a brawler; and whoever is led astray by it is not wise."

Monument Square in Baltimore was a center of political activity and the site of countless speeches and rallies. The monument honors those who defended the city in the War of 1812. The brick building at left was in 1864 the headquarters of the Eighth Corps, U.S. Army. (Maryland Historical Society.)

have please pardon. I think the strength of your argument favors a negative answer, did you not wish me to understand it thus? Is this sufficiently plain, and do you understand me? if not, ask me any questions you like, and I will take pleasure in answering them the best I can. Please consider the question and I shall await a decided answer with anxiety. Please describe in your next your feelings the night you received the hasty note to gratify me.

As the pleasant weather of Spring approaches I grow more and more weary of being confined in an Office. I want to be out in the Country were I can enjoy liberty and sweet Country air, rather than pent up in this (would be rebellious) City. I think that an adventurous life in some wild Country would suit me exactly as I like to be in the midst of excitement. I fear that I cannot content myself at home when the war is over. My time will not allow me to write longer and I will close. Please accept this and think not that it is a delayed answer on my part, and reply as soon as convenient and

Believe me as Ever Yours— W. G. Dunn

P.S. Please excuse the style of this letter for my pen is miserable, my ink more blue, and my arm most nervous and written in quicker time, with a still stronger love for you. Walter Dunn

Jarvis U.S.A. Genl. Hospital
Baltimore, Md. April 25th 1864

Dear Emma

I regret very much that I am obliged to write this under so late a date. Since I received yours, there has been so many changes and my time has been completely occupied that I have scarcely had time to think, much less to write. I received yours on Sabbath evening, and at the same time received one from Eld. Rogers.

Yesterday, my friend, Charlie Deskler with many others, was sent North to make room here for the released prisoners. Charlie and self were on our way to church, when he received an order to be ready to start for N.Y. at 2 P.M. and as he had some preparations to make, we turned back, consequently I did not attend church twice yesterday as usual, but once. For several weeks past, him and I have attended church togather and taken a walk on Sunday evening, just as regular as Sunday came, now he has gone and I will have to select another congenial heart with whom to while away the hours of Sunday. I told him that if he should chance to get in Newark Hospital, I would give him a letter of introduction to some of my friends who frequently visit that place, and should such be the case, if agreeable, I will give you an introduction by letter to him. You will find him to be a very pleasant and agreeable person after you get well acquainted with him.

Since I wrote you last this Hospital has received two hundred and sixty four, paroled prisoners, just from Richmond Va.[60] The majority of them are reduced to mere skeletons by ill treatment and starvation. Several have already died and many more will follow soon. It is hard to listen to their stories, of their treatment while in the hands of the rebes. When I think of their situation and of the "butchery of Ft. Pillow"[61] I have a feeling of revenge that I cannot controll. I have not before favored retaliation but now I say retaliate— in every respect; turn man for man. I hope that measures will be taken to revenge all the "cold blood" that was shed at Ft. Pillow. I feel somewhat encouraged to night for I have just had a talk with Dr. Dickson, our Ward Doctor, in refference to the performing of the opperation in my shoulder and he spoke quite encouraging. I am in hopes that I may soon join my Regiment—and bear my part—in the comeing campaign. I think that Richmond will fall soon and I want a hand in it. Things indicate a vigorous Spring campaign, which, in my oppinion will crush

---

[60]From Belle Isle (see note 63 below). Prior to 1863, prisoners-of-war had been exchanged on a regular basis through an informal cartel, but in 1863 Secretary of War Edwin M. Stanton proposed that the exchanges cease, on the grounds that they aided the Confederacy more than the Union. Prisons soon became overcrowded and conditions unbearable. Sometimes, but not always, the worst medical cases were shipped back across the lines.

[61]Fort Pillow, Tennessee, on the bank of the Mississippi River, was garrisoned by 557 Union troops, 262 of them black. On a raid of northern communications posts, Confederate General Nathan Bedford Forrest sent 1,500 men against Fort Pillow, whose Union commander refused to surrender. The Confederates swiftly took the fort, and Union casualties numbered 231 killed, 100 wounded, and 226 captured. The ratio of killed to wounded was highly suspicious, and numbers of Federals testified that many of the men were killed after they had surrendered. Confederate authorities hotly contested these assertions, but the "massacre" at Fort Pillow remains controversial to this day. Casualty figures from E. B. Long, *The Civil War Day by Day: An Almanac, 1861–1865* (Garden City, N.Y.: Doubleday & Company, Inc., 1971), 484.

the very heart of the rebellion and compell the rebellious to surrender.

I attended the Sanitary Fair last Tuesday evening. It is progressing finely and bids fair to be a grand success. I noticed in the papers to day that Gen. Grant got a very large majority of the votes over McClellan for the [award]. He is the man to have it. The N.Y. Fair realised a very large sum and I hope that Maryland will not be behind, in proportion to her size.[62] I did not see President Lincoln as I expected, my business would not permit my absence.

Dear, Emma I deeply sympathise with you in your suffering and if I could, I would bear your sufferings willingly. I would recommend that you take out of door exercise, as much as practicable when you are able, such as riding on horseback. Yes I will promise you that I will not drink one drop of intoxicating Liquior for one month. You heard me express my opinion, in case, I should loose a limb or be, in any way disabled, and I trust you will not hold yourself bound from what has been said. Have you any objections of telling me who and how many you have had to make you such generous offers? Why did you accept mine when you refused others on the same grounds that you rendered objectionable to me, at first? I fear, you have accepted one, who is far less worthy than those preceeding him, and may yet regret it. I hope that such will not be the case. I will leave you to judge that. I will write no more about this at present for I cannot express myself as I would like to in account of being very tired. For several nights past I have had considerable less than natural sleep, being disturbed by the afflicted and distressed victims of Belle Island[63] and to day I have been unusually busy driving the quill hard all day and I hope you will not think I

---

[62]The Maryland Sanitary Fair raised a little over $80,000 for the Union war effort and the medical relief of the wounded. New York and Philadelphia raised over $1 million each. Schoeberlein, "A Fair to Remember," 482. The reference to Ulysses S. Grant and McClellan is unclear. The former had recently been made commander of all Union armies.

[63]Belle Isle, a Confederate prisoner-of-war camp for enlisted men in Richmond. Officers were imprisoned in a tobacco warehouse nicknamed "Libby Prison." Following the raid by Kilpatrick and Dahlgren, and prompted by severe crowding and fears of a prisoner insurrection, Confederate authorities began transferring Union prisoners-of-war out of Richmond at the rate of four hundred a day to the new and soon-to-become infamous prison camp at Andersonville, Georgia. The worst medical cases were sent north, to Baltimore and other places. See William B. Hesseltine, *Civil War Prisons: A Study in War Psychology* (Columbus: Ohio State University Press, 1930), 132.

am growing cold, for I am not. I will probbably feel more in humor for writing next time, and then I will endeavor to write as I feel. Remember that still waters runn deep. Please accept and reply at your earliest opportunity and believe me to be as ever

Your true Friend W. G. Dunn

Office of Coms'y of Musters
8th A. Corps. Baltimore Md.
May 18, 1864

Dear Emma

Having a few leisure moments, I will endeavor to improve them in reply to your last, which I received last evening, and also comply with your request. You need never fear that I have any difficulty in reading your letters, if I did, I do not know what I would do with some of the writing I have to contend with in this Office. Do not think that I am about to reply to your challenge for you will be disappointed if you do. I have been quite busy to day with the pen and I feel but little like writing or doing anything else. Feeling as I do at present, I would rather accept a challeng to meet some one, with the less powerfull weapon, the sword. I think I could use it to a better advantage.

The news are still encouraging, but I have seen nothing of the surrender of Beaureguard. This evenings Clipper[64] reports that Gen. Crook (Union) has had an engagement with Morgan and gained a decisive victory, and captured Gen. Jenkins who is mortaly wounded. Gen. Sigel has met with a (one horse) repulse, loosing six (6) hundred prisoners and four (4) peices of Artillery, small loss.[65] Grant is being largely reinforced and will soon move upon the enemy with such a force that will make the Southern Confederacy tremble. On Sunday evening nearly two (2) hundred of the wounded from the late battle were admitted into Jarvis Hospital, among them, was one of "C" Company of the "Gallant and Bloody Eleaventh." He stated that the regiment went in the fight with two hundred and eighty and came out

---

[64]*Baltimore Clipper*, a former Know-Nothing newspaper, now with Unionist leanings.

[65]The engagement was the Battle of New Market, Virginia, in which Gen. Franz Sigel's force of 5,500 Federals fell back before an advance of a motley Confederate army that included 247 cadets from the Virginia Military Institute.

with less than seventy.[66] Col. McAllister had received two wounds, had two horses killed under him, mounted his third and was still in command of the Regiment.[67] Oh I only wish that I was with them. I would gladly endure the fatigue and sufferings that I might do my part in this final strugle. I cannot feel that I am doing my duty to my country, but still I cannot help it. It is impossible for me to get back with my regiment. Have you heard from John Hardy?

You have led me in a mystery which I cannot fathom and I beg a more detailed explaination. Who are the parties and for what object did they wish to know my address? You may be assured, should I receive a letter or letters bearing ficticious names, I will give them the notice and reply, such letters deserve. From what has come under my observation, I apprehend no mischief and should that be their object, I shall be prepared to meet the worst. Please tell me their names and the circumstances that I may have some grounds on which to defend myself. I will inform you should there be anything said concerning you and I wish you to tell me should you hear my name on the lips of Gossip. Should I receive a letter bearing a ficticious name, I will surely reply in such a way, that a seccond letter would not be required to give the person to understand my opinion of him or her.

I will tell you why I wished to know if Will. Van. Winkle was one of the five when I have a good opportunity to speak with you face to face.

Our Anna has left us, she has gone to housekeeping in Howard Street with her husband. She did not do the cooking but had the oversight of it only. She was quite a good looking young lady with blue eyes and a pleasant and inteligent looking countenance but not so

---

[66]On May 12, 1864, the 11th New Jersey took part in the assault at Spotsylvania Court House and was at the center of some of the heaviest fighting of the war, at the Bloody Angle. In the initial assault, Union forces captured two Confederate generals, Edward Johnson and Marylander George Hume Steuart, whose home in Baltimore had been turned into Jarvis hospital. For fourteen hours, Union and Confederate troops hugged opposite sides of the Confederate breastworks, desperately firing to keep the other side's heads down. The musket fire was so heavy it brought down an oak tree twenty-two inches thick on the Confederate side. According to Marbaker, the 11th New Jersey lost about seventy men, killed and wounded. See Marbaker, *Eleventh New Jersey Volunteers*, 176.

[67]It doubtless seemed that way to this soldier after two savage battles. McAllister had had the horses shot out from under him earlier in the Wilderness fighting. Robertson, *Letters of General Robert McAllister*, 414.

musical. Have you had your hair cut off yet? Do you think of sending
me that picture? Enclosed you will find one of Eld. Rogers letters to
me. I cannot say whether it is the one I promised to let you see or not
as I disremember which it was. It is somewhat soiled by carrying in my
pocket. I received another from him a day or two since. I must close,
hoping that you will answer immediatly. Grant is well and so am I.
Please accept, and Dearest Emma believe me to be as ever, your friend
and Protector

W. G. Dunn

P.S. Address me Box 1203 Baltimore Md. untill farther orders.
You need not be particular about sending me the Waverly for quite
often we have from two to three at once in the Office. I will forward
you the "Companion" tomorrow morning. Do you suppose, your father
will favor our nuptial? I hope you did not understand me to mean
anything by the way I spoke concerning the unanswered one, did you.
I wish that you was here so that we could walk out the pleasant evenings and enjoy a pleasant chat in the Parks.

Walter

Office of Coms'y of Musters
8th Corps. Baltimore Md.
June 1st 1864

My Dear Emma
Could you see me just now, it would be a sufficient appology for
my — which may seem to you — long delay. The past few days of
sickness and fever have given me a Ghostly appearance and I can
assure you that my feelings compare with my looks. Since Sabbath I
have been quite unwell, lost my appetite, and accompanied with a hot
fever, makes me feel miserable. Yesterday and Monday I kept my bed
and would today if prompted by my feelings. The fever has abated
today leaving me very weak indeed, and a plentifull lack of ambition. I
am under medical treatment and hope to recover very soon.
Your last dated May 22nd was received Sabbath evening. It reached
the Hospital Thursday. I think you misunderstood my address or I
made the mistake in giving it to you. I intended to have you address
me Box 1203 (P.O.) Baltimore Md. not to the Hospital for I have

Civil War Baltimore as seen by the Union garrison at Fort Federal Hill overlooking the harbor. (Maryland Historical Society.)

moved from the Hospital and am staying at No. 34 North St. After this please direct to said Box Baltimore, Md. care of Major Wharton.

A young man who I recommended for a clerkship from the Hospital is here with me and we are quartered togather in a room directly over the Office. We have a very pleasant room and only two of us occupying it. I like it much better than Hospital life. We are bound to have gay times, at least you would think so could you step in and see us. (There is a bar room in the same house but it troubles us but little.)

No I would rather you would not read Eld. Rogers letter to those ladies nor let them see it even. I did not wish for anyone to know that you had it, please keep it shady and when you get through with it you may send it back if you please.

There were several questions that you asked me in your last, which I will answer in my next.

My feelings will only allow me to acknowledge the receipt of yours and trusting that you will accept and reply soon I will close.

I am yours truly

W. G. Dunn

P.S. Say nothing about my sickness for I do not wish mother to know anything about it at present. Please excuse this scratching and consider the circumstances under which it is written. I will try and do better next time. I am convalescent.

W. G. Dunn

Chief Mus. & Disbg. Office
8th A. Corps, Baltimore, Md.
June 8, 1864

Dearest Emma

Your letter, bearing the sad tidings of your illness, came to hand this morning. I will not write a long letter this time, as you requested, for my time will not permit.

I am happy to inform you that my health has greatly improved since I wrote you last. I have again resumed my duties and, although not entirely recovered, I am much better than I have been for a week past and do hope that you may have entirely recovered ere this reaches you. I deeply sympathise with you, Dear, in your sufferings and would willingly relieve you by suffering myself were it possible. The greater part of the time of my short existence, I have been blessed with good health, having only enough ill health experience to lead me to exclaim "Oh Disease, deliver me from thy torture." But we must be content and not complain, for whether in ill or good health we must remember that all comes from the hand of an All Wise Providence and our trials and afflictions here are to show us, our frailty and weakness and fit us, more perfectly, for an happy hereafter. May they not be without effect.

I am glad that you have as much kind attention paid you by your many friends. I have the assurance that you will not lack care which is very essential to the comforts of the sick and feeble.

What a vast difference there is, in being sick among friends or among strangers. I have experienced that difference and hope that you may never.

I suppose that Eld. Rogers conversation while with you was very encouraging, was it not. I can almost imagine what he would say on such an occasion. I have not yet answered either of his two last letters, don't you think I deserve being shot?

You stated that you had your hair cut off— do you think it a benefit to your head? I hope it may be. I had mine clipped off short last week.

There are no news of importance to-day. The last we had from Genl. Grant was, "all going on well." Gen. Hunter has possession of Stanton[68] a very important place to the rebels. The papers are flooded with the proceedings of the National Union Convention which met in this City yesterday at 12-M. The renomination of Abram Lincoln for the Presidency is without a doubt.[69] I am just realising the fact that I will be old enough to vote next presidential election, and if soldiers are allowed to vote, Honest Old Abe will receive one additional vote. I have heard several of the Delegates speak, among those I heard, were Gov. Todd, Dr. Dorsy and Gen. Carry of Ohio and Ketchum of Pennsylvania. They all harmonise in sentiment. They are to have a grand Mass Meeting to night in Monument Square about one block from this Office, I think I shall attend.

Evening————

I have just returned from the grand Mass Meeting. The attendance was very large indeed and it was impossible to hear or even see the speaker. When I left, Parson Brownlow[70] had the floor and I judged from appearances that he intended to keep it a while. I never saw so many people togather in Baltimore. The rain is begining to fall quite fast and I think it will scatter the crowd.

Mr. Mackey, (my room mate) is quite ill with a fever to night. I tell him it is his turn this week. I am acting as nurse. He is a very patient, patient.

You wished my opinion as to the propriety or impropriety of

---

[68]Staunton, Virginia, in the Shenandoah Valley.

[69]In the National Union Party's presidential nominating convention, Lincoln received 484 ballots and Gen. Ulysses S. Grant 22. Missouri then changed its vote to make it unanimous. The convention nominated Andrew Johnson of Tennessee for vice president, in place of Hannibal Hamlin.

[70]A vocal Unionist agitator in Tennessee who would later be elected its governor.

keeping an engagement from the knowledge of the parrents I would say that He or She might act their own pleasure about it, either inform their parrents of the exciting fact or keep it a secreet. I think it would be well to let the parrents know should there be any doubts as to their approving of the "Union." No I had no doubts as to any opposition from your father, particularly, I only asked the question for satisfaction. No indeed, you need entertain no fears of my thinking any question you may see fit to ask out of place, for our intimacy will not allow me to think thus. Anytime that you wish information on any point, do not be backward in asking and if I can I will answer and give you the desired information. I harbor no fears of any opposition on the part of my parrents. They were informed through some unknown chanel that we were engaged when I was at home on furlough shortly after being wounded and said nothing opposing it. They knew that I was a frequent visitor at your home, both times when of furlough and also before I enlisted, but never discouraged my visiting you, which they would have done had there been any desire to check our intimacy. I think that they will both favor and encourage our "Union." Act your own pleasure as to informing your parrents, but please make it known to none other. Is this satisfactory and do you understand me? It is nearing time to retire and I must close. Please accept this with much love and Dearest Emma believe me to be your true and promised companion

Walter G. Dunn V.R. Corps

P.S. Please reply as soon as possible for I am anxious to hear from you.

I think that they are getting very eloquent at the meeting. I can hear the speaking from my room.

Baltimore, Md.
June 13, 1864

Dearest Emma

I was not a little supprised (agreeably however) upon drawing the drawer of my writing table this morning, preparing to commence the business of the day, to find in it a letter, bearing the familiar hand writing of one whose letters have long been the source of much pleasure to me, and now, more than ever before, do they furnish that pleasure, whose equal cannot be derived from any other source. Your letter arrived yesterday but I did not get it until this morning as I was not in the Office yesterday after its arrival. I was truly glad to hear from you and thank you kindly for your prompt response. I regret that I cannot answer yours, as promptly.

I am glad that you keep up such good courage in your illness. Judging from the tenor of your letter, you are quite cheerfull. Nothing is better for the sick than keeping up good spirits. I have found it so in my experience among the sick and wounded soldiers. I am glad to hear you express yourself as a possessor of that strong and high hope in Christ; with that to support you, you can brave all the dangers that human nature are subject to and resist all temptations of the wicked one and finaly when your allotted time, here, expires you have the assurance of a blessed hereafter Dear Emma, cling to that hope and as you near the grave, Christ will make it brighter and brighter untill it is no longer a hope, but a blessed reality. I have not ceased to remember you in my prayers, nor will I, feeble as they are, yet God may in his mercy, answer them by a speedy restoration of your health. I claim an interest in yours. My health has greatly improved since last I wrote you. My patient also is quite well. I would like for you to try some of the milk toast I made for him. I would like to hear what you would say about it.

Yesterday P.M. I attended chapel. Text, Matthew 5::17,18.[71] I spent the evening with the family of Col. Johanes (of the 8th Md. Vol. Infy.). Misses, Taylor and Imes came in and we had a very pleasant time indeed. The bell is ringing. I must go and get my beefsteak. If you will say that you will come to tea, you may have a seat beside me, not as they did at Clarks, once on a time).

Evening

I have regained my appetite, and now I can do my part at the table. We have exelent living for soldiers. Our rations are prepared by two experienced cooks. I was weighed a few day since. My weight is all of 150 3/4 lbs. — just my weight one year ago shortly after being wounded, so you may judge how I look now. I would have weighed a considerable more when I was at home last. The weather is very

---

[71]"Think not that I have come to abolish the law and the prophets; I have come not to abolish them but to fulfil them. For truly, I say to you, till heaven and earth pass away, not an iota will pass from the law until all is accomplished."

pleasant. Splendid evenings for walking out. My room mate insisted upon my going out walking with him to night but I will finish this first and walk out afterward. I wish that you were here to walk out with me, occasionally, but wait until this cruel war is over. I must close, requesting an early reply. I hope this will find you much better than when you wrote me. May the richest of Heavens blessings be yours, is the prayer of one who holds you very dear.

Walter G. Dunn V.R. Corps

I received a beautifull bouquet a few evenings since, donor unknown.

Please excuse the mistakes and blurs for I have been driving the quill double quick, all day and my arm is very weary. Walter

Answer soon as convenient and oblige your friend W. G. Dunn

Baltimore, Md.
June 25, 1864

My Very Dear Emma

Your letter, dated June 22nd was received yesterday. Accept my most sincere thanks for the large amount of genuine pleasure it afforded me while reading it and also for you kindness in responding so promptly to my previous letter.

Tis a beautifull Sabbath morning, would I were in New Market long enough to attend church, you cannot imagine how I would enjoy it. It is my desire that the hope that you expressed, in refference to attending church today, may be realised.

The weather is uncomfortably warm, rather inclined to be hot, and that, even is a faint expression of it. I feel as though I would like to get in somebody's Ice house, and there remain untill this Summer is over.

Last evening I had a nice long ride on horseback. It was the first time that I have drawn reins on a horse since the morning after the Leap Year arrangements. Major Wharton wished me to go to Camp Carrol[72] and give Capt. Courtney (of the 11th Regt. Med. Vol. Infy.) some instructions in refference to the muster in of the Regt. I had a

---

[72]An army mustering and training camp in the southwestern portion of the city, on the grounds of the Carroll mansion and near the B&O railroad yards.

splendid horse and as I rode into Camp, I was saluted and addressed several times as Lieutenant and as I dismounted one of the boys came out of the Office and held my horse untill I had finished my biz. I could not had been treated better had I been a Brig. Genl.— but saying nothing about that, for they are new troops and rather green. I had a very pleasant ride and would like to have such business every night. After my return from camp my chum and self went to South Street Wharf to see the Itallian Vessell, "Julia," burn. She caught fire early in the morning and being laden with a large cargo of Coal Oil it was burning nicely. It was a splendid sight after dark. There were seven or eight lives lost besides several burned so badly that their recovery is very doubtfull.

I did not visit the Fort last Sunday evening as I expected. The weather was so very warm that I did not go to Chapel in the afternoon, where we were to meet. I called on some of the ladies in the evening who were to go, and after apologising for my non fullillment of promise, took a very pleasant walk and was made the recipient of a Bouquet and had the promise of another, very soon. The donor is going out in the Country to spend the Summer. I believe that she is at Annapolis now visiting her brother, a Lieut. in the 1st Md. Regt. who is sick in [the] Hospital. I had a very pressing invitation to accompany her there, but could not see the go.

My roommate has said but little about taking a Commission in a colored Regt. of late. He is opposed to having colored troops at all and when I ask him why he is so anxious for a position among them, he keeps still. The last he told me was that he was very anxious to go and was waiting on my decision, which I have not yet made. I should judge from what you said, that you rather oppose it, am I right in understanding you thus. I know I would meet a great deal of opposition on the part of Mother. If I decide in favor, she shall not know it for a while, but I hardly think I shall make such a decision at present. I shall wait and see the result of this Campaign, if successfull, I shall give it up entirely, but if Grant is defeated which will prolong the war for some time longer, I shall be very apt to decide in favor. I'll lay the subject on the table for the present.

I did not mean to speak either very delicately or very plain upon the subject, regarding that request. I wished to express my desire with as few words as possible and not be obscure to you. I heartily approve of your proceedings in the case. I think we perfectly understand each other. If there is anything obscure to you make it known and I will endeavor to enlighten you.

Your request, regarding your promise shall be complied with, to the utmost and I beg your forgiveness for useing it as I did. We have so many strangers to deal with in the Office, that a promise or a statement is considered worthless, without it is given under oath. Do not understand that to be necessary in this case for I consider your word as good as an oath and will endeavor to remember, when I am writing to you that our correspondence is of a Civil, not a military character. (Carried forward to sheet No. 2)

Evening
While writing you this morning I received orders to report to Jarvis Hospital to meet a Board of Officers, concurred to investigate and correct an error in my Descriptive List and as that prevented me from finishing this, then, I will now add a few words before mailing.

One year ago to night, at this time, if I mistake not, I was in your company. Do you remember it? My chum and myself have just returned from taking our evening walk. This evening we went out Gay St. to the Market to see the pretty Market "Girls" please do not get jealous and there we had lots of cherries and Ice cream. Do you remember the "Cherry pit Battle" which was fought, by two powerfull opponents, without a decided victory on either side, "on or about the 20th of June 1863"? I was reminded of it to night while eating cherries. The Fourth of July is fast nearing. I have not yet decided where or how I will spend it. I would advise you (had you asked my advise) not to take any part in a Fair or anything of the kind, under the existing circumstances, viz, that you have ill health and not able to stand the excitement.

In your last letter you signed yourself thus "Mary E. Randolph." I believe that requests are now in order, if so I would request that when you write to me, you sign your letters by the more euphonious and sweet name, of "Emma," think you I am not getting particular? Such is my style.

If those reports concerning Eld. R. are founded on facts, I very much disapprove of his proceedings. Please keep me posted as well as you can.

One of our Clerks (a citizen) has this evening, received the saddening news that his only son was killed in an engagement before Petersburg. He had served nearly three years and reenlisted as a Vet. Vol. The father takes it very hard.

You asked had I ever any inclinations to leave the Sabbath. No I have not. I believe it to be the day appointed by God and shall endeavor to observe it, as such. I must close and retire. It is already quite late. Please excuse the many imperfections for the heat makes my arm very nervous, accept; and reply at your earliest convenience.

In much love, I am still your most Sincere Friend, and future Companion.

Walter G. Dunn   V.R. Corps

Plainfield, New Jersey, on the eve of the Civil War. Firemen parade down Front Street in 1859. (*The [Bridgewater, N.J.] Courier-News.*)

Part II: "Sitting by the Cool Window"

Early in July 1864, Robert E. Lee sent General Jubal A. Early and a small Confederate army north, down the Shenandoah Valley and into Maryland with the intention of threatening Washington and Baltimore. Part of the original plan was to capture the prison camp at Point Lookout, releasing and arming twenty thousand Confederates held there. When swift Union reaction made that maneuver impractical, Early settled for a thorough disruption of communications and a threatening march on Washington. Confederate cavalry swept north around Baltimore, cutting railroad lines and causing a mild panic but accomplishing little other than burning the governor's house. The "invasion" passed quickly, leaving as one of its few casualties the ashes of Emma Randolph's letters written during 1863.

Emma's earliest surviving letters show just how serious that loss was. In her tiny, precise hand, looking sometimes "like a crab going to war," as her impish sister jested, the other side of Civil War life comes to light. This was the war at home. The men Emma knew balanced the urge to volunteer—spurred by the loss of friends and brothers, by guilt, and by the taunts of young women—against the grim reality of the army. Some enlisted. Others looked for ways around the draft. Women feared for husbands and lovers in the army. Some grieved when the dreaded message arrived. Some took solace in their churches, others were driven away.

For Emma herself, life in New Jersey revolved around her large family in Plainfield, the Seventh Day Baptist Church in New Market—services, Sabbath School, fund-raising events—and the normal busy round of family visits, trips to the beach, and ice cream socials. Even without reminders from the eloquent and strong-willed Reverend Lester Courtland Rogers, Emma knew that life was perilous and short. Each spring she contracted a serious illness in her lungs, and she suffered frequently from chronic headaches. Medical care was primitive, the doctor to be avoided whenever possible.

Then, too, her attention increasingly turned to Baltimore.

"Dear"

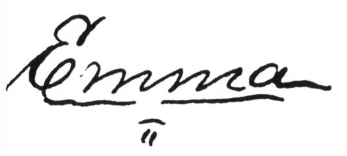

Baltimore, Md.
July 14, 1864

My Dear Emma

Yours of July 6th was duly received, after several days of disappointment. Oweing to an unexpected visit to the suburbs of this City by a party of "Harry Gilmors raiders"[1] and circumstances connected therewith, I have been unable to write you before. Do not consider the object of my delay to cancel yours, . . . as I pardoned you for your delay, thus do I hope to be pardoned.

This City has been in a very critical condition, surrounded as it has

---

[1]Colonel Harry Gilmor, of a distinguished Baltimore family, led a band of Confederate "irregular" cavalry. On July 5, 1864, he was part of an "invading army" under the command of Jubal Early that crossed the Potomac and threatened Washington. On July 9, Early encountered a Union force hastily assembled by General Lew Wallace at the Monocacy River, near Frederick, and defeated it. As elements of the federal Army of the Potomac rushed northward from Virginia to defend the capital, Confederate cavalry under the command of Bradley T. Johnson broke off and began cutting railroad lines north of Baltimore. Johnson sent Gilmor on a march to cut the Philadelphia, Wilmington and Baltimore Railroad northeast of the city, which Gilmor managed to do after stopping at his Baltimore County home along the way. After menacing the capital for two days, Early withdrew to Virginia on the fourteenth. For a detailed account of the operation, see B. F. Cooling, *Jubal Early's Raid on Washington, 1864* (Baltimore: The Nautical and Aviation Publishing Company, 1989).

been with bands of lawless robbers,[2] when it was defenceless and its mail and rail communications all cut off from the outter world. For several days past the City has been the scene of the most intense excitement, but now is quiet and I think all danger over as the enemy is reported retreating toward the Potomac. On Sabbath evening Brig. Genl. Lockwood, Comdg the "Civil Forces" for the defence of the City, established his Head Quarters in our Office and a good portion of the time since the street in front has been crowded with troops. It would make you laugh to see the awkward appearance of some of the "Civil Forces" that have been daily reporting here. Yesterday the "Negros" reported by "thousands," armed with picks and spades for throwing up fortifications. Last evening at 5 o'clock the "Militia" was ordered out. The order was for all loyal men to turn out and the disloyal to leave the City. A large number have already reported to these "Head Quarters" and gone out to the front. It will take about five times as many such soldiers, as it would of Veterans to guard the City, for in several instances, a single volley of musketry has broken and made them run.[3] The raiders burned Gov. Bradfords house,[4] a short distance from the City, and I do not see why they did not enter the city, as there was nothing to prevent them. It is useless for me to write more on this subject as you will get all the particulars in the New York papers. I have been out to the "front" only once. I volunteered to take the "countersign" to Forts No. 6 & 7[5] for one of the "Orderlies" if he would let me have his horse, which he appeared as willing to do as I was to go. I had a gay ride over hills and ravines and enjoyed it heartily. I have been

---

[2]The reference to "lawless robbers" is aimed at Gilmor, whose troops had acquired a reputation for brigandage after robbing a train and its passengers in the Shenandoah. See Kevin Conley Ruffner, "'More Trouble than a Brigade': Harry Gilmor's 2d Maryland Cavalry in the Shenandoah Valley," *Maryland Historical Magazine*, 89 (1994): 389–412.

[3]Walter is probably referring to the Battle of Monocacy, where raw Union troops acquitted themselves reasonably well in a holding action against seasoned Confederate veterans. He does not refer to the fact that in Washington military officials believed they could defend the city with invalids and hundred-day men.

[4]Bradley Johnson burned the house of Maryland Governor Augustus Bradford, a few miles north of Baltimore, in retaliation for the Federals' burning the house of the Virginia governor in Lexington before rejoining Early outside Washington.

[5]The forts surrounding Baltimore were numbered.

employed as clerk in the Adjt. Genls. Office, consequently have not seen fight. I volunteered to go out to the front several times, but one of the Staff Officers told me, my services would be of more advantage in the Office, he being my superior, I obeyed him. I am glad to learn that you had such a fine time on the Fourth. The history of my doings on that day would differ greatly from yours. In answer to your question, the Baltimorians do celebrate it as a day of independence. In the morning my chum and myself took a walk to see what was going on in the City. Feeling quite ill after dinner I went to bed and slept soundly untill supper time, after which I went to Holliday St. Square, and saw a fine display of Fireworks, thus did I spend the Eighty-Eighth birthday of our National Independence. I declined an invitation to visit "Druid Hill Park"[6] on the Fourth with a party of ladies and gents and on Friday I received a note of invitation from the same party to visit the Park that evening, but I did not receive the note untill after the hour appointed for meeting at the depot, and as a matter of course I could not go, such is my luck. I have accepted the invitation to go out in the country. I expect to go on Sabbath afternoon and return Tuesday, as soon as the raiders relieve us of their non-welcomed presence. I wish that you were here to go with me but as that is impossible I will wait untill this war is over and then if our lives are spared we will have some pleasant trips togather. Please inform me who "Aunt Em" and "Cousin Hannah" are. You stated that you had been weighed, what is your weight?

I think that Plainfield must be past all redemption when the ladies are obliged to make their "beaux" from their own sex. I think, for the benefit of Plainfield and the people of N. Jersey in general, that it would be a nice plan for the State authorities to call home some of their Soldiers, I mean those who belong to the "Veteran Reserve (Invalid) Corps" what think you of it? If you are about to turn "beaux" I will know where to get one when I come home.

I rejoice to learn that Dannie Ayres, before his death, gave good evidence of his acceptance by "God," what a great amount of satisfaction it must be to his friends. I sympathise with you for the loss of your friend, Mr. Force.[7] It must cause sad thoughts when you reflect on the

---

[6]A magnificent park north of the city that had opened in 1859.

[7]Possibly a relative of Emma's cousin, Susie Force, who would marry Lew Dunn, another of Emma's cousins, in March 1865.

past, that you have been accused of being the cause of his enlisting, which some would say was the cause of his death.[8] Susie and your cousin Lew Dunn are very intimate; are they not?

I have heard nothing about Tom Titsworth and Will Smith being captured. I cannot credit it.

I suppose that Hattie Dunn[9] has returned from Alfred Center[10] has she not? It is reported in this City that there is a "great riot" in New York City.[11] I have not seen a New York paper since the 10th, have you heard anything concerning it? I have already exhausted the time allotted for the writing of this letter and must close by asking you to excuse all imperfections in general for I have written this the way that the 11th Regt. Infy. Md. Vols. retreated at the Battle of Monocacy[12] a few days since, (double quick was no name for it). Please answer immediately and oblige one who holds you very dear and is anxiously awaiting your answer.

With much love, I am yours,
W. G. Dunn

N.J.
Plainfield Union Co
July 18th 1864

My verry Dear Walter

I have just finished reading yours of the 14th which I received

---

[8]From the beginning of the war, women played a prominent role in inducing men to enlist in the army. Although community pride and competition with other towns boosted recruiting, women through encouragement, scorn, and what Gerald F. Linderman calls "sexual intimidation" drove men to war. See Linderman, *Embattled Courage: The Experience of Combat in the American Civil War* (New York: The Free Press, 1987), chap. 80. Embittered Union veteran Ambrose Bierce wrote scathingly of their effect in his chilling short story, "Killed at Resaca."

[9]Harriet M. Dunn, of Plainfield, attended Alfred University from 1862 until 1865.

[10]Alfred University.

[11]The report was erroneous.

[12]The 11th Maryland Infantry was a one-hundred-day regiment mustered in on June 16, 1864, in Baltimore. Thrown into the Battle of Monocacy against a seasoned Confederate army under Jubal Early, they became part of the general Union rout as Federal forces fled all the way from Monocacy to Ellicott's Mills.

about 7 this evening for the third time, and agreeable to request "answer immediately" have seated myself to have a nice little chat with you, through the medium of the pen. To be candid I would much rather *you* would *surprise* me (as I dreamed last night you did). I should like it better. But as like Emma (ha hum) going in the country with you and your friend is an impossibility, we will let present circumstances rule, and have high hopes for the future life and health permiting shall we not?

This is my second attempt to write. Tis about nine (9) O'clock. Maggie dear Gracie and Jennie[13] has had a romp in my room, and it was impossible for me to accomplish any thing while they were having such a frolic. Maggie is so full of mischief. Jennie has learned her to say Mont Harrie Lew and last but not least Halt for she does not in her broken language use the letters W. and S. It is laughable to hear her pronounce some words, Walt and Shell particularly. Gracie and Maggie's good night kisses are still warm upon my lips and they (after Jennie had made Maggie say "Emma say somthing bout me") has all retired, leaving me *all alone*, but my sweetheart is nary with me. I can not write much to night, as I do not feel as well as usual. I fear that I can not *half* repay you for the amount of pleasure your letter was the means of affording me. My head aches worse than it has since my illness. Oh! for the "gentle hands." They would be welcome now I assure you "Dear" but I will do my best to interest you. If I do not succeed, you may take the will for the deed — will you?

Let me tell you firstly that I have been verry much excited lest those "pesky raiders" as Granpa calls them should take Walt prisoner, but I see he is not, do not know if his heart will be if he goes out in the country retreating with one of the pretty Baltimore Ladies. Shall want you to tell me how you enjoy yourself and what kind of a place it is you go to if it is not to tedious. I hope you will have a gay time. One week ago Sabbath day your sister Mollie came home with me from church. In the evening Lew came out and I accompanied them home. Our folks expecting to come down and spend a part of Sunday with us at

---

[13]Emma's sisters. Jennie was born in 1847. Maggie was born on September 5, 1861 and would die, unmarried, in 1888. Grace "Gracie" Fitz Randolph was born on May 3, 1863, the day Walter was wounded. She later married Isaac Harris. They had a son, Walter R. Harris, who gave Walter's and Emma's letters to Ruth Bailey about 1948.

your house with Eld. Rogers family. Oh! I shall never forget that visit to
"your home." You would liked to have been with us, would you not.
Cousin Joel and Lew[14] were busy in the Hay field in front of your house
so your Father said "the women would entertain the dominic." Instead
of that he entertained us nicly. He — Eld R. rather got the best of me.
Mary said somthing as though she would like to live in New Market or
Plainfield. "Emma dont you think that Mary has a verry pleasant home
indeed?" asked Eld. "Yes. A verry quiet pleasant home" I answered.
"You think that you could live in a place like this so far from friends
and be happy do you?" he asked again. Oh certainly I should like a
change I said, not seeing what he meant. "Well, then" he said and his
eyes sparkled, I think it would be a verry good change for Mary to take
Emma's brother and Emma one of Mary's brothers. They had quite a
laugh at my expense, Aunt Sallie Randolph[15] included since I spent the
day with Eld. Rogers at your home. I love him better still. Last Sabbath
twas communion at N[ew] M[arket]. Eld. Rogers preached the first
time since he fell, text — Hebrews 8th Cpt. part of 9th verse. Eld.
Bailey[16] has had the nuralegia and could not preach. By the way Eld. B.
has resigned his ministerial charges and will not wait upon them
longer than Oct. The most part of the community are quite thankfull
that he did so.

I sympathize with you to think that you did not get your note in
time to meet the part[y] at the depot on the 4th. I'm sorry you was sick
in the afternoon. I guess you walked to far with your chum. What kind
of a looking "Soger" is he? Has he a nice moustache? By the way are
you sporting a moustache? One reason you are a favorite of the Lady
your going in the country with! I think you do not have "white gloves"
as you did one time when you wrote me, to "cultivate your
musentonchet." [?] If you have any "Carte de visite"[17] taken please
remember "your Amme."

---

[14]Walter's father, Joel A. Dunn, and brother Lewis.

[15]Emma's aunt.

[16]Elder James Bailey (1813–1892) was the pastor of the Plainfield Seventh
Day Baptist Church from 1853 until 1864. In that year he "closed his labors
with the church at Plainfield" and went to Alfred Center with his wife and two
children, then to Walworth, Wisconsin.

[17]A visiting card, literally a card presented when calling on someone.
They generally contained a photograph.

Rev. Lester Courtland Rogers,
leader of the Seventh Day Baptist
Church in New Market, N.J.
(Seventh Day Baptist Historical
Society.)

You want me to inform you who Aunt Em and Cousin Hannah are. Well now, what a question, I'd tell you. Aunt Em is Aunt Em, Father's sister.[18] Cousin Hannah is Mother's neice. Ha ha, that is kinda funny too. I think I hear you say I reckon so too, how to speak plain. I do not remember how I spoke of said persons, please enlighten me. I write so much nonsense that I do not wonder you what some of it means but realy I cannot call it to mind. It seems an age since I wrote one or received one from your own Dear self, but as I have answered immediately I hope you will do the same. May I look for one Sabbath Eve? Pa has been to the city of New York today and sayes all is quiet. No signs of a riot. I hope there won't be any!

You asked my weight. It is 128. The friday before I was taken sick, sunday, my weight was one hundred thirty-seven and a quarter pounds. The second time I was up town during my convalescence, I weighed 120. You see I'm gaining what I lost. Father thinks I will not gain my good looks untill I let my hair grow out, and do it up in the old fashioned way. I think about keeping it cut off for about 3 years, what think you on this subject? My cousins are verry anxious for me to have my

---

[18]Aunt Mary Randolph, born in 1838, was the sister of Emma's father, Barzilla J. Randolph.

"humbly face" printed on some cards. I think if I have any taken it will be a miniature and for miself to look upon when my hair has gone grey.

Yes I do think it would be advisable to call home some of Veteran Reserves, more especialy the "Invalid" weak armed ones. Yes you know where there was a good "beaux" when you come home from the war. But wether you will find me here or not is to be decided for the Ladies tell me I make a good one. Some of the charming ones may propose. It's Leap year and as I have not latly been in the habit of saying no to requests. I do not know what may happen but I guess your tired of this. The "Ladies" have all returned from A[lfred] C[enter]. Hattie is looking quite well, and so is Judson[19] and Wardner[20] Titsworth. Jennie has been talking in her sleep. She said she did not know what time she would die. I thought perhaps her dream was not pleasant, so I woke her. Did you dream when you was sleeping on the fo[u]rth? Several times I wondered where you was, but no answer. Did you go and take dinner with that Lady last Sunday? I was eating chicken in *my old place* at your *Father's right hand.* Hope you enjoyed your dinner as well as I did mine. I will stop. Please write soon and now good night. May angels guard you while you sleep, safe till the morning light. Then I have faith to believe that our heavenly Father will guide you and answer the prayers for your safe return "To those who love you truly and" dearly tis my prayer. Dearest Walter, remember me as yours with *everlasting Love* Till *Death*

Emma

34 North St. Balto. Md.
11 P.M. July 21st 1864

My Truly "Dear" Emma

Yours of the 18th inst. was duly and gladly received.

You asked if you might look for an answer, Sabbath night, certainly

---

[19]A. Judson Titsworth, of New Market, attended Alfred University throughout the war.

[20]Wardner Carpenter Titsworth was born in 1848, the eighth child of Isaac Dunham and Hannah Ann (Sheppard) Titsworth. He was a member of the New Market Seventh Day Baptist Church and attended Alfred University from 1863 until 1866. In 1877 he accepted a pastorate at the Farina, Illinois, Seventh Day Baptist Church, and in 1883 became the pastor of the First Seventh Day Baptist Church in Alfred, New York.

you may look, but I cannot say that will not be disappointed. I will do all that lies in my limited power in order that you may receive it according to request. Please accept my thanks for your prompt reply and if convenient, be full as prompt in replying to this one.

If you fear that your letters fail to interest me, I think I have ample reason to fear the same on my part: Had your letters failed of that once the greatest object of my correspondence, I would have discontinued it long since. Believe me "Dear," that your letters are very interesting and pay me well for writing you- when they fail to do that I will inform you. Please, in the future, let me not hear you say anything more upon that subject neither entertain any fears of the kind.

You need not "dream of being supprised" for should such happen, I would be as much supprised as yourself. Do you remember what I said when at home last March that I had no desire to come home again untill I came home, there to remain. Yes, we will let "present circumstance" rule, for my part, I do not see how we can avoid it.

I have just returned from President St. Depot,[21] where I went with my chum who has received a furlough this P.M. and is now on his way to Catskill N.Y. where his parrents and friends reside. He has gone for fifteen days and how I will miss him for his departure was so unexpected and sudden, both to himself and me. At noon to day he had not the least idea of going. Time worketh miracles. In answer to your question, he is quite a good looking sort of a fellow, minus a moustache although two years my senior. I formed his acquaintance in February, since then him and I have been very intimate. I recommend him for a clerkship in our office and obtained an order to that effect. He has been my roommate since May last, during which time we have spent many happy hours togather. Although we are very intimate and warm friends, yet politically he is my foe. I think you would laugh to hear some of our arguments on some few subjects that we differ most upon.

Those pesky raiders have left "My Maryland"[22] and all is quiet once

---

[21]The Baltimore terminus for the Philadelphia, Wilmington, and Baltimore Railroad. It was also the place from which, in April 1861, the 6th Massachusetts Volunteer Militia began its journey across the city that resulted in a substantial riot and the first bloodshed of the Civil War.

[22]The reference is to the song by James Ryder Randall, written in 1861 and popular in the Confederacy, which excoriated the government for coercing Maryland to remain in the Union.

more. The raid is proving itself to be a complete failure. Their main object was to plunder which our forces are daily compelling them to burn and give up.[23] By the time they reach Richmond they will have but very little more if as much as when they started besides an army demoralised by long and continued marches. The news of to day are not important. There seems to be a general lull in Military affairs at present. From Petersburg we have the usual news viz. all quiet except occasional Artillery duels at long range and exchanging of shots by the Sharpshooters.[24] From Georgia the news are such as lead us to expect more and better in a few days. What the result may be I cannot say, but I have a strong faith in the ultimate capture of Richmond, Petersburg, and Atlanta.[25]

You said in your last that you had not been in the habit of saying no to "requests made to you." May I ask if that is the reason you replied in the affirmative to a request I made you, on or about the 13th day of April last?

I would have liked to have been home very much when you were visiting at Fathers house but still I think it was better as it was, for if you had insisted upon having my place at the table there would certainly have been some quarreling—and as I am your superior in strength you would have to yield, but as it was you ate your dinner in peace and quiet. I should not object to a chicken dinner myself just now. It has been a long time since I saw a chicken even. But why is it that you never come to Fathers house when I am at home? You are not afraid of me are you? Although I bear the name of a soldier, I am perfectly harmless, bear that in mind will you.

---

[23]The object of the Confederate raid of 1864 was to draw Union troops away from Lee's front. Additionally, Confederates had hatched a plan to march around Washington and liberate twenty thousand Confederate prisoners held at Point Lookout in southern Maryland, a plan they were forced to abandon.

[24]Walter's former commander, Robert McAllister, might have disagreed. From the Petersburg trenches he wrote his wife, "We have but little amusement here. In fact, we have been so hard worked that until now we had neither time nor inclination to be funny." See Robertson, *Letters of General Robert McAllister,* 467.

[25]On July 17, John Bell Hood replaced Joseph E. Johnston as commander of Confederate forces around Atlanta. Whereas Johnston had conducted a careful defensive strategy, Hood immediately took the offensive. On July 20 he suffered a repulse at Peachtree Creek.

I am glad to hear that you are gaining flesh so rapidly. If you continue at that rate, you will soon regain all that you lost. My weight is 154 lbs. just what it was at Alfred Center with the addition of a heavy beard.

I thought your Aunt Em lived in New Brooklyn with her Father. Is Daniel R. and his wife on the farm yet? I feel anxious to get on a farm again. When I come home I will make a great revolution in affairs on the farm. I will change every thing and begin my farming career on a new basis. But I have already written more than I intended, such as it is and now by asking you to excuse all imperfections and accept and reply at your earliest convenience, I will drop the curtain of silence untill I hear from you again. Untill then remember me as yours with long and abiding love.

W. G. Dunn
V.R.Corps
"Good night"

Plainfield Union Co N.J.
July 24, 1864

My Verry "Dear" Walt

Yours of the 21st was received Sabbath afternoon instead of evening. Many thanks for your kindness in complying with my "perhaps to[o] urgent request." I was truly right glad to see your hand writing on the envelope when Eugene gave me it, and told me I will if I read it and for the identification of the company. Pa Ma Maggie Grace David R.[26] and his wife Aunt Marys brother and myself was the company that came to Jerseys[27] spending the afternoon. After reading your verry interesting letter I felt just like sitting down and answering immediatly, and started for my hat but they would not hear me to coming home. I remained untill after supper. I came home about dusk and went out riding, went down to New Market to attend the young peoples prayer meeting held at Eld Rogers. Just as Mr. Codington helped me to alight or attempted to the pony got frightened and came near upsetting me. And then perhaps you would not have "This

---

[26]David Rogers.

[27]Jersey Ann Randolph, Emma's older sister, was born in 1840. She married Eugene Runyon on August 6, 1863, and on December 19, 1864, they had a son, Walter Grant Runyon. Jersey died in 1897.

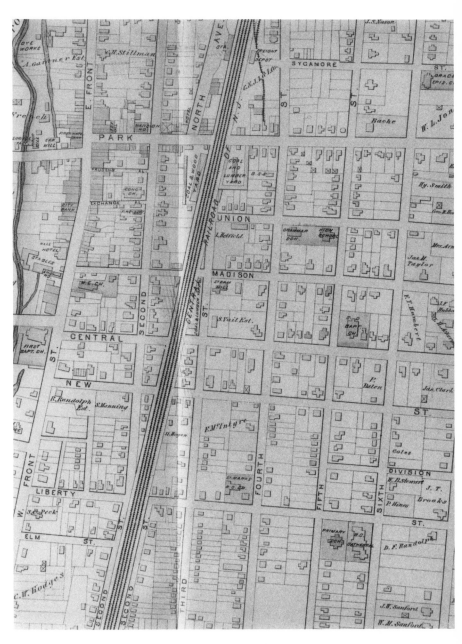

Period map of Plainfield. (Courtesy, Alexander Library, Special Collections, Rutgers University.)

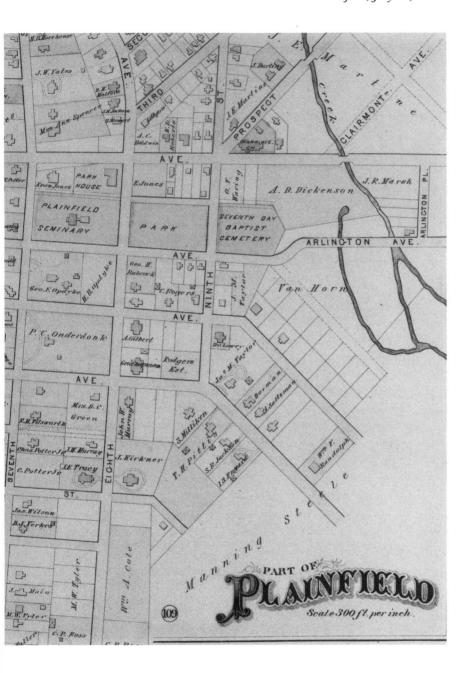

PART OF
PLAINFIELD
Scale 300 ft. per inch.

Emma" to love. Dont you say "its a pity it hadnt." It was some twenty minutes before he was able to quiet the animal enough for me to reach the ground. We were detained so long a time that I did not go in the house but sit on the "stoop" untill the meeting ended. We could hear all that was said, and verry interesting time we had too. Judson Titsworth did speak verry highly of those who love the sweet privelege of the Sabbath and the prayer meeting. The little band who are going from our Church were most earnestly prayed for "and that peace might reign over us and our loved ones return to us as better men and faithful Christians."[28] I have not attended any of the meetings before that evening but shall endeavor to in the future.

Dearest Walt pray for the prayer meetings as well as for your "friend Em" will you? Coming home we stoped at cousin Aurelias[29] and Vermont[30] out on the "Piazza.". . . While we were there the meeting folks passed and we drove verry slow or rather I did, and by the time the Titsworths family were at the house we reached their gate. I stoped and serenaded Jud sing[ing] "Rock me to sleep Mother" and "Gone to the War." They all came out and asked us to come in but biding Jud a hearty "Good Night" I drove on home to Plainfield, got some Ice Cream, serenaded Dave and Sallie[31] and then came home. This morning Aaron Clark the young man who lived with us last winter came to see us. I went down to let him in and accosted him in my old way and not he said untill I smiled and said "How are you?" Hardly did he know me. He thinks I'm "greatly changed." I'd not think so. What is your opinion on the subject?

This afternoon we have been down to Eld Rogers spending the afternoon. Oh we had a verry pleasant visit indeed. You cannot imagin what a nice time we did have, "but the longest day will have an end" and the shortest one to[o], and the time was came for us to return

---

[28]Probably a reference to those who had gone into the army. Friends and families regarded army service as an experience that strengthened character but worried lest the soldiers pick up bad habits such as drinking, gambling, etc. See Linderman, *Embattled Courage,* 87–89.

[29]Aurelia J. Ayres (b. November 6, 1846), married Walter's brother, Lewis C. Dunn. She was Emma's cousin.

[30]Vermont Fitz Randolph, born January 20, 1844, would marry Emma's sister Jennie soon after the war.

[31]Friends Dave and Sallie Johnson.

home. Maggie, Lester and Dannie had fine times, as well as the old
folks. Mrs Rogers Mother is at the parsonage helping Mrs Rogers get
ready for her journey west. I do not think she takes after her Mother in
the least, perhaps the reason I cannot see a resemblence is because
I'm not acquainted with Dick Westcott. I was verry anxious to understand a remark made by Kizzie Potter,[32] and so [asked] Eld R. who she
meant, after telling me he did not understand either. "Emma where
did you hear her speak of it"? he asked. He caught me nicly so I owned
up. He said he heard a horse making a time, and was going to come
out but he did not hear anyone scream, and he did not think it worth
while untill he heard a noise. He spoke rather reprovingly to me and
told me to bring him in next time. But Good night.

Second Edition Monday Eve
　　Yes Dear Walt I do remember what you said when was at home the
last time. Although I'd like to see you again so much yet I would much
rather have you stay for good when you do come. And it will suit me
just as well and better should the war end next fall as a year from now.
It would not [disconcert] you in the least should you have the chance
to [illegible] your family on a new [illegible] farmer! Oh I shall have
fun when those new fangled farming operations get under headway
laughing at you. I think it will be much more amusing than listening to
[to]days discussion on the everlasting topic "Politics" although it must
be quite amusing to hear a young Walter talk on said subject. I for one
can tell how interesting he can converse and write on the subject.
Dont I Emma?
　　No siree I am not afraid of you if you weigh 154 lbs. and wear a
"heavy beard." Nary a once. But I'll tell you what I would do should
you ever interfere with my place at your fathers house at the table. I
would be tempted to "smack you in the mouth" as Emma Bryant[33] says,
and ask your Mother to make you mind. Now I suppose you say I could
not accomplish as much but let me tell you your father told me he
likes to have me sit by him and I think he would let the youngest have
their way. Will you bear this in mind! So it has been a long time since
you seen a chicken even. May I be pardoned if I ask when you have

---

[32]Keziah D. Titsworth married W. Riley Potter, who was in the army.
[33]A cousin living in Newark.

seen one uneven! The verry best reason in the world why I cant go to
your Fathers [a small sketch of the house is in place of the word] when
you are home just because you never asked me. Now I'd say that [is] a
good answer! And is not that a perfect image of your home! You did
not know I was taking lessons in sketching, did you? Not I either but
do not laugh at it to much.

I'm glad to hear you express a wish to get on a farm again but
never mind.

Yes Uncle Dan and Aunt Mary[34] remain on the farm. Uncle Dan
takes the [illegible] I thought I had mentioned in my letters previous
to the one I wrote just after the fo[u]rth of August Ems moving up to
Plainfield and taking [up] dressmaking. She with cousin Julia live up
in the house just the other side of Laign Hotel.[35] She has small but
verry nice rooms and gets along finely. They were here with Uncle Dan
and wife, Willis [?] Gail [?] Jersey and Em [?] was over and we had an
Ice cream supper. Ollie is quite a good hand at making cream and we
had good luck friday evening.

Ollie has gone to Elisabeth City to pay the money down that
exempts him from this draft only. We were much surprised to hear he
was drafted but he will never go he says no matter if he is drafted
again.[36] I hope and trust he will get along all right to day for I would
tremble for him should he be forced into the army. But I hope he will
not be. I could give him up willingly did he volunteer but being
drafted is diferent. I'll keep out of it.[37]

Here I am on the last side of my paper and was hardly aware of the
fact. I will answer one more question, then stop this scribling.

Now you "naughty boy" do you suppose it would be right for me to

---

[34]Probably Daniel Fitz Randolph (1830–1910), Emma's father's brother,
who married Mary Lucretia Randolph on June 7, 1864. Emma also had an
Aunt Mary Randolph, her father's sister, born in 1838.

[35]Laign's Hotel, at Front Street and Madison Avenue in Plainfield, was
built in 1828 and owned by John Laign. It was a village meeting place and a
popular hostelry for travelers on the Old York Road.

[36]On July 18, 1864, Lincoln had called for another 500,000 men. Ollie,
like a great many of those subject to the draft, apparently paid the $300
commutation fee, thus buying exemption.

[37]By 1864, after the slaughter of Grant's summer campaign in the
Wilderness, Spotsylvania, and Cold Harbor, Northern war fervor ebbed
seriously, as reflected in Emma's remark.

answer diferently from what I meant, when I answered such a request as you asked of me on the 8th of April last! No Dearest Friend, my own heart answered. And believe me Walt to be candid in what I say. I studied my feelings toward you carfully before giving answer, for I think it is something that should not be lightly broken, and easily laid aside, and rudly as Eld R. has served Louise.[38] I see her Sabbath evening walked down main str[eet]. I was teasing her about Lew for I heard he called there not long since, but her sad and weary manner checked me. Louise is looking verry verry bad indeed. The doctor has forbid her sewing, but I do not think the Doct. can cure the disease that is [gnawing] at her heart. But I hope and pray that the bruised reed will not break but will rise and shine and be the means of much good, but I must close. Hoping you will excuse all mistakes and answer as soon as possible and remember as still your own true and still loving

Emma Randolph

N.B. Jennie and you just balance weights — remarkable.

34 North St. Balto. Md.
July 31, 1864

Dear Emma

I am in receipt of yours of the 24th inst. which arrived duly. I would gladly comply with your request if it was in my power, but as it is impossible, I trust that you will accept this tardy letter and "take the will for the deed" will you not?

The past few days our business has been more than usual, my time being nearly occupied in the Office, togather with the uncomfortableness of the weather, which has been very warm, indeed, is the reason I write you under this date.

The fear of another invasion by the "Johnnies" is creating quite an excitement in this City. It is reported and I doubt it not, that the "rebels" occupy Chambersburg Pa. with a large force.[39] It is not believed that they can remain there long, and I think that they will give

---

[38]Probably Louise Johnson, engaged to Mr. Miller, a widower.

[39]Confederate cavalry under the command of John McCausland demanded a ransom of $100,000 in gold or $500,000 in currency from the town of Chambersburg. When it was not forthcoming they burned it in retaliation for the depredations of Union forces in the Shenandoah.

Tier's Pond, a popular recreation spot, where Emma sometimes went for ice cream. (Plainfield Public Library.)

us a call on their return. I hope that they will, for I think they will receive a "warm reception," even if we could not keep them out of the city, which they could not hold if they should capture it. During the late raid, a very small force could have taken this City — and even now I do not think that they would meet much opposition for all the troops defending it are new and green and what are they to contend with — the "Veterans of Seserhia"? This City is better able to repulse a naval attack than an attack by land. Time will tell the result.

"Sitting out on the Stoop" is the way that you attend Prayer Meetings is it? I judge that you do not profit much by such attendance. I would advise you in the future when you go to church or Prayer meetings that you drive a trusty horse, such as "Old Pat." I am glad to know that your health permits you to enjoy yourself as well, as the tenor of your letter indicates. I hope you may prove successfull in your endeavors to attend prayer meetings in the future. I think that much good originates from, and would earnestly reccommend a regular attendance of such places.

If your Sketch represents fathers house as it now is, I say that time has wrought a very great change in it since I last saw it. No, I should judge that you are not taking lessons in Sketching or penciling, by your examples, or otherwise you are not very proficient in the branch.

I have just one year from today to serve my "Good Old Uncle Samuel," that is not very long is it. I suppose that you think I am like some of the Thirty-day men, when they had served one day, said that they "only had twenty-nine more." Two years as a soldier and never in the Guard House. I must get in this year in order that I may experience the full life of a soldier.

While conversing with Major Wharton a few days since I asked him if it would be convenient for me to go home on furlough about the 1st of October, he replied, "certainly," I would rather you would go now, for we are not as busy now as we will be then. I received a letter from my "Chum" since he reached home, and he writes of having such "pleasant times," that it has almost made me wish that I was home. My mind has changed some in reference to a furlough since I received his letter. I have no particular desire to go home now, for I think it will be pleasanter when the fruit is ripe and the weather cooler. I will wait untill the "busy time" is over which will be about the first of November and then, if my life is spared I think I may visit my home in New Jersey. Keep Shady

Did Ollie succeed in getting his exemption? I fear that he did not: If I understand the Conscription Act the "Commutation" or "Three Hundred Dollar clause" has been stricken out and unless a person is exempt for "Physical disability," over or under age or Alienage, he has to go or furnish a Substitute. I hope that he was successfull.[40] I should not like to have either of my brothers drafted. I believe that I am the

---

[40]Walter was correct, the "Commutation clause," the means by which a man selected for the draft could excuse himself by paying $300, was repealed in the summer of 1864 for the reason that too many had taken advantage of it and too few had reported for duty. One of the reasons for including a commutation clause in the Enrollment Act was to keep the price of substitutes below $300. Such was no longer the case. See Eugene C. Murdock, *One Million Men: The Civil War Draft in the North* (Madison: The State Historical Society of Wisconsin, 1971), 197–202.

only representative of our branch of the Dunn family in the Army, and an awfull poor one at that. How are you?

Do you pretend to give as a reason for not visiting at fathers when I am at home, that I never asked you. I am sure that I never asked you to go there when I was not at home. If that reason has kept you away when I have been at home, why has it not the same effect when I am absent? I think I see your object, it is to avoid a collission at the table, knowing that I am your superior in strength, now acknowledge that to be a fact will you? Expell those fears and the next time I visit Uncle Joels[41] "Mansion," please be so generous and kind as to favor his family including his now absent son, with a call. Please understand that the above invitation only takes effect when your "Obdt. Sevt." is at home, will you consider the matter "ha haw."

In your letter you have a sentence which reads like the following. "I am glad to hear you express a wish to get on a farm again—perhaps—but never mind————." I would like for you to finish those broken sentences.

Yes, you may be pardoned when you asked when I saw one "uneven _____"

The weather is so warm and uncomfortable that I cannot write more and must close.

My hand is so unsteady I doubt whether you can read this. Please accept of this scratching (for I certainly cannot call it writing) and answer as soon as convenient.

From your absent yet True Friend
Walter G. Dunn
V.R.Corps

P.S. I am ashamed of the style of this letter and if I was not so lazy I would burn it and write another. W.

Plainfield Union Co N.J.
August 3rd 1864

My Dear Walter

I was the happy recipient of you[r] last kind favor yesterday. You may take this as a fact that I was verry much disapointed upon going to

---

[41]Walter here referred to his father.

the P.O. Sabbath Eve and not get a letter from you, but I will take "the will for the deed" seeing I cannot help it.

I'm quite happy to inform you that we are having a verry cool evening, Plainfield having had its face washed by a few light showers, but not sufficient to wet the ground enough to do much good to the Potatoes. The weather looks rather stormy, and I think we will have a dull day for "fasting and Prayer." It's so cool and comfortable it reminds me of the winter.

Now you hope they, the pesky Rebs, will take Baltimore do you? I do not for I'm afeard I would miss my Letters coming from someone who wears "Brass Coats and Blue Buttons," for Em's sure they would choose the good looking "Sogers." The next thing after hearing that Baltimore was taken I should expect to learn that you was prisoner but I hope this will not be the case. I must leave you now untill sometime tomorrow. Good night

Fastday

Here I come to bother you with some more of my trash, but you said you liked it and of course must ha[ve] more of it. It has rained alternately, one minute and sunshine for the next five, all day. Granfather[42] and Mother have been spending the day with us. We have not fasted much I can tell you. I have not been to Church, should go this evening but we expect Louise and Sarah Johnson and Susie Force to call. Should like to go as it is union prayer meeting, but Susie told me they were coming. So "curly head" advised me "to drive a trusty horse to prayer meetings" one like "Old Pat." Now I'd not know of another such an one, consequently I'm to understand I had better drive "Patriotic" or stay at home rather than drive one that is not gentle! Am I right? Hey! It seems impossible for me to attend the meeting. Eld Rogers and Mr I. D. Titsworth[43] both of them have made

---

[42]Emma's grandfathers were Jonathan Fitz Randolph (1797–1876) and Archibald Dunn.

[43]Isaac D. Titsworth was born in Piscataway in 1805, one of the ten children of Lewis and Keziah (Dunham) Titsworth. He was apprenticed to Randolph Dunham to learn the tanning and currying trade and later worked for Randolph. In 1831 he married Hannah Ann Sheppard. Isaac, along with Thomas Stillman, laid out many of the streets of Plainfield. The *Sabbath Recorder* reported that Isaac gave seven sons and sons-in-law to the ranks of the Union armies. When one of his sons was wounded he applied to Secretary of War Edwin M. Stanton for permission to visit the boy. Stanton refused on the

me offers that I might go home with them after morning service, remain to Sabbath School, attend Evening meeting and they would see that I come home. Now was not that generous? I do not know wether they meant to or send Judson or some of the younger ones. I think Jud would prefer making his own arrangements. He attends quite regular. Yes I do think one year is a good long while. It will not seem near as long if you come home once again. You do not know how glad "Emma" is that you think diferently on this subject. I must not write what I would for it might spoil you. Depend upon it Walter Dear you will get—well you know—from B.J. Big boy as W.D. calls M.E.R. I shall not come to New Market to see you. You might not come to see me—quite so soon—but I promised to forget I can surely know you when you are back for then I have not any time only the present. Now I shall look for your coming or something certain for you tell me Major Wharton is "certainly" willing for you to come on "North now or in Oct." and if you do not come, I shall think you do not want to leave your "Chum." You seem so attached to each other. I think I should like him too, for his letter changed your mind. I will keep "Mum" but my "smiling countenance" is not near as "shady" as it was before I received this bit of news. I should much rather you would come now, we could go to "Florida"—you could see your school mates—get Ice cream, ride in a grocery wagon, walk down past the old familiar place. And I suppose you think that is a verry poor programme. I would say, I would call as you wished on Uncle Joel and "his now absent son," but as I do not think it will, I shall not give my promise so to do. Yes I will consider this matter.

Where did you get your cold? Or have you had it since that never-to-be-forgotten night. If Pa should ask you now "What you want"! would your answer be the same! This evening I was out diging around the roots of some flowers and I jumped up and went to see if I could stand under the tree, but not verry handy— You perceive I remember you at all times __ __ __ __ Friday evening I had just put little Maggie to bed and kissed her, I verrily believe for the 5th time, when there was

---

grounds that there were too many such requests, whereupon Titsworth applied to President Lincoln, who reportedly said, "If this man has given seven sons to fight for their country, let him go to the boy." I. D. Titsworth died in 1897, a deacon in the church and the owner of several large tanneries.

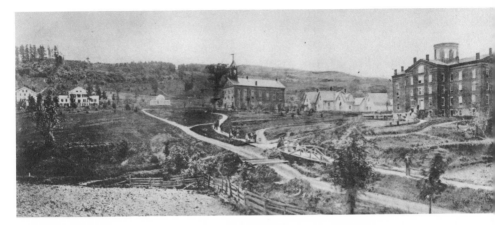

Alfred Center in 1866. Much building occurred in the years after Walter attended school there. (Herrick Memorial Library, Special Collections, Alfred University.)

a knock at the door, and down I went in a hurry. I thought the knock was familiar, had no idea but that it was some of the children, but what was my astonishment to see my old friend Mollie Bogart. She stayed untill monday morning and then returned. She is to send for me in Oct. and wants me to stay a month or six weeks. She has vacation at that time and lots of fun. Do not expect to. You should like to. Eugene[44] is going to leave the store next week and again Em is needed. They try to make me think that they cannot do with-out me.

As long as I did not receive an invitation from you and not expecting to next time, and the other members of your family gieving me such "invites" is the reason I have not let your not inviting me keep me from visiting your home and family. Is that satisfactory? No I shall not take "that to be a fact." You will remember that in the "Cherry Battle" we both quit equal victors and as you have a lame shoulder, I shall not own you as my superior in strength, untill a trial. Now do you "[week for stay?] " "Hey"! __ __ __ __ Yes. Ollie did pay the three Hundred Dols., raised by the county, and had no trouble much with it. He did

---

[44]Eugene Runyon was married to Emma's sister, Jersey Ann. He ran a grocery business in New Market with William Shotwell and Alexander Dunham under the name "Shotwell and Co."

not wish to get exempted. He thinks that looks "sheepish unless unfit for duty." I wish he had got a substitute[45] and then he would not stand the next draft of our portion of the 500,000 men [which] have been raised by Capt. Hubbard['s] volunteers. As usual Union County is ahead. Dont you wish you had him?

Walt, please receive my thanks for the Waverly. I received it and have read the peice penciled, and liked them verry much, the one "In love with a portrait" especialy. Did you think while reading it "one and only one true love." I wonder if "Josie" copied her answer. I shall know that paper for it is verry interesting indeed. You marked an advertisement—you recaled—do you know the lady or did you notice it because she said "Soldier Prefered" is that it?_____ Well the girls did not come consequently I have had my time to myself, and can go to bed early, hoping that you will excuse this poor attempt to answer yours—and write and let me know when you expect to come. I will close.

And May Heavens richest blessing Ever be yours is the sincere wish of one who is truly yours.

Emma Randolph

"Good night" and sweet dreams

P.S. I hope you will get this sabbath evening — for I think of you often then.

N.B. Do not forget to inform me of when you are coming, and I will have my face washed and clean. I wish you were here now. I could enjoy a chat with you. I wish this was to be the last letter I was to write you before you come, and we shall speak "face to face." Are you going to inform your folks of you intention of comeing "North" for a while? Or do you intend to surprise them as you did before? I do not know what I should say should I go to the door come evening and find you there. The first one I would say would be come over to show you the way, for you will remember we do not live on second str. but over on the corner of Sixth and New Sts. — quite a walk from town I bet you but I will stop. Please write soon as convenient, and oblige

Emma

---

[45]A man subject to the draft could avoid military service in three ways, by physical disability, paying the commutation fee for the draft in question, or hiring a substitute to serve in his place. Brokers furnished substitutes, who frequently deserted and hired themselves out again.

Baltimore, Md.
August 9, 1864

Dear Emma

I take pleasure in acknowledging the receipt of you last, which with its due arrival, afforded me much pleasure. I received it Sabbath morning, instead of evening, which was quite as agreeable. I hope that you will not allow yourself too much disappointment when you fail to receive my letters at the expected time, for my circumstances will not allways permit me to write as soon after receiving yours, as you request. You may look for an apology for this delay, but believe me "Dear" Emma, that only causes of great importance prevent me from writing to you, although I do not always state them, believe me to be candid.

I have also received the "Plainfield Union" for which kind favor consider me very greatfull. You wished to know why I penciled that advertisement, it was because the advertiser was a "country lady," which I "prefer." I prefer the "Waverly" to the "Companion" and if I mistake not, you said that the latter with the exception of the former was your favorite, if so I will send you another Waverly tomorrow and if you do not take it I will send it regular. Please inform me which of the two above named papers you prefer in your next.

The weather is still very warm and dry. It seems like an age since we had rain, but I feel thankfull that there are strong indications of it tonight.

My "Chum" has returned, his leave of absence having expired. He states that he had a very pleasant time indeed. He attended several parties, where there were three or four ladies to one gentleman, that I think is too much of a good thing, what think you? I fear I would not survive a furlough, should such be the case when I come home. I do not wish you to allow anything that I have said in reference to a furlough, prevent you from visiting your friend Miss Mollie Bogart for my visit home is more dubious than certain. The Chief Clerk in the office has left, and another one about to leave. I fear that I shall not be able to come north untill still later than the time I named in my previous letter. Yes I intend to keep it from the knowledge of my parrents untill I am certain that I can go and what time. Please do not say one word about it, for my prospects for a furlough are very poor, below par.

I attended chapel, sunday evening, the exercises were very interesting. I wish that you could have heard them. The Hospital Chaplin has gone on a visit and a stranger addressed us, which I think was an improvement. I did not learn his name.

Do the ladies who have been attending school at Alfred Center and Jud, expect to return? I judge from what Hattie Dunn said, that she would not. I often think of the year I spent at Alfred and wish that I could spend another such, but my school days are past, never to be recalled.

I suppose that the Saltwater fever begins to rage does it not? It is about time. If you go, as I hope you may, I hope that you will enjoy yourself. I would advise you to go as often as you can, for I think that it will be benificial to your health. I would like to go with you just once. I think we would have a pleasant time. Do you remember the last and only time that I was with you, especially the way that Little Dave carried on while we were going home. Many of the pleasant hours spent while on furlough with you are as bright in my memory as ever. I hope soon to add many more to their number.

Mother informed me that Eld. Rogers and wife expected to go West on a visit, have they gone yet, and who will fill his place in the pulpit? He will be very much missed, will he not?

On the corner of Sixth and New Sts. — do you think that I would need a pilot to find that place in as small town as Plainfield is, no, no. If I would, I do not know but I would have been lost about a dozen times, in the Monumental City.[46]

It is growing late and I have written enough trash therefore I will close. Please excuse my delay and write me as soon as you possibly can. Excuse all imperfections, for they are very many on account of my great haste. May Heavenly Angels hover arround your pillow, and your dreams be very pleasant, in the wish of one who "loves you dearly" and "truly"

W. G. Dunn
V.R.Corps

---

[46]Baltimore has long been referred to as the "Monumental City" after John Quincy Adams so dubbed it in a toast.

Plainfield Union Co N.J.
August 15th 1864

My Dear Walter

Your last kind favor and verry welcome one I received in due time. I'm verry sorry I have to write under so late a date. One reason is vis. that I know what it is to wait for an expected letter. It means so long a time before I hear from you again. The delay is not meant to retaliate, "believe one to be candid" will you?

The weather is verry warm to day but it is not quite as dusty as it has been owing to one having been blessed with a little rain on Sabbath evening last but not enough to do much good, only sufficient to lay the dust and made yesterday a verry pleasant day for a trip to "Florida." Thursday evening I received your Letter and had company to spend the evening the same ones I expected past evening and several others. Friday evening I remained home from Prayer meeting to write to you, but two of my cousins called and stayed untill quite late. Sabbath evening I went with our folks to New Market to meeting. Went to "Dear" Uncle David Dunns[47] with Sarah Titsworth.[48] Eld Rogers has gone. And Rev Thomlinson preached from the 3rd Chap. of Rev. 20th verse.[49] Verry good discourse but I do not like his style of delivery, and I found Uncle D. or none of the rest of them liked his manner of speaking. We had a nice sing before the exercises began. Mr. A. J. Titsworth[50] taught the bible class of which I'm a poor member. When there Mr. Martin Titsworth made a short farewell address, his remarks being chiefly of the influence of the Christian Communion in the army. He returned that morning. In the evening Nate Davis, Fannie Eisher, Sarah, Lucy, Mart, and myself went over to brother Titsworth to attend prayer meeting. We had an exelent meeting. Mart spoke much nicer in the evening than at S[abbath] S[chool]. About the time I intended to leave the meeting and go to meet the 9.20 train, it comenced to rain, so I remained. After meeting was out we had

---

[47]Emma's uncle.

[48]Sarah A. Titsworth of Plainfield attended Alfred University from 1863 to 1865. Although her time there postdated Walter's, she was known as one of Walter's "Alfred Friends."

[49]"Behold, I stand at the door and knock; if any one hears my voice and opens the door, I will come in to him and eat with him, and he with me."

[50]Judson Titsworth.

some singing and music on the organ. Mean while Judson and Mart were tuning Guitars and then they favored us with some beautiful music. I asked J. to please sing "The Vacant Chair." He said he was most happy to be able to comply with my request. Thinks I hope about a request to write the name "Emma" instead of somthing els. So you see "Dear Walt" I verry often think of you, when I'm where we might enjoy ourselves together, but fate has ordered it otherwise. And we may be happier when we meet, for you will feel that you have done your duty, and I, well I do not like to say much, but I shall be proud and happy to acknowledge you as a friend but the friend will not know how "dear" you are to me. You perhaps cannot imagine how I long to see you . . . more, and look into your "true eyes" and clasp your hand in mine. Now I expect you to think I'm going to write a "love Letter." Excuse me, Walt. I cannot help expressing myself.

We went back to Uncle D. on the foot-step, or rather the horse did. I have never seen it light[n]ing as it did all the time while we were going and rain I guess it did, and Em had to hold the curtain and consequently I was pretty much wet. We got there about 11 oclock. Went to bed early. I promised the girls I would tell them my dream at my house. I did so for I dreamed Judson T. had come to my fathers house to get me to go to New Market to practice singing for the picnic. The girls all laughed and said they would tell Josie Copp if he did. I think they may inasmuch as he asked me if he might come up after Miss Randolph on Tuesday Eve 16th, before we left his home, while assisting me through the rain to the carriage. I do not know when we shall have the picnic probaly not untill he (A.J.) leaves so I understand he leaves next week. I do not know where he is going. I will after to morrow evening. Sunday morning I had their invitations to go to "Salt water," but refused them all, and remained at Sarahs expecting to come home in the afternoon as I had an engagement in the Eve. but Uncle David could not come, for we heard a carriage looked out the window and who should it be but Mr and Mrs Joel Dunn and daughter come to spend the afternoon. They were verry busy getting Lucy and David Titsworth ready to start for A[lfred] C[enter] this noon but nevertheless we had a verry pleasant visit indeed. After supper your father heard me speak of going home. He said Yes certainly I could go home with them, he would like to have me to. And he would offer me the inducement of going to salt-water with the young folks thursday

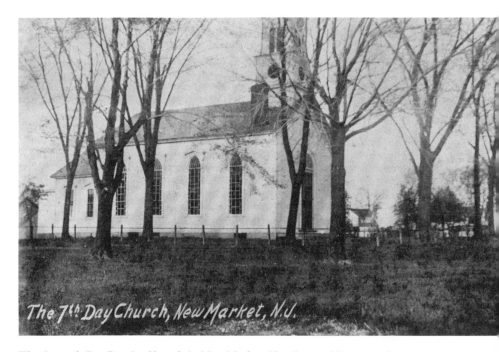

The Seventh Day Baptist Church in New Market, New Jersey. (Courtesy, the Seventh Day Baptist Historical Society.)

next. They all enjoyed a hearty laugh at my expense. He was so kind as to take me as far as Uncle Jims[51] where Ma was to meet me but you will see how they do not remember me long, for Ma went around by Grandfather and never even once thought of me waiting at New Market for her. But when "Emmas" gone for good, then they will know what a plague is gone. Howard Giles and Jennie Randell[52] were at cousin Aurelias, and we went home with Jennie. Got all the Apples, Plums, and Pears, we could carry in our pockets, and went back for Jud and Mart said they would come and serenade us. We to took a walk over the little brige thinking we could hear them when they came. We thought we did, and went to see them but we were mistaken. It was

---

[51]James Ayres was the husband of Hannah Ann Ayres, Emma's mother's sister.

[52]Jennie Randell married Charley Randolph on November 2, 1864, at the New Market Seventh Day Baptist Church.

Andrew Smaley Coriella. They insisted upon our going four in a buggy and serenade the Miss Davises, and go we did. No more got turned around toward New Market when we meet Jud and Mart, Nate and Fannie. They had been to our house, and were on their way to serenade Sales and Lucy "four in a buggy." Was most to many to ride far, and we drove to uncle Jims and Smalley, helped Aurelia to alight, and th[en] Emma had the ribbons and off we (Howard and Em) went to expect the invite to accompany then the Sales, and they had Guitars. And Walt they did sing beautiful. I did wish you could have heard it. Among the peices Jud sang was "Yes in a Horn." We had quite a chat with them. Heard that Fannie while in bathing at Florida, fainted away and Mart took her up in his arms and carried her ashore, and it took some time to bring her to. We returned to Uncle J. and I remained all night and come up on the train he went to N.Y. on but this is enough of this. The "Waverly" I received on Sabbath. Please receive my thanks for it. The "Waverly" is my favorite, but Walt I'm afraid it will not be convenient to you. If it is I would be happy to receive them from you. Yes I think your Chum had too much. I do not think there was much "Leap Year" arangements there at those parties. You need not fear that you will not survive a furlough. I can not go to see Mollie B, so I shall be at home to greet you when you come. None of the ladies but Lucy return to Alfred. I wish I could go for about 3 years. I know I should like it.

Yes we miss Eld Rogers verry verry much indeed, and I shall be delighted to hear him preach once again. I do not know that any particular Reverend sir fills his place.

Yes indeed I should dearly like to go to "Florida" once with you. Last wednesday evening I spent the evening with Little Dave up to Susie Thomas. He brout me home in his buggy, and we got to talking of the time we had so much fun coming home eating "sharks." He wished you were here to go with us this season but not untill next year. It does not seem possible you are to return then. I can hardly realize it. I have not been down to "Salt water" yet though I've not had less than half dozen chances. The young folks go on Thursday next. Your Mother told me I was to go, but I think she will miss it this time. I promised Lew along in the winter I would go to "Salt water" with him and Little Dave and his Sallie. I do not think he will hold me to that promise. Your Mother said that she had not heard from you in over three weeks. Why is it? they wish to know when I had heard from you, so I informed them, although I confess I did it reluctantly. Maggie is waking and wants "Mamie to turn a bed" so I must close, hoping you will excuse all mistakes and they are many. I will try and do better next time, make my Letter more interesting. Please answer as soon as convenient and oblige one who is most truly yours with Love

M. Emma R

N.B. So you think you will not need to inquire to find our house. You need not be to confident about not knowing your way, for if I mistake not, I remember of a certain soldier who stayed away and had to inquire the way somewhere in the Monumental City. Do you not remember the time? I shall be impatient to see you. Do you want to see me as I am? Or rather do you want to look at my picture "with my cut off." If you want to verry bad just let me know will you! You will not be jealous if I go to New Market with A. J. Titsworth will you? If you are just let me know in time and I will stay at home. "Your" Emma

Baltimore, Md.
August 20 1864

"Dear" Emma

I doubt not but you are wondering why I, of late, am so delinquent in replying to your letters. The reason, which I will state, is from no lack of a desire to be prompt, but the heat has such an effect on my shoulder, coupled with my duties, which are not so arduous but of such a nature as oftentimes to incapacitate me entirely, for writing letters. I trust you will consider my circumstances, being an invalid, and pardon me for my delays accordingly. Will you?

I received your letter of recent date in due time and, although tardy, read it with interest. I have no Thunder Storm adventures or serenading expeditions to write about to make my letters interesting. I might write about a promenade down Baltimore St. one Sunday evening recently, in search of an "Ice Cream Saloon," but my time will not permit me to give the particulars, besides you are unacquainted with the place and I fear it would fail to interest you.

Tis Sabbath, P.M. I suppose that you are at this time attending Sabbath School in the little country church in New Market, are you not. If you could see the papers that are strewn on the different tables in this office and the business appearance of things, you could scarcely imagine even that this day is kept by some as Sabbath. I should like to be in New Market, listening to Bible instructions.

If I continue at this rate, I will have this completed by Monday morning. It seems that there are more calling on business when I attempt to write a letter than any other time. Captain—— has just called, to correct an error that he made several months ago, and of course, I had to search over papers that were filed away in March. It is real provoking. I gave him a peice of my mind, which he will undoubtedly remember when he makes out his muster rolls again.

I was very agreeably supprised on Thursday evening, upon meeting an old Alfred acquaintance. He heard that I was in the city and called to see me. He is a brother of Amanda Langworthy[53] and had just returned from a furlough to Alfred, so I was quite well posted as to how matters stand at the above named place, the first news that I had heard from there since last April. He is at West Hospital[54] in this City, with another old acquaintance of mine. I saw them both last night, and talked over, our boarding school adventures.

You wished to know why I did not write to my mother. One reason is, I seldom write more than one letter before I get an answer, and the reason I stated on the first page of this letter is another. In the same mail that I received your last. I received one from mother, also one from Cousin Eliza Nichols.[55] I immediately answered mothers, and told the cause of my delay, as she asked me if "I could under any reasonable excuse for not writing." I cannot say whether or not she will consider it reasonable.

We too have been blessed with occasional showers for a few days past. The weather is very cool and agreeable, tonight.

As to when I shall receive my furlough, I am, as yet unprepared to say. I think however that I will make an application about the 20th of Sept. and will probbably be at home between that time and the 1st of October. I have had the promise of the necessary approvals, and I

---

[53]The sister of one of Walter's Alfred University friends.

[54]G. H. West's Buildings Hospital, located near the B&O's Camden Station in Baltimore, opened on September 19, 1862, immediately following the Battle of Antietam.

[55]Walter's cousin.

anticipate no trouble in the least in obtaining a furlough. I believe that Maj. Wharton would do anything in his power for me. He has paid me several compliments, through my company Commander. I like him very much, and an officer that I like, I will please if I can.

Yes I would very much like to see you, but as that is impossible at present, you will oblige me greatly by forwarding me a picture a representation of the original. Please do not fail to comply with my request, at your earliest opportunity.

Why did you ask me if I would be jealous if you went to New Market with Mr. A. J. Titsworth. Did you ever see me exhibit a jealous spirit? Certainly not, for what have I to say who you shall ride out with? I am glad to learn that you are enjoying yourself as well as your letters indicate. May you continue, thus to do, is my desire. My time compells me to close. Please accept this dry and tardy letter and reply immediately if convenient.

I am with much love

Yours, Truly
Walter G. Dunn

I have the last number of the "Waverly," which I will mail, Monday.

Plainfield Union Co. N.J.
August 22nd 1864

Dear Walt

Agreeable to request I will answer your kind and much looked for Letter that I received to day immediatly. My poor head is aching verry badly indeed, but not knowing when I shall get another opertunity I will improve the present one and trust you will excuse all imperfections and remember I'm not verry well.

There is not much news that I know of, nothing going on at present, the rain excepted. It has been showery about all day. You was "muchly" mistaken thinking I was at Sabbath School about the time you was writing me. Although it was a verry pleasant day none of us attended Church. I was enjoying a good nap about that time, but awakened time enough to go to the "Office" but nary a letter from "W." This after noon after mail was changed I run over to see if there was anything in "114" and there it was. And right glad I was to see the "well known hand writing" I do assure you.

So you gave that careless Capt. "a piece of your mind." Oh how I should liked to have steped in and heard you. It would be fun for me. Since I wrote you last I have been to "Florida" twice. Last Wednesdsay I was to fulfill an engagement with Mr. C. that Ma made for me when I was at New Market with A.J.T. About eleven tuesday Eve Ma told me he had been here wanting me to go to Salt water, and she answered for Em. Just as "luck favors the brave" we did not go untill thursday and then Little Dave, Sallie and Louise Johnson, Ollie and Susie Force (cousin Lew D. intended) Cousin Tom Harris[56] to be and Susie Dunn Mr. Cadington[57] and Emma all went in buggies. We took a sail in a row boat, came home by Rahway, got some refreshments, got home about 7 Oclock. Had quite a pleasant time. My head pains me so I shall have to lay this aside for to night. I think if I had some "gentle hands" to bath and soothe my head it would feel Oh so much better, but remember "1st Oct." And now "good night, I hope your dreams are sweet, and angels are guarding you while you sleep" tis the wish of Emma

Tuesday Afternoon

Walt are you glad I'm going to write more of my nonsense? First let me know if your not and I wont write so much next time. I have caught cold, and do not feel natural. You must not expect one of Ems old Letters. I received a Letter from Mollie Bogart the same time I received yours. Now isnt this blue Ink just the style! Well here I am up to the "Shop" and it is wednesday 2 P.M. Ma has been quite sick, and of course the duties wher heaviest on my Shoulders. That is another reason I have had to lay this aside so many times, but please do not blame for it. This afternoon it is verry warm, and I do not feel much like writing. I have some Coats that are ready to be stiched but this time I will take "pleasure before duty." Between every half dozen words, I have to jump up and "pass some military pants." Here are some vests so "au revoir."

Well again to tell you the news. Judson T[itsworth] has concluded to go to the War, instead of College. I was at New Market last evening to let them know I could not attend the picnic and there I learned the news, he goes next Monday. We had a verry pleasant time going to

---

[56] Thomas S. Harris, son of Mary C. Harris, married Susie Dunn.
[57] Probably William A. Coddington. Little is known about him.

Undated postwar photograph of Walter Dunn's home in New Market.
(Courtesy, Jeannette Fitz Randolph Duryea.)

New Market last tuesday eve. We got home about Eleven. While
looking over my pack of pictures he spoke of you and told me what I
had heard before vis. that Walt Dunn was the favorite at Alfred Center
and they missed him verry verry much. So you see Dear Walt, you are
still remembered. I did not tell him that he was "prefered" here. I
asked him (Jud) where you was. He told me pretty correctly but said "if
that old fellow had answered my letter, I could be able to inform you as
to just how he is now." His brothers intend going to school when they
return, and he believes you do to. Now do you? I just received the
"Waverly" and with it a good Letter from Cous Jont. I have not heard
from him in some time, and right glad was I to get it. He says every
hour seems a month and every month a year. He anticipates "Lots of
fun, when he gets to home and loved ones." My prayer is that he has

been spared so long that he may still be favored and return in safty to his loved ones. I wish you were coming "there to remain." The picnic has gone to Chimney Rock to day. I hope they are enjoying themselves. The mail closes in five minutes and I must stop. Please excuse the mistakes, and except this poor attempt and answer soon as convenient, in haste, from

Truly your Friend
Emma

Baltimore, Md.
August 27th 1864

My Dear Emma

Time in its onward march, has again placed me in your debt, a letter. One week ago, this very hour I wrote you, since then I have received an answer, which has added much to the pleasures of the past week. I wish that you only knew the pleasure that accompanies the reading of a letter from my friends at home. You can never realise it, untill you are deprived of the privaleges and enjoyments that home and a large circle of friends afford and, tis my wish that you may never be called upon to make that sacrifice.

Yours, bearing various dates was received in due time.

The duties of the day are performed and the Office vacated with the exception of myself, so I will endeavor to improve the hours of solitude, by conversing with you, through the medium of the Pen.

I was pleased to learn that you had such a pleasant time at "Florida." I think I could enjoy myself hugely on such an excursion, as it has been a long time since I realised any such enjoyment. But wait untill the 1st of Oct. or later.

I received a letter from Mary E. Dunn to day, she stated that she has been to "Florida" twice. But I must stop and hear the news which seem to be quite important.

The evening papers state nothing definite, but represent military opperations, as progressing successfull. A few days since I had a long talk with an Officer belonging to the 2nd Corps direct from Petersburg. He places all confidence in Grant and says that the campaign will end with the ultimate capture of both Petersburg and Richmond, and he doubts not but the unconditional surrender of Lees army, which is not only his opinion, but the opinion of the soldiers in general.[58] If such be the case, have we not reason to hope? Let us take courage and despair not, for with men, in whom so much confidence is placed, to lead our armies, we will certainly, sooner or later gain the reward, Peace, which when gained will be prised according to its cost.

Of late you have seldom spoken of your headache. I was hoping that since you had your hair cut off, that it had ceased to trouble you. I would advise you to apply cold water freely, as I have found it a relief.

I was somewhat disappointed when I received your last that it did not contain your picture. I judged from your previous letter, that if I expressed a wish for it, you would send it. Have you one for me? If so please forward and oblige.

If Jud has received information of my intention of attending school when I return from soldiering, he has been misinformed. Such is not my intention. I have not yet decided what I shall do. I should not be supprised if "1856" [1865?] should find me in the Navy.

You stated that Jud had concluded to go to war. Do you know what Regt. he is going in?

The time for the "Draft" is fast approaching. Is New Market doing anything in the line of recruiting?

I doubt not but Jont is anxious for the expiration of his term of service. As the time draws near the anxiety increases. I presume that Will is equally as anxious. Have you heard from John Hardy[59] yet?

In your previous letter you said that you could not go to see your friend Mollie Bogart but would be at home to welcome me when I came home. I hope that what I said in reference to receiving a furlough does not prevent you from visiting her. My visit home is quite uncertain. I hope you will visit your friends regardless of me. One of the clerks in this Office expects to go to New York (his home) next week on a leave of absence of three days. If business will not permit me ten days, I will not come at all.

A young officer who has been transacting some business connected with this office, met with quite an accident a few days since. While riding in the City Passenger Railway cars he slipped and fell, the

---

[58]After a series of bloody battles in the Wilderness, the Army of the Potomac and the Army of Northern Virginia settled into trench warfare along a line from Richmond south to the railroad hub at Petersburg, Virginia.

[59]A friend missing in action about whom nothing else is known.

Emma's friend, Kizzie Potter, who was married to a man in Walter's company. (Courtesy, Jeannette Fitz Randolph Duryea.)

car running over his foot and mashing it terribly. He was on his way to a "Pic Nic" at the time of his accident. He was on leave of absence which expires on Monday next at which time he was to report to his Regt.

Am I right in supposing that you are at Sabbath school at this time? If you are, I can assure you that there is a vast difference between our present situations. Imagine me at church tomorrow evening.

(I think that this dry document will certainly weary you and in order to try you no longer I will close, by asking you to excuse all imperfections as my ink is poor, my pen more miserable and myself a most awfull letter writer, when combined make what is more properly called scribbling.) Please accept from one who is still yours in love

Walter G. Dunn

P.S. Be sure and answer promptly and send me a picture without fail.

W.

Plainfield August 29th
1864

Dearest Friend

I'm again the happy recipient of an interesting letter from you. Although I cannot know what it is to enjoy the privalege of speaking with you "face to face" I will through my friend the "Pen." I am verry glad if poor me can be the means of affording you the least bit of pleasure. I can write you with a better heart, if you enjoyed the best one I wrote you: For candidly I was ashamed to send it.

Let me tell you I know what a pleasure it is to receive Letters from a Friend that is "deprived of the privalege and enjoyment that home and a large circle of Friends affords him." I can assure you Walt, I prize them verry dearly. I believe I have now 39 of those "precious missives" from Baltimore, as Mr. A. Dunham[60] calls them. He told me not long ago that he would not bring me over any more letters from the Office because I would not tell him what was in them. And sure enough this morning after mail was distributed he walked over to get the Letters. He came hurrying back "Em there is one for you but it is from Baltimore and I wont get it." I thought he was trying to fool me but he said he asked for it, thinking it was for my Father but it was for me and from Baltimore and he told them to put it back. And sure enough it was just as he said for I run from the shop and asked the Post Master and he said Mr. Dunham meant have some fun. I guess he didnt.

It has been a beautiful day, so cool and pleasant, and this evening it is splendid. Star light, it reminds me of an evening that we took a walk up second up Peace to Main street and so on and on. Do you remember?

Jennie sits in the other rocking chair sleeping quite soundly. She has no pillow. I should think she would prefer the sofa to dreaming in a chair. I wonder if she is dreaming of a hat. Ha hom. How I would like to be sitting by the "cool window" to night. I have not been in it since we moved, but have got as far as the door, several times forgetting but what we lived there still.

The war news though disastrous to both armies, seems to be pretty good for our side. Oh I hope and pray that the confidence placed in

---

[60]Abram Dunham was on the Seventh Day Baptist Roll of Honor for wartime service, but little else is known of him.

Grant is not misplaced, but that he will prove himself able and worthy the great trust.[61] I think that I should go about crasy to know that Peace was proclaimed throughout the land. Yes I do think we have reason to hope, and I fell verry much encouraged and hope you do to.

I did not wish to give you to understand that I had any of my "facsimiles" for I have none at this time. I wrote you about them. I was intending to have some taken and wanted to know which style you prefered. Granpas folks laugh at me so much I have nearly decided not to have my "Cards" taken untill my hair has grown out which I do not intend to let it do untill about two (2) years from now. And our family to[o] seems delighted to tease me. Oh Walt you do not know what a looking "monkey" this is writing to you, they tell me I'll surly break the Cameras. Dont you think I'd better wait than run all that risk? Hey!

I thought Jud was not right in reference to your returning to school. So you think of reenlisting in the Navy. I do not see what their is to attract so many to the Navy. Jud and three or four more of the Alfredites are going in the above named department. Please tell me what the diference is that is more favorable will you? Speaking of the Alfredites reminds me of the company that I suppose are now enjoying themselves at Mrs. Aggie Dunns,[62] this evening namly, next edition.

2ond Part

Mr's Hubbard,[63] Rogers,[64] Green,[65] Burdick, C. Thacher, Jud, and two more gentlemen from Alfred that I do not remember their names,

---

[61]In the ten days prior to Emma's writing, the Confederates had driven Union forces from the devastated Shenandoah Valley, but Federal troops had gained control of Mobile Bay and had cut the Weldon Railroad, a vital supply line to Petersburg and Richmond. The fighting was bloody, but Union forces had indeed gained important strategic advantages. Nevertheless, Union war spirit was very low. President Lincoln had advised his cabinet that he would probably not be reëlected and that their duty was to "save the Union between the election and the inauguration." See E. B. Long, *The Civil War Day by Day*, 556–59.

[62]Aggie W. Dunn, of Plainfield, attended Alfred University for the 1862–63 term.

[63]Probably Captain J. Frank Hubbard, who later married Mrs. Belle Titsworth in 1866.

[64]Probably David Rogers of New Market.

[65]Probably Joseph A. Green of the 11th New Jersey. He was mustered in as a substitute on September 2, 1864 and was discharged on June 6, 1865.

Hattie Dunn, Amanda Rogers, Mary Bailey, Sarah Titsworth, Ernie Albertie, Sarah Coriel, and Mrs. Josie Copp.[66] I presume they are having fine times, talking over the scrapes they have had at the "old University." Dont you wish you was there, in the midst of them? I suppose Jud and Josie will have a scene to night as Josie goes to morrow. I would be a mouse in the wall just for a little while if I could. I was at Sabbath school as you imagined. After morning service by Eld Morse I went home with Cousin Real.[67] Jud taught the bible class, and Rea Morse, Uncle Jim, and Jud got into quite a discussion. Jud delivered a farwell address, and he did do finly. I'll bet you I do not know how he could have such good command over his feelings while he was speaking of his intended departure to join his brother gone before.[68] He spoke so deeply there was not a dry eye in the congregation. His folks feel verry badly about it. Kizzie Potter is feeling worse because her husband has gone to war, without biding her goodbye. Jud sayes she does not eat scarcely enough to keep her alive. Oh when is these partings to be over? Jud called to Aurelia's to see me after S.S. [Sabbath School] to make an engagement with me and he did so. I went to prayer meeting at his Fathers house and we had an exelent time. I remained untill the clock struck nine and then I left, J. accompaning me to the Depot as I supposed to take the last train for Plainfield but he came all the way with me. And I must tell you of what happened when we got home: there was a horse and buggy tied under one of the trees, and sounds from the house as though they were enjoying themselves hugly. So of course I must do something wrong (so I'm allways doing). I told him Judson if he would unhitch the Poney we could have a ride, and he, to[o] willingly, did so, and off we went, but not without hallowing to them so they might know who had it. And we was off and stayed not over twenty minutes, and was on our way home.

---

[66]No further information on Burdick and Thacher is available, but like the others who gathered at Aggie Dunn's, they were probably classmates who attended Alfred University at various times during the war. Hattie Dunn, Amanda Rogers, Mary Bailey, Ernestine Alberti, and Sarah Coreille were from Plainfield. Josaphine M. Copp lived in Portville, New York. Sarah Titsworth was one of Walter's "Alfred friends."

[67]Possibly Aurelia J. Ayres.

[68]Judson Titsworth, about to enter the Union navy, is bidding farewell to his friends as he follows in the footsteps of a brother who had joined the army.

Pat was prancing along nicly just before you cross the railroad there by Hatties, when Pa steped out and said, Em is that you. Yes sir was my answer and introduced A.J. He asked me if I just come from New Market. I told him a few minutes ago in the last train. How asked he. "In the Cars" said I and thinking he was looking for the Buggie, I told him we had borrowed Lews buggy. Oh how he answered, he does not know it. The poney started and Pa said "Emma you ought not to have did so." We came home as straight as possible, and Oh my stars, what a time. Never will I forget it. Jennie asked us if we had met Lew's horse and B. and as soon as J. could he informed them how it was. We waited for Lew, Ed[69] and Mont to come back not thinking but Pa would see them up town. Jud was in a hurry so I told him to go and I would take the blame for it was my fault, and he did. Pa came down in a few minutes. Jennie and me sit on the stoop enjoying ourselves finly. When he gave me just such a scolding a never want again. Lew had gone to Brooklyn, Little Dave to Rahway, Ed and Vermont to your house and one of Lews buggies to Scotch Plains. They had telegraphed to Elisebeth City all to head off the "Thieves." Oh dear me I cannot help but laugh yet when I think of it. They did hear us hallow to them and then some of them thought it was stolen not dreaming in just fun. Pa could not have and Ollie was not speaking and what to do we did not know, when the Idea poped in my mind to go get Ollie and Pa did so and he started after bringing father home in the direction Lew had gone, and met him coming in to head quarters to see what progress had been made. Oll told him the straight of it and Lew he said was not angry at me but was provoked at Mr. Titsworth. I have not seen any of the party concerned to speak with them. Since Jud does not know what a time we had he is thinking it a nice little joke unless he has seen some of the persons concerned. He was to call on me one of the three evenings, Tuesday, tonight, or to morrow night. I'm glad he has not called this Evening for I have been able to answer immediatly as you requested me, and as I should like to do allways. What do you think of our Skedaddle? We need a good blessing for it you think! dont you? I have no doubt but Lew is angry at me verry, and I do not want his ill will. We were getting along so nicly. We were the subject of conversa-

---

[69]Ed Dunn, of Newark, would be drafted the following March.

tion in many places. The last news which I suppose you have heard is that we are engaged and only playing off. I wish that people could mind there own business and let others alone.

Yes Cousin Jont seems verry anxious to get home again. I wrote him about four times as much as I have writen you. In the morning mail I bet you he will laugh when he gets it if he ever does. It is the 4th I have sent him and he has never received it. I hope he will this one. He has not heard from John Hardy in a long time. Jont wrote that they are busy Skirmishing all the time and two more of his company had been taken prisoners. He supposed they had gone to keep poor John company. Yes the time for the draft is drawing nigh, and I believe New Market is doing nothing at all. We have our Quota filled, and I'm so glad. They are expecting a hard time in the City at the time of the Draft. I'm glad I do not have them. Pa has come down from up town and has filled his pockets full of sweet harvest apples. And they taste delicious, how I wish you was here to eat some with me. Do you have plenty of Fruit? What are Peaches selling at now! They are selling here for $100.10 [$1.10] a basket, quite high now, but it is time you stoped . Ollie sayes he sees me crossing it and dont like it, and I dont either.[70] I will stop my scribling and seek response, for I feel the need of it verry much this letter looks like dont it. Please excuse the numberless mistakes, and answer soon, yes soon as possible. Now good night, from your Friend.

Emma R.

Baltimore, Md.
August 31st 1864

My "Dear" Emma

Yours is at hand and in order that I may repay you for your very prompt reply, I will, in accordance with your request answer immediately, although I shall be very brief, as my time will not permit me to write much. Please accept my most sincere thanks for your prompt, lengthy, and very interesting reply to my last.

I was not aware that we had exchanged letters thirty-nine (39) times, since I was ordered to this City, which was one year ago, the 3rd

---

[70]Emma has begun writing across the side of the letter.

day of last July. I suppose from the manner in which we have carried on our correspondence, viz that each letter you write as canceled by one from me that I have received as many of the most precious missives as you have, but I have at present comparatively few of them. When I entered the Hospital I thought I would preserve all your letters, and did untill the late raid, when I thought it prudent to assign them to the flames. I can assure you I did it with regret but knowing the threatened condition of the City in its defenceless hour and knowing that all correspondence found in a government office would be subject to a very rigid examination by a band of lawless ruffians, I concluded that you would justify my proceedings, and acted accordingly.

In reference to your "Skedaddle" as you term it, I consider that neither you nor Mr. A.J.T. are deserving censure from the very fact that your motive was innocent. Resulting as it did, I call it a capital Joke and not very expensive. After reflection, I think that Lew will exonerate Jud of all censure. It will be queer if Lew does not miss his horse and buggy not a few times when I reach home on furlough. Prepare for some pleasant evening rides then, if the roads are good and weather favorable, as I intend to make up for all lost time, and much more. You cannot imagine how I would appreciate a repetition of some of the evening rides we took togather in the Summer of 1862, especially the first one, after my return from A.C. Do you remember looseing your hat in our way from New Market to Plainfield? I anticipate much pleasure when I reach home. I trust my anticipations will be realised. I shall not attend any "Leap Year parties" if I know it. How are you 2nd day of March 1864.

Last Sunday, P.M. my chum and self, visited Greenmount Cemetery of this City. My visit caused many solemn reflections which I trust will be deep and lasting.[71] I have since thought how soon will my body lay silent in the tomb, if I only felt myself prepared for that great change, I would welcome it at any moment. My visit to so solemn a place taught

---

[71]Greenmount Cemetery is a historic cemetery in Baltimore. Cemeteries were highly regarded as places of reflection and in fact became "cultural institutions." For a recent discussion of the "culture of death" as it played out in the Civil War period, see Garry Wills, *Lincoln at Gettysburg: The Words that Remade America* (New York: Simon & Schuster, 1992), chap. 2.

Greenmount Cemetery in Baltimore, ca. 1860. (Maryland Historical Society.)

me a lesson, with which by the Grace of God I hope to be profited. Pray for me to that effect, will you?

Not long since, I promised Adj. Norris, 11th Md. Vol. Infty. that I would assist a clerk of his in making out copies of five rolls of his Regt. to place those lost in the Battle of Monocacy. This evening the clerk came arround and we commenced our task which went on very favorable untill he told me that he used to live near Plainfield, which introduced a conversation, and oh— what a lot of mistakes. I found out that he was acquainted with I. S. Dunham, Elias Pope and many others of Plainfield with whom I am slightly acquainted, I have not the least doubt but he is acquainted with your Father. I did not ask him. It seems so good to meet those who are acquainted with the scenes of childhood and talk about that "place home" the dearest spot on earth. He is acquainted arround New Market and New Brunswick and it seemed almost like meeting an old friend. He is to call again tomorrow evening when we will have another review of the past, but not untill after our work is accomplised as it is too much trouble to correct errors.

A Wholesale Coal Merchant in this City, of my acquaintance, gave me an invitation last evening to go on a fishing excursion with him next "Sabbath" day. I think I will not go as it is about the first of the month when our business is very brisk. I would just like for you to see what a job I have on hand, all to be accomplished as soon as possible after the month begins. I imagine I hear you say deliver me.

Sept. 1st 1864.

You ask why so many prefer the Navy. I prefer it because it is a life of more adventure and excitement than the branch of service that I am now in, besides getting rid of long marches. I have not decided to reenlist in the Navy or the Army, it depends altogather upon the progress of the war when my present term expires.

My duties compell me to close. Please accept and overlook errors and believe me to be as ever

Your loving friend
Walter G. Dunn
V.R.C.

P.S. Please oblige by answering promptly. If you call this interesting it is more than I do.

Yours untill again
W. G. Dunn

Peaches are so very cheap that they do not taste good. "35 cts. per bushel"

[Part of a letter written Sept. 5th 1864]
"Second Edition"

Good Morning, Walt, how you was this fine stormy morn? I hope youre enjoying among other blessings, good health: Do you feel verry well? Please tell me for I think youre not well as usual. Now be "candid frank" are you? I think you are to much confined writing in that Office, and hope your anticipated visit Home will help you. I'm looking forward anxiously for the first of Oct. I'm all prepared for some pleasant rides in moonlight evenings. I think it ought to have been time gone, instead of lost time, for I think the time had been as profitbly spent as could be under the circumstances. You say, I cannot imagine how you would enjoy a repetition of some of the evening rides we took together in the Summer of 1862. I shall be compelled to contradict you, for I can mind that. Yes I do remember loosing my hat, and the Ghost and driving in a ways, to let the others pass. I do hope you will have pleasant weather, good roads and a good time to talk of to your Chum. I do not know of any thing going on then but I know that Miss Vandelia Baker is to be married, next wednesday next, may she be happy. I do not like the looks of her intended husband but I will not judge from appearance. I expected she would be the next one out of our congregation to "throw herself away."

I'm verry glad to know that you have met with one who is familiar with some of our friends or acquaintances at Home. I should think you would both enjoy to chat, and it is no wonder it was the means of your neglecting your vis. Does he know me? I think it would have did you good to go on an excursion. Am sorry you could not put by the press of business. I should like to see the job you have, but I think if I was there I should look at the jobber, instead of the work, mightnt I? Dont you want a clerk to copy! I know one who I think would like a job. I see him here they call him Walt.

I am feeling quite happy about the War and do sincerly hope the navy will not get or want any more Vets or Volunteers. The draft has been postponed. Oh what glorious times it will be when the cruel war is over. We will have or I will have a grand time when the "Jonnies come marching home." If I'm permited to live untill that happy time. But I have no doubt I'll feel sad for those who look in vain for their loved ones. It will be a dear bought Peace, but I hope never to live to see another war. Miss Louise Candit sayes give him my love, so I endeavor to please my company. I come up and locked me in my room but they will not stay down stairs and I have to stop to answer a question about every word I write. You must not think you would get used to them in my missives __ __ __

Going to the "home of the dead" seems to influence you to sad thoughts as well as myself, for I have had just such thoughts questionings and longings as you speak of having, upon visiting Greenmount Cemetery. I hope it will profit you more than I fear it has me, but my Dear friend, I will and have remember you especialy, that you may always be ready with your Lamp trimed and burning and that the messenger may be welcome when he shall come to bear your spirit Home. Do not forget me. You do not — do you? I trust your prayers are not few on my behalf for I need them, but I must close. We are having verry pleasant times and although I enjoy the friends that are present, I can not or would not forget the absent one who is dearer than all to me and who I hope soon to see, tis the wish of one who is

Yours till Death
M. Emma Randolph

P.S. Please write soon as convenient, and tell me how youre geting along with bis and the prospects of your having a furlough and when do not forget

your caring Emma

Baltimore, Md.
September 14th 1864

Dear Emma

Your last which was received on the morning of the 7th is before me. I regret deeply that my duties have prevented me from answering before. At the time I received your letter we were busy moving our Office, togather with the more than usual rush of business, has completely occupied my time, both night and day. I trust that you will consider my circumstances, pardon me for my delay and accept this, though tardy letter, as it has been impossible for me to write you under an earlier date.

This evening being very much fatigued with the confinement that my duties demand and desiring some out of door exercise, I accepted of an offer, from a friend to take a ride on horseback. I rode out

Charles St.[72] to the Country where I enjoyed a good long ride and returned feeling much benefited (for I have not enjoyed very good health for a few days past) by the pleasant exercise that horseback riding affords. I never before appreciated it as I do now and I would recommend that as a very healthy exercise for you. I met several ladies out riding this evening, it is very fashionable here. Do you ride out often?

On the morning of the 6th we received orders to pack up and prepare to move, which was soon done and everything ready to load on the wagons. The chief clerk being at Monocacy on duty at that time, the superintendence of the job fell upon me. I had six men to load and four to unload the wagon which kept me busy keeping them at work. We finished Friday evening and although, I had but little to do, more than see that it was done, I was completly worn out. After attending to my duties in the office, Sabbath day I felt so bad I concluded to go to the Hospital and on my way there I met an acquaintance, who said he hardly knew me, I had changed so, he said I looked about played out, so you may judge that I felt miserable, as my feelings corresponded with my looks.

The Office is much more pleasantly situated now than before. It is on one of the most fashionable streets in the City.[73] The building is large and more commodious and the change had made a great improvement, but the beauty of it is, that there are two very pretty looking young ladies directly opposite, who have quite a habit of sitting in the windows where they can be seen. I presume that they have an idea of "making love" to some of the fellows in the Office, I hope I may not fall a victim.

Last Sabbath I made an application to be relieved from duty here, but Maj. Wharton to whom I applied would not hear to it, he could not spare me. He has been trying to have it arranged so that he might retain me untill my term of service expires, so it seems that he holds my services in high appreciation. I like him but I dislike the duty, it is too confining for me. I prefer a life of more excitement. One of the

---

[72]A major north-south thoroughfare from Baltimore's harbor to the countryside. In 1864, Baltimore was geographically a much smaller city than it is today, and the "country" was much nearer to town.

[73]Walter's new office was located at 31 Calvert Street, on Monument Square.

clerks is about to be relieved, and I expect I will take his place, charge of the department of Comsy. Musters,[74] a more responsible position than I now occupy.

My prospects for a furlough are very obsure at present. As one of the clerks is about to leave and as we are driven by our business, I think it would be improper for me to apply for a leave of absence at present. I have had the promise of one whenever I wish it, but I think it advisable to wait a while. I can probbably inform you better next time, as to when I will visit New Jersey. I hope it may be soon. Had we not been so busy, I should have been home last Sabbath. I will live in hopes of having a merry time when I come, whether sooner, or later.

I am glad that you are enjoying yourself as well as your letters indicate. While you were enjoying yourself so well on Sunday evening, I was also having a pleasant time. My Chum and myself made one of our weekly calls at No. 6 Oregon St. where some of our lady friends reside. We had a pleasant time indeed. The evening flew swiftly by and at midnight a proposition was made by one of the party to have a game of Euchre, but I did not favor it at the late hour and proposed that we adjourn which was seconded by my chum and about 1 A.M. after spending an evening that we will all remember, we bade them good bye (one of them probbably for the last time as she was to start for home the next day, several miles from here) and returned to our room to sleep away the few remaining hours of the night.

Dearest Emma, I am glad to learn that when you are enjoying yourself in the company of others, I am not forgotten. Accept my most sincere thanks for the assurance that I am a subject of your prayers, and believe me Dear Emma, you are not forgotten, but earnestly prayed for by me. I would give anything I have for an interview with you this evening. I long for another furlough that we may repeat some of those pleasant spent hours of last March, especially those about midnight. I shall come home as soon as I think it advisable.

Tis growing late and as I am quite weary, besides having a very lame arm, I will close. I cannot express with the pen, what I would wish to. I will wait untill I can speak with you. Please accept this with the promise to be more prompt in responding to your next, if my time will permit. I presume that you are at this time sleeping soundly, and I

---

[74]The Eighth Corps Office of Commissary Musters.

hope having pleasant dreams. That you may be protected from all dangers and harm and be ever found waiting on the Lord from whom you derive your very existence, is the prayer of one who loves you with his whole heart and who is bound to you by the ties of affection.

W. G. Dunn

P.S. Please excuse the style and mistakes as I have written in a great hurry. Address as before.

Walter "Good night"

Office Comsy. Musters
8th Army Corps
Balto. Sept. 26th 1864

Dearest Emma

The anticipated pleasure of reading your letter, which I received Sabbath morning was mingled with sorrow by the tidings of your illness. I regret that you are still the object of so much suffering. I sympathise with you deeply and if it were possible, would endure your sufferings myself that you might be relieved, but I can only pray for you which I do earnestly that you may recover speedily and again enjoy the blessing of heath of which I am happy to say through the kindness of my Heavenly Father, I am in perfect enjoyment.

I knew not what was the cause of your unusual delay. I thought I wrote something in my last that offended you and as I had been so delinquent, you would delay the answer of my letter in order that you might return "ill for ill." I am glad that such was not the case. I freely pardon you for your tardy response and trust that ere this reaches you, you will have so nearly recovered that you will be able to reply immediately as I am very anxious to learn the state of your health at as early a date as possible.

Last evening I attended the Presbyterian Church on the corner of Charles and Fayette Sts. with a friend of mine. Text Hebrews 6::20 — an exelent discourse. The Choir music was without exception the best I ever heard, and I enjoyed it very much.

I was as busy as a bee all day yesterday, which is unusual for me. Sabbath evening Major Wharton recd. an order to have a certain job completed by this (Monday) morning. He came to the office early yesterday morning and sent for me before I was entirely dressed (being Sunday I did not rise very early) and from that time untill church time in the evening I was as busy as I could be. It is rather hard when a person cannot have one day out of seven to rest. What think you of it? We are very busy indeed at present and will be for several days. Major Wharton asked me this evening when I wished to go to my home in New Jersey. I told him I would like to go a soon as I could be spared, he said I might go as soon as this present job was finished (which will be in a few days) for said he "if any one deserves a furlough, you do." If I can make out the semi monthly report on Friday (being the last day of the month), I will start for home Friday night so as to attend church Sabbath day. I shall be governed by our business as one of our clerks has been ordered to his Regt. there is a great deal for me to do.

"to be continued"

I was aware that Father and Mother talked of going to R[hode] I[sland] I know not how long they expect to remain there. I think it very strange that I have not heard from home for over two weeks. If Jennie is at Fathers house, that accounts for it as Mary or Lew could not find time to write. If such is the case wo be unto her when I get home. If they do not write soon, I will just for spite.

The news are very encouraging this evening. It is reported that Mobile has surrendered unconditionally to Admiral Farragut. I hope it may prove true. Gold is falling very fast and everything is of an encouraging nature.[75]

I feel very little like writing, being much fatigued with the duties of the day. I hope soon to be able to have an old fashioned talk with you face to face which I prefer to writing. I desire that you answer immediately, that I may hear from you soon should I be disappointed in getting my furlough and even if I should not, I will receive it befor Friday night. I do not promise you certain that I will come then, nor can I for I am unable to tell what time. If I have time I will drop you a

---

[75]Admiral David G. Farragut had won the battle of Mobile Bay on August 5, closing Mobile as a Confederate port and paving the way for land operations against the city. The last Confederate fort fell on August 23, although the city itself remained for a time thereafter in Confederate hands. The price of gold rose on bad war news and fell on signs of optimism.

line Thursday morning that you may receive it Friday. In it I will state whether or not I can get off the above mentioned night.

Please comply with my request and reply immediately. Excuse all imperfections and accept this hastily written letter from your true and loving friend.

W. G. Dunn

V. R. Corps

Written in great haste.

Explanations given, if required, when I get home next Sabbath night probbably.

Walter Dunn received his furlough and returned home to New Market, though when and for how long is not certain.

Part III: "Badly Worsted by the Change"

In mid-October 1864, Walter received a furlough and returned home to New Market for a brief stay, which included long visits with Emma. Doubtless they shared the growing excitement of the presidential campaign of 1864. A war-weary North, saddened and embittered by the long casualty lists that had emerged from Grant's bloody Wilderness Campaign and the resulting stalemate before Petersburg gave serious consideration to the opposition candidate, former Union General George B. McClellan. In states like New Jersey, where Peace Democrats carried significant strength, not even William Tecumseh Sherman's spectacular capture of Atlanta was enough to turn the tide clearly for the incumbent Lincoln, and both sides dug in for a battle at the polls. Walter, remembering his friends in the 11th New Jersey, who had suffered terribly in the Wilderness and at Spotsylvania Court House, voiced his ardent Unionist views and, like many soldiers, returned home again briefly to vote.

On his return to Baltimore, Walter encountered a surgeon with whom he had worked who examined him and said it was now feasible to remove the troublesome bullet from his shoulder. Walter happily agreed to an operation he was soon to regret, as once again he found himself immersed in the blood and filth of hospital wards overcrowded with wounded from the recent battles. When his letters home suddenly stopped arriving, Emma grew increasingly fearful, even as her own health again weakened.

Dear

Emma

Baltimore, Md.
Oct. 20th 1864

My Dear Emma

Pursuant to promise, I will improve this my first opportunity in informing you of my safe arrival to this City at 4::20 A.M. Monday.

I will give you a brief history of my trip which is as follows. About 6::30 P.M. Sunday Lew and myself started for New Brunswick enjoyed a very pleasant ride and reached said place in time to witness a considerable excitement, caused by the burning of the R.R. Bridge. The alarm was given and a large crowd gathered at the Depot to witness the anticipated illumination, which, however resulted in nothing more than a fright and a little smoke.

Being very anxious to return to this City in the train which was then about due, I felt somewhat disappointed, fearing that the bridge would be so damaged as to render crossing unsafe, but at "luck favors the brave" my anxiety was driven away by seeing the train crossing the bridge and fast approaching the Depot, about twenty minutes after time. Soon after its arrival, I bade farewell to my friends who were there, and steped aboard as the train was moving off. I was not long in procuring a seat and making a pillow of my Carpet Bag. I got in a very easy position and was soon sleeping soundly. With the exception of being awakened occasionally by the Conductor, I slept the trip through, not seeing Phila. nor any other of the most important places allong the line and finaly woke up as the passengers were vacating the cars in this City. I enjoyed a good sleep and felt much refreshed. A few moments walk brought me to this office and I set about for an entrance by pulling the bell to the tune of "Yankee Doodle" which in time arrived one of the boys, when I got in and commenced routing them out of bed. I would like for you to have heard the sport we had that morning and the different questions that were asked me. Since my arrival, we have been in the Office every day as regular as before I went home, although I must confess, it went against my feeling the first two days. The boys tell me that Maj. Wharton enquired about me nearly every day, asking when my furlough would expire. One day he brought his fist down on the table, hard enough to shake the house and said I would rather spare him three months any other time than now. But he got allong without me, and no bones broken, so I think I will let him try it again soon as I met Dr. Dickson to day on Baltimore St. and he told me to come to the Hospital in a few days and he would opperate on my shoulder.

I received your letter. Did not I obey well in sitting in fathers seat in Church? Most certainly I will excuse the style. I think we might lay asside all formality as our intimacy does not demand it. I have been taking an inventory to day of the things in the Office and am very tired, and on those grounds I ask to be excused for not writing more. Please accept this brief and tardy letter with the promise of more next time. Please reply as early as possible. This leaves me enjoying good health, may it find you the same is the prayer of one who loves you sincerely. Dearest Emma believe me to be as ever, yours,

Walter G. Dunn

Did you not think I was "lovesick" last Sabbath night? I presume I acted thus, Did I not?

Little did I think when I told you I would write you in about a week, that it would be as late as this, but this is my first opportunity and I beg you to pardon my delay, which was not intentional by no means. Allow me to ask an immediate reply as I am extreemly anxious to hear from you. I hope you are in better health than when I saw you last. I am enjoying myself hugely and I hope you are the same.

Yours, Walter

Address as before (Box 1203, care of Maj. Wharton Balto. Md.)

Plainfield Union Co. N.J.
Oct. 25, 1864

My Own Dear Walt

Your kind and ever welcomed Letter I did not receive untill last evening. The reason why you shall know presently.

I'm verry glad you had such good luck in reaching Baltimore in safty, and had such a good sleep you needed it.

Immediately after you left me the last evening you was here, I retired to bed and you will laugh perhaps when I tell you I did not sleep any untill the clock told me it was five A.M. Do you know what time it was when Lew came?

I did not go out untill tuesday evening and then I went with the rest to the "grand meeting at the Wigwam."[1] I had the pleasure of standing the whole time from 7 P.M. untill about 11 A.M. and then had the exquisit pleasure of remaining in doors untill last Sabbath evening. I dressed with intention of going up to the meeting as I was verry anxious to hear Eld Rogers political speech, but Ma spoke and said she would rather I would not go. It was such a long walk so I remained at home, took a couple of Pillows and struck a comfortable "posish" on the Sofa and dreamed of happiness and then was aroused from the presence of Past, Present, and Future by a knock at the door and there was Vermont and Mr. M. Smalley. Mont said he had come for me, that Harrie had cut his big toe nearly off. Calvin[2] had let the Horse run away with him and throw him across the fence hurting him some. Lib had been to Newark to spend a week and had come home sick, and they wanted me to come down and stay a few days. I told Mont that Ma wont not hear to it at all. I told I would go if she is willing. He sayes "where is Ma?" and upon his learning that she was at the meeting he started for said place, and he soon comes back telling he had seen Mother and gained her consent and at half past 10 we were out. I was coming home monday evening but did not come untill last night, which is the cause of the delay. I had a very pleasant visit indeed. Harries cut has laid him up, and Monday night we went up to New

---

[1]The Republican Party nominated Abraham Lincoln in the "Wigwam" in Chicago in 1860. In 1864 towns in New Jersey and elsewhere built "Wigwams" in which to hold Republican meetings prior to the election.

[2]Emma had a brother named Calvin Randolph.

Market to hear the speaking and I guess he sent word through Lib for Nan to come home with us and she did, and was verry attentive to him. I think all things are fair for you to win the "Oysters."[3] The second of Nov. Charley Randolph and Jennie Randell, David Rogers and Julia Bridsell are to be married at the Church at New Market 9 Oclock A.M. Is not that new? Joy is with them.

Mr Walter G. Smith[4] has been discharged come home last Sunday morning week ago. I was just for seting myself to write you when Ma informed he wished to see me. I have not answered his last letter that I received when I was sick in June. Mrs. Martin Dunn is verry low with inflamation of the Lungs is not expected to live. Ellis[5] who is still at Westerly R.I. has broken his leg in two places, he is doing as well as can be expected. I do not know of any more news. I guess that is enough, for it is all bad news I have told you. I hope I will have better next time I write. And I hope of having it fullfilled that I shall feel better when you hear from me again. I know Dear Walt that this is not interesting, but please excuse this poor attempt for I tell you I'm not feeling or looking better than the "last night." If any difference, my head pains me considerably more. I have not had anyone to tend me tonight. Oh, how I miss you Walt. You dont know. You cant half imagine. My feelings compell me to close. I hope your prayers will soon be answered for I'm so tired of this, but I endeavor to endure to the end, for I know "tis all for the best."

Are you coming home to vote? All the rest of the Jersey boys are. So I understand. Things are verry livly here now indeed. Please remember the Soldiers dinner will you? and "pitch your tent." Please tell me when you expect to have the ball extracted. Oh I shall be glad when it is out and I know you are anxious but do not forget the loving ones at home think of you always, and as prayers have already been answered they can hope for the future. I'm one of them.

As Ever, Your Emma

---

[3]Walt and Emma have apparently made a bet with Dave Randolph and Sallie Johnson over who will be the last couple to be married. The winner will receive a quantity of oysters or an oyster supper.

[4]Walter G. Smith was not on the original rolls of the 11th New Jersey and was probably a member of a different regiment.

[5]Ellis J. Dunn.

Baltimore, Md.
Oct. 30th 1864

My Dear Emma

Sunday, 10::30 P.M. I imagine you will think it rather a late hour to write a letter, but as this is my first opportunity and probbably the only one I will have for several days to come, I will endeavor to improve it. Your very interesting and longed for letter of the 26th inst. was duly received, the reading of which was accompanied with more than usual interest as your illness when I left, caused me to be very anxious, indeed, to hear from you. I was about to write you again, to ascertain the cause of your delay, fearing that you were sick and unable to write, but I was gratified to learn that such was not the case, still I regret that you were feeling quite ill at the time of writing and earnestly hope and pray that you have recovered and now in the enjoyment of perfect health, which I am blessed with at present.

I judge that Mrs. Randolph places a very high estimation on your nursing qualities by sending so far for you to nurse her "poor boys." I think I can reccommend you in that capacity. Do you remember the night at Clarks? I have abundant reason to be thankfull to you for you kind attention that night, depriving yourself of pleasure as you did, to relieve me, nor was it without effect for I began to amend immediately after the application of the cold water.

As to my coming home to vote, I do not expect to. Men are being sent home from nearly all the Northern states for that purpose but if a man belongs to New Jersey he cant go, as the state has made no provisions for her soldiers to vote. Her State Legislature would not pass a Bill, where by her soldiers could be represented at the Ballot Box and of all that has been done for the soldiers, that little contemptible state has done the least.[6] Nearly every state has their agents to visit the Hospitals and administer to the wants of the sick and wounded, but is there any one to enquire about Jersey men? No, nary an agent and whats more we dont care to see one, as long as our good old "Uncle Samuel" furnishes us with plenty of hardtack and Greenbacks. I lived

---

[6]Many Northern regiments were permitted to vote in the field in the presidential election of 1864, but not New Jersey troops. The Democrat-controlled state legislature, fearing strong Lincoln support among the soldiers (although many were known to support former General George B. McClellan), refused to send agents to collect their ballots.

Baltimore in the 1860s. (Maryland Historical Society.)

The soldiers of the 11th New Jersey took a straw vote among themselves and gave Lincoln a narrow majority. Democratic presidential candidate McClellan narrowly carried the state by 7,301 votes. For an account of the election in New Jersey, see William Gillette, *Jersey Blue: Civil War Politics in New Jersey, 1854–1865* (New Brunswick: Rutgers University Press, 1995), 287–91. For the 11th New Jersey's reaction, see Marbaker, *Eleventh New Jersey Volunteers,* 228–29.

in New York nearly one year and I shall claim that as the state in which I reside, I shall own New Jersey no longer for she is not in the Union, nor never has been.[7] I think I have said sufficient on that subject and will therefor give vent to my feelings no longer.

Last Friday evening, Mr. Mackey and myself called on our friends in Oregon Street and had a very interesting game of Euchre, also added two young Misses to our list of young lady acquaintances. One has recently come home from Petersburg Va and is inclined to be on the red and white principal.[8] She does not like to hear any one say rebel, she thinks that confederate sounds much better, but she did not object to playing with Union Cards. She has two brothers in the rebel army, and her parrents being rebels, I think is the reason she is. She was very sociable and we had a very pleasant time indeed, leaving there about 1 A.M. Sabbath morning.

Em, give me a long merit mark for I have been to church three times to day. This morning I went to the Charles St. M.E. Church. Text. 1st Corrinthians 1st:: 22, 23 and 24th verses,[9] at 3::30 this evening I attended Chapel, text John 5::40[10] and at 7:30 this evening the Union Square M. E. Church, text unknown as I did not get there quite early enough to hear it. There was a funeral sermon preached at the Chapel for two bodies. At the Hospital they bury soldiers at the rate of two and three a day. There is a large number of severely wounded at Jarvis from Sheridans army and they are dying very fast.[11]

---

[7]Walter, who resided in New York while attending Alfred Center, here reflected a common theme, doubt about New Jersey's wartime patriotism and loyalty to the Union.

[8]Throughout the war, but particularly in its later years, the Union army's provost-marshal's office in Baltimore expelled suspected Confederate sympathizers across the lines into Confederate territory. Not surprisingly, some probably returned without notice. Red and white were Confederate colors, and women wearing them were targets for deportation.

[9]"For Jews demand signs and Greeks seek wisdom, but we preach Christ crucified, a stumbling-block to Jews and folly to Gentiles, but to those who are called, both Jews and Greeks, Christ the power of God and the wisdom of God."

[10]"You search the scriptures, because you think that in them you have eternal life; and it is they that bear witness to me; yet you refuse to come to me that you may have life."

[11]On October 19, 1864, General Jubal Early's Confederate armies surprised Union forces at Cedar Creek. Union General Philip H. Sheridan rushed back to his command from Washington and inspired them to a

I am sorry to hear that Ellis Dunn has met with such a misfortune. Did you learn how it hapened?

Yes, I too wish, the parties that you named much joy as they are about to enter the state of matrimony. May the hours of prosperity and happiness ever shine bright on their paths, and you think that things look favorable for me to win the oysters. I have thought so for a long time. Keep the oyster supper in view.

I cannot say when I shall have the ball extracted as the Surgeons are very busy now at the Hospital and I hate to trouble them when so many cases are suffering much worse that I am. I shall have it done the very first opportunity. I told one of the lady nurses, who (by the way is both young and goodlooking) that I expected to be a patient in the Hospital soon and asked her if she had an empty bed in her ward, she said she had none now, but would make one for me any time I should come and would be happy to wait upon me. Is not she very kind?

Dear Emma you said that you missed me very much, you cannot miss me any more than I do you, that is impossible. I have dreamed about you several times since I returned and oh, such pleasant dreams. I only wish that I might realise them soon. If you were only here to night I could tell you how much I miss you, not only with words but with my actions as I have a keen desire for a good hug, but that is impossible under the circumstances. Be sure and not forget the second Sabbath night in August next.[12]

I have much more I would like to write, but I fear that I have already wearied your patience therefore allow me to bid you good night and retire as I must get up by 7 tomorrow morning, which is rather earlier than I have been in the habit of arrising, since I re-turned from New Jersey. However before closing I will ask you to excuse all imperfections and miserable writing for I have written in great haste besides feeling quite dull, by being up quite late the past few nights. I am resolved to do different, stay in nights, go to bed early and arrise early, and hope to feel brighter when I write you again. I fear that you will have some difficulty in reading this, if you do send it

---

successful counterattack. Union losses were 644 killed, 3,430 wounded, and 1,591 missing in what was the last major battle in the Shenandoah Valley. Figures from E. B. Long, *The Civil War Day by Day*, 585.

[12]The date of an anticipated buggy ride with Dave and Sallie Johnson that will mark Walter's return home.

back, and I will send you a translated copy of it. Dearest Emma, that you may be speedily restored to the enjoyment of perfect health is the sincere prayer of one who loves you dearly and who will always be true to the object of his affection (I wish you knew my feelings to night.)

I am ever yours in love
Walter G. Dunn

My arm is very nervous to night, please excuse the awkward shaped letters. Walter

"Substitutes"

I am quite ashamed to send this, but circumstances compell me to.

[Drawing of a star] "Evening star" of the West

I have about a dozen soldiers, who if they are allowed to go home to vote will accept your Mothers offer to dine.

An Invalid

Write immediately (or quicker) as I am very anxious to hear from you.

W. G. Dunn

Plainfield Union Co. N.J.
Nov. 1st 1864

Dearest Walt

Good morning Youre well: How am I? I do not see how I can help feeling much better after such a dear missive as I have just perused: believe me Walt. It is verry interesting and to get another just like it. I'm going to answer by return mail, "business permitting" (haw) for I'm acting "Chief Book Keeper" at the "Office": our former Clerk having met with quite an accident getting his foot mashed under the Seventh day evening excursion train. Dr. Stillman[13] says it will have to be taken off just above the ankle—to bad.

---

[13]Dr. Charles H. Stillman was Emma's family physician. Born in 1817 in Schenectady, New York, he attended Union College and later received his medical degree in 1840 at the College of Physicians and Surgeons. In 1842 he moved to Plainfield and became a member of the Seventh Day Baptist Church. Called the "Father of Free Public Schools in New Jersey," he was the superintendent of schools in Plainfield for all but two years between 1847 and 1866 and was a surgeon for the Central Railroad of New Jersey. In 1872 he would become Plainfield's mayor. Medical knowledge at the time was far from advanced, and his treatments nearly cost Emma her life.

Dr. Charles H. Stillman, Randolph
family physician. (Courtesy,
Plainfield Public Library.)

Friday Evening last while you was enjoying yourself with you[r]
Baltimore friends I was in a comfortable position on Ma's bed watching
the little ones. How sleepy they grew waiting to see cousin Jont who we
expected to come and stay all night with us. He came, but not untill we
were all asleep and dreaming. Will and Jont looks first-rate. He, Jont
went to Church at New Market with us. The folks stared at us some
when we took our seats. And I was surprised to see Mr. Able
Titsworth[14]—he is at home to vote, and is looking better than I ever
seen him. Ada Green is visiting Kizzie now. Mrs. I. Titsworth thinks it
happens lucky that she Ada has come while Ables home. So think I.
don't you?

The Soldiers came just in time last thursday evening to get their
supper at "Aunt Ems" and go to the meeting with the Plainfield Clubs
at West field. Pa says they had a grand time friday evening meeting at

---

[14]Abel S. Titsworth, four years older than Walter, had enlisted as a
corporal in Company D of the 11th New Jersey in August 1862. In September
of the following year he became a hospital steward.

the "Wigwam."[15] Sabbath evening excursion train to Elizabeth City—
verry large meeting and Pa said and so did Mont, Lew and all of them
that they never seen dwelling houses trimed and illuminated as those
they paraded past and—came home about eleven. Jennie and your
humble Servant sit up (or rather took the sofa) to wait for them. (Pa,
Mont, Lew, and Oll). We of course fell asleep, and the first thing I
heard, "Em wake up and see 'Walt' dont you know Walter Dunn is
here!" I answered So am I. They laughed at that and Em (haw) was
"wide awake." Pa went to bed but Ollie dident go and do likewise nary
a once. You know he likes to sit up with me. But they out stayed him
and a happy time we had. After Jennie and I went and took another
nap slept about half hour after they Skedaddled, and 3 A.M. before we
retired now I have not told you how long they stayed. How about those
drinks that was bet on the "last night"! Hey!

I received a letter from Cousin Emma Bryant this morning with a
pressing invitation to come down to Newark and have the Grand Dr. to
perscribe. Ma is verry anxious for me to go. Pa is willing but Em (I) do
not feel quite as ready to grant their request. And I know Pa does not
know how to spare me: for you must know I'm good for scmthing if
Mrs. Randolph would send so far for poor me.

Last evening there was a grand procession and a large turn out of
Cavalry. Cous. Jont was Capt. Will 1st fruit [lieutenant]. They had a
splendid tramp. Your Uncle Isaac Dunns house was luminated and
several others. I with all my Cousins was at the "Wigwam" to hear the
great and honorable speaker Col. Montgomery from the South. He
kept the audience in "roars of laughter." I got home about 1 P.M.
taking an extra cold with me. Tomorrow Evening is an extra meeting.
A speaker still more humores than the Col. Sabbath Eve. is to be
another Cavalry Show. The ladies are to prepare wreaths of Evergreen
to trim the poneys. Our Grace is to be the Goddess of Liberty.

Oh! I wish you were here to attend some of the meeting. By the
way New Jersey (so the speaker said) is in the United States, and is
going for the Union.[16] Now dont you wounded "Sogers" want to see an

---

[15]Emma referred here to the excitement and enthusiasm leading up to
the presidential election, which was held a week later, on November 8.

[16]New Jersey had been the butt of derision for its Democratic sympathies,
many in the nation believing that the state was controlled by Copperheads.
Republicans and War Democrats constantly struggled to refute the charge.

agent from said state. Now I'll bet you would look at me should I come, and I think I'd have to for I do not know about that young nurse. I hope you will come and vote. Be sure if you can and we will welcome the Soldiers to dinner.

I think some of going down to the wedding, to see how its done. Yes! I will keep the Oyster supper in view.

But what about those "Substitutes"?[17] I am verry anxious to know wont you write me about them? If you do not, I believe I shall ask Little Dave.

It is nearly night. I'm sorry I could not send this in the after noon mail but there has been so many in and my books bother me, and you will please remember how this was writen when you read it. I find this does not agree with me for I go home with a throbbing headache. You would laugh could you hear some of my dreams. I'll bet our dreams resemble each other. I understand the "evening star" but I do not like that kind, do you! My feeling[s] compell me to stop. Oh how I wish you was coming up to see me to night, but never mind spaces there is between us or how far apart. I think of you always, and remember you as my own Dearest Friend, the one I expect to find "True as the Stars." I have confidence that such you will prove. Good night. Please write soon to your own true and still loving

Emma

Please excuse this. My head pains me verry much. Please write so that I can get it Sabbath Eve. and troublesome Em.

Plainfield Union Co N.J.
Nov. 16th 1864

Dear Walt

Having a few spare moments I will make an attempt to write to you. I could not write you yesterday for I was not verry well, and had more business to attend to than any day I have been at the store, so please take the "will for the deed."

Feeling to much indisposed to walk down home to dinner. I have taken it here in the shape of an Oyster Stew. (how are your stews for four) Theres two bets.

---

[17]Emma referred not to those who sold their services as soldiers in the draft but to a minor mystery Walter has made in his letters regarding "substitutes."

There is no especial news that I know of unless it is that snow fell here yesterday to the depth of an inch. But to day the sun has caused it to (nearly all of it) skedaddle. I understand they had sleighing up at Albany. I realy did think we would have to get the sleigh out. It seemed so much like winter. To day is verry pleasant. Could I have a part of the ride I had last Sunday morning, I should feel better. But as that cannot be, I will be contented.

I see Clark up in town this morning. I had a notion to ask him if Walter had gone back, but did not. We were in to R. Dunhams and there was a couple of women in the store talking up for "Little Mac"[18] and making sport of your Uncle Ruben Titsworth[19] for being out with a party of "Lincoln men" as they called them. After they left I asked Clark did he know them? He said, "no we dident want to. As they came from of the mountains, we all thought they dident know any better."

How is Mr. Stevens? Did he look for you before you came. I suppose you arrived at Baltimore safe, and by this time have regained lost sleep. I have had a good oppertunity but my head has pained me verry much this week and it is some time before I can go to sleep, after going to bed. The hands are coming in quite fast and if I send this to day I will have to cut it short.

This morning I called the Dr. for Jennie has been quite sick for a day or two with the sore throat. I hope it will not be any thing serious. He (the Doctor) felt my pulse and was about to prescribe somthing for me, but I told him I did not want any of his attention, but had called to request him to go down to the house and see Jennie. He said "that if I did not care he guessed that I did not want his medicine and he would go and call on Jennie 'the Fatty'" as he calls her.

I must close, hoping your health is good. Dear Walt do not think I'm brief and cool for could you only know how much I love you, you would not harbor such a thought. It is verry lonly since you went back. I hope for the time when you will not be so far away from one who loves you dearly and will love you to the end. Remember me as yours till Death

Emma R.

---

[18]Democratic presidential candidate George B. McClellan.
[19]Reuben Titsworth married Walter's aunt, Susan Dunn.

P.S. Plese write soon. And tell me all the news and about the Substitutes.

Baltimore, Md.
Nov. 19th 1864

My Dear Emma

I cannot, with the pen, express the longing anxiety that preceded the reception of your brief yet interesting letter of a recent date, which I rec'd. in due time. The interest in, and the pleasure coupled with the reading of you letters, are increasing as each letter proves to be the source of more gratification than the one preceding it. You cannot half imagine how cheering and full of encouragement your letters are to one who oftimes feels sad and lonely, but when he receives one of your precious missives, a gleam of pleasure can be seen on his countenance, showing that joy is "Substituted" for despair, and, on the other hand, imagine the disappointment when they (letters) fail to arrive when due. Do not accept this as flattery, but believe me Dear to be sincere.

I have just returned from a ride on horseback. I never enjoyed a gallop of about four miles better than I did this evening. On my return I called at the A. G. O.[20] to see Mr. Stevens but was disapointed, he not being there. I saw his cousin (Mr. Armstrong) who told me that he was much better. He called here to see me on Thursday morning and looked very bad, his face was very much swollen with the toothache caused by a heavy cold. He was sick in bed for several days, but has now, nearly recovered and again resumed his duties.

Mr. Skinner, the writer of the letter that I read a portion of to you, called here on Tuesday on his return from a furlough home to vote. I asked him how he voted, he replied, "Through the influence of your letter I voted the right way, for Abe. Lincoln." He was formerly a supporter of McClellan but now he says "I see where I was wrong and no 'true soldier' will endorse the principles of 'G. B. McClellan'." We had a hearty shake hands over the victory. My Democratic chum said that he did not vote at all, and that he is very glad that President Lincoln was reelected, I am also.

Yes I reached Baltimore safe at the time I expected.[21] I took the

---

[20]Adjutant General's Office.
[21]Evidently Walter Dunn, like the other clerks mentioned, was given a second furlough that he might go home to vote.

11::30 A.M. train from New Brunswick, reached Trenton at 12::40 P.M. where I remain untill 10::15 P.M. and arrived in this City at precisely 5 A.M. on Tuesday. The cars were crowded when I got aboard and I was obliged to stand up most of the way which was not very pleasant. I must confess that I felt quite rough for a few days but I now begin to feel natural once more. I have made very long nights since I returned, going to bed about 9 P.M. and arrising between the hours of eight and nine A.M. by that method I have gained sufficient sleep to make me feel ordinarily bright.

Tis growing late—allow me to lay this asside untill tomorrow, as my eyes are getting quite heavy. How often, tonight, I have thought of where I was one week ago, with the Sofa drawn up to the Stove. Oh, if I could only enjoy tonight the pleasure that I realised one week ago this very minute, how happy I would be, but I must drive away such feelings, knowing that circumstances seperate us for a time, but as time rolls on and we are again permitted to enjoy each others society, we will then more highly appreciate it, because we have been so long deprived of that unequaled pleasure.

Sunday Nov. 20

If I mistake not, I promised to inform you previous to having the opperation performed.[22] I dislike to speak about it this time, from the very fact that I may be disappointed as I have been before. I am not positive, but I have taken some very important steps toward having the opperation performed tomorrow. I have made an application to that effect and obtained a leave of absence from the Office. I also spoke to that nurse for a bed in her ward. She said that there was none vacant at present, but she would have one vacated for me—how kind. I shall use all the means in my power to bring it about tomorrow, and if I fail, you may be assured that it is not my fault.

I intended to go to church this evening but the rain will prevent me, as today will pass for a "right smart" rainy day.

I feel sorry that your head aches so much. I wish I could bathe it with cold water. I hope and pray that you may feel better when you receive this.

---

[22]The operation to have the ball removed from behind his shoulder.

I am aware that there are two bets at stake. I think that we are good for our "oysters" don't you?

I have had my moustache and Imperial[23] shaved off, the boys tell me I look ten years older. Now are you old enough to get married? I will tell you about the "Substitute" in my next.

Have you had the ratification meeting in the Wigwam yet, if not when do you expect to hold it?

I have already exhausted the time allotted to the writing of this and therefore I must close, hoping that you will write very soon to one who loves you with an undying love and has bright anticipations of the future. Dearest one that you may be in the enjoyment of good health is the sincere prayer of your devoted friend and future companion

W G Dunn

P.S. Address me Jarvis Hospital Balto. Md. Write soon and a long letter as you are accustomed to do. Write often and oblige. Walter

(I must tell you what I imagined or rather dreamed in the cars. While traveling between New Brunswick and Trenton I sat were the sun would shine in my face which was very agreeable as the morning was quite cold. I tried to get asleep which I suceeded in doing without much of an effort. I was dreaming and woke up saying, "Emma, you have a very hot fever" the sun made my face feel so warm. I laughed right out, when I woke up and thought of it.)

Walter G. Dunn

Plainfield Union Co. N.J.
Nov. 28, 1864

Dear Walter

Tis monday morning, I have looked in vain for a letter from you. I can endure suspense no longer. Walt what does it mean. Are you sick! Have you had the operation performed on your shoulder? Are you angry with "your Emma." Have I displeased you? What is the matter. I have not heard one word from you since you went back. Have not you received the letter I mailed to Baltimore the wednesday — as you left — monday! Cannot you write me. If to sick, please get some one to

---

[23]Moustache and goatee.

Card from a Newark substitute broker. (Courtesy of Ruth Washburn Bailey.)

write for you. You cannot imagine how anxious I am to hear from you.

I have received two (2) "Waverlys" since [the] Election. Please remember me as "thankful Em" for such kind favors. Will you?

Not knowing but youre displeased at something (not meant) I do not know how or what to write. Could not write much any how, one reason, I never do write what I consider much sense, another time will not permit, as I am verry busy and must have this go in the next mail.

The fall meeting (Great) at New Market was verry good I understand. I was not able to attend, quite a number of strangers was present.

I was to meeting last Sabbath morning. Eld. Rogers as usual preached a very good sermon. Text Judges 5 Chapter and well I do not remember the number of the verse, but it commences with "Curse ye Meroz."[24]

After meeting Uncle Reubens family came home with us and took dinner. In the afternoon we all attended the funeral of Mr. Hooker, distantly related to us. I spent the remaining hours of the Sabbath on

[24]"Curse ye Meroz, says the angel of the Lord, curse bitterly its inhabitants, because they came not to the help of the Lord, to the help of the Lord against the mighty."

the sofa. I supposed of course I would get a letter Sabbath Evening, but was again doomed to be disappointed. You know the old saying "nothing surer that Death and disappointment."

How did you spend your "thanksgiving"? Oh! how the weddings did come of[f] on that great day. I presume you have heard that Will Van Winkle and Annie Dunn was married on "thanksgiving" Eve. May they be happy! is my wish. I must close. Please let me hear from you soon and tell me just the cause of this long silence. Write soon to your own loving

Emma R.

Haddington U.S.A.
General Hospital, Phila. Pa.
Nov. 30th 1864

Dear Emma

Although not in your debt, I consider it a privalege to write you a few lines, informing you as to my whereabouts.

Last Monday, I with many other cripples, was transfered from Jarvis to the above named Hospital, situated near Philadelphia, Penna. The transfer was a matter of choice to me, but I can assure you that I got badly worsted by the change.

I left a Hospital where I lacked nothing for comfort, while here everything comfortable is lacking. I never before saw such a comtemptible, ill begotten, long forsaken chance of a place, as this is. I cannot describe it, nor will I say anything more about it, as I cannot say anything good.

According to my anticipations when I wrote you last the opperation was performed on my shoulder successfully. The wound, which is very sore, is doing as well as I can expect. I am not entirely over the effects of the Aether as I took such a large quantity. Dr. Dickson told me I took enough to kill nine men. The Steward who administered the Aether told me I took 16 oz. of Aether and 4 oz. of Chloriform, more than any man has ever yet taken at that Hospital. It leaves me with a headache from which I have suffered almost continually since the opperation. The ball that was extracted is a Minie Ball[25]

---

[25]The cone-shaped soft lead bullet used in most Civil War rifles. Walter's guess that it hit a tree before striking him is plausible, but it may also have flattened in striking his bone.

some flattened at either end. I presume it struck a tree before wounding me.

The Doctor here chose me for a Wardmastership in this Hospital, the same day that I came here, but I declined it as I am anxious to be returned to duty at the Office as soon as my wound heals. He asked me several questions, and after finding out that I lived so near here, said he would reccommend me for a furlough. If I accept it, it will be to get out of this place. I am determined to leave here soon, if I cannot by fair means, I will by foul.

You must excuse me if I do not send a "Waverly" this week as it is impossible for me to obtain a copy here.

I have not yet received an answer to my last. I presume it is at Jarvis Hospital. I sent for it to be forwarded here. I may get it tomorrow with my other mail from that place.

I cannot write more at present. Please excuse me for taking this liberty and write me immediatly. Consider me situated among strangers with nothing to read to while away my time which hangs very heavy. Accept my love. Ever yours

W. G. Dunn

P.S. Address me, Haddington U.S.A., Genl. Hospital, Ward O, Philadelphia, Penna

Excuse the style as I have written this on my bed.

"At The Office"
Plainfield Union Co. N.J.
Nov. 30th 1864

My Dearest Walt,

Now if I should come quietly up to your bedside and lay my hand on your forehead would you say "Emma what do you want"? How dearly I should love to greet you this morning with something besides the pen. I think if said Nurse should happen to see me would think she would have to step back: Don't you?

It is a beautiful morning the sun shines so warm. There is a gentle breeze. The roads are good. Granma says "It's Injun summer" and the folks seem to be enjoying. It makes me sigh to think of those who are forced to remain in doors. I think a gallop on horse back this fine day would help any ones health.

Not having time to write tuesday I wrote to you wednesday and waited anxiously an answer to my brief letter. I received one "Waverly" but nary letter from Walter. Another Waverly Pa got out the office monday morning (27) and threw it at me, my looks asked for a letter and my heart and hand too but I was again doomed to be disappointed: Then I looked at the directions on said wrapper and the writing confirmed my fears that you unable to write me from some cause perhaps you was displeased with your mate. So after considering I took my pen and did something I never did before (If I remember aright) vis. write the second time to you without receiving a reply. I suppose while I'm writing this (the third) the second one is in Box 1203 at the office: perhaps you have received it and are considering where your letter of the 19th inst. is. I will inform you the verry previous missive is here on the desk. As Jennie says "by some hocus pocus" I did not receive it until, well the first thing I heard this morning was "Emma did you know that there was a letter in Pa's pocket for you." The answer I gave Ma was "Ma please don't say that for Pa told me last night Walter had the ball taken out and how do you suppose he can write. No! Ma did not know it." She came out of the hall in to my room and lay your dear [letter] on my pillow. I was wide awake then and sooner devoured the contents. How long Pa has carried it in his pocket I don't know. You may laugh when you get my second missive yet I did not ask you half the questions I wanted to. Enough though.

Ah! my Dear I shall be compelled to dispute with you for saying "you cannot half imagine." For if you do not know it others do that Em can have a smiling countenance as well as you! I shall most certainly think your learning to flatter. If you substitute a countenance of pleasure for one of dispair but speaking earnestly now, the feeling is mutual for sincerly Walt every one is dearer.

I'm very thankful that you have writen to me the last letter I should get while that "Pesky Rebs" ball was in your shoulder. And also thank my heavenly Father that he has permited you to live through (it could not help being) the painfull operation of extracting the ball from your shoulder. How I should like to be with you and not let you get sad and lonsome. I was thinking of you at the time you was writing me and I was lying on the sofa thinking of the pleasures gone and trying to drive the "blues" away with bright hopes for the future. I wish I could write you what my thoughts of the future has been for the last

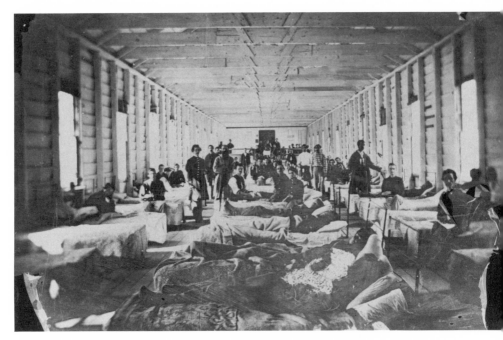

Photograph of an unidentified Civil War hospital ward. (Maryland Historical Society.)

week but it would cause you many sad thoughts and give you pain for you have told me you did not like to hear me speak so. I love you too well to cause you for a moment to feel unpleasant. I shall endeavor for your sake Dear Walt to keep a good heart, and not get discouraged: I know I'm naughty but feeling as I have this week I cannot help it. I have been alone all day (for it is after 4 PM) and I'm afraid I shall not get to the shop to morrow. I'm so wearry. I feel like having some one to take my head and lay it on his shoulder (not the wounded one) with gentle caresses sooth the pain [in] my head and let me sleep for a little while as I did one night for I'm verry tired. I must finish and go home. Please excuse me for writing and giving vent to my feelings thus Dear Walt. I will try and do better next time. How are you getting along? "Aunt Eliza" told Pa yesterday at the vendue[26] (Uncle Reubens)

---

[26]Public auction.

that you had [the] ball taken out your shoulder, and was geting along finly. Is it so? Tell me just how you are? Please will you! If you cannot write get some one to drop a few lines for I shall long for an answer. And to hear about the "substitutes" I'm verry anxious. I know you will tell me in your next for you have said so. But I must close for I cannot write any more. I will write again to morrow if I feel well enough for I know how cheering it is to receive a few lines from a friend.

That you may be tenderly cared for is the wish of one who holds verry dear. And my prayers though feable are in your behalf. That he who cares for us all will watch over and in his good time remove these afflictions and bless us both with health. If it is not to be so, may I meekly say "Thy will be done." Good night.

Ever yours, with much love

E. Randolph

Plainfield Union Co. N.J.

Dec. 5th 1864

Dear Walter

Good morning and how is the cripple this fine day? I hope you are improving. Is it so?

I received your last kind and believe me verry welcome letter friday evening. Pa gave it me while we were sitting at the supper table. I was very glad to hear from you, but sorry to learn that you are in such a mean Hospital as I think it must be. Els you would not use such language to express your opinion.

How dearly I would like to step in and take you prisoner and remove you here to "Randolph Hospital" to keep me company. What do you say to that arrangement my Dear? Do you think you would be much "worsted" then.

I suppose by this time you have received your mail from Baltimore and in it you ought to get two missives from me, one that was directed to Box 1203 and one to Jarvis.

I have tried to answer this last one several times but have failed in the attempt. I shall be ashamed of this I know writen as it is with a lead pencil not that I mean to reprove you for writing with pencil. No indeed Dear Walter. News from one I love is just as good to me wether formed with pen or pencil.

I dislike to own I'm to nervous to write with the pen. If Gracie did look over my shoulder yesterday and say my writing "look like a crab going to war," causing me to throw it down in despair this is my reason for using a pencil.

It is beautiful weather now, and if I wanted to please my Doctor I would be out riding now, it's being nearly the middle of the day but as it requires quite an effort to get up and down stairs I think it will be better for me to remain in doors today. To morrow (tuesday) I suppose they will do with me, as they please. Cousin Jont says he is coming after me in the buggy and drive carefull for they must have Emma or the circle formed by the family gathering at Grand Fathers to morrow afternoon and evening will not be complete. Do not think Dear I'm verry sick for I'm not although the Doct. has attend me for a few days, his treatment causing me to feel worse than I should had he not been called. I shall give up to him once more and if his present plan of treatment (which seems rather severe to me) does not produce a permanent cure, I shall give up all hopes and induce others to give me up.

Dear Walt you [would] smile could you see me now, the position Granma says "poor Emma" while I think it is Fat Emma. Granma says "Tell him you pitied him and felt so deeply for him while suffering with his wound that the Doct. has went and put Spanish blisters[27] on Em and now she can sympathize with him" truly: you have it in Granma's words.

I wish that you would accept a furlough and get out [of] that miserable place. I'm very anxious to hear about the "substitutes" and I would like to see how you look "ten years older." Oh you naughty fellow. If you come, you know the penalty if you had that nice moustache and — well the Imperial I did not care anything about — but come! Possibly I may relent, see what the inducements are. I shant promise.

If I was able to get out I would send you something to read. I will try as it is.

I must close for I'm verry tired indeed. Remember me in your

---

[27]A poultice made of ground green southern European blistering beetles ("Spanish flies") and applied to wounds and burns to draw the infection to the surface. It was also used to apply medicine, the logic being that by stimulating the capillaries the medicine would move more quickly through the system. Old style medicine lingered into the Civil War years in that many doctors still treated patients by trying to balance the four fluids (cardinal humors)—blood, phlegm, choler (yellow bile), and melancholy (black bile).

prayers Dear Walt. I have plenty of leisure time and my thoughts are with one I love devotedly who is now suffering "all for his country." Ever wether waking or sleeping you're not forgot. My heart is full of love for you Dearest. I would love to lay my aching head on your shoulder and give you ___ but the moustache on the inside you will find one. Write soon. Good bye Dear Walt.

Your Em

P.S. Lew and Mollie was up to see me last thursday (Dec. 1) Evening. She told me how you was and where you was. Please write soon to your own

true Loving Emma R.

Augur Genl. Hospital
Alexandria, Va.
Dec. 9, 1864

Dear Emma

I have received two of your letters, bearing their respective dates of Nov. 28 and 30, the former I received last Tuesday and the latter last Sunday. You will please pardon me for not replying before as I have been traveling since Monday morning not remaining in one place long enough to write you. I wrote Mother a few lines, while I was in Washington, using the top of my hat as a writing desk, I felt too miserable to write to you at that time and even if I had written you, I fear, as you requested, I do not think that you would like to read it. I felt rough and could have given you a hard description of my feelings as my wound had not been dressed for nearly three days and I can assure you it was very painfull and I had been two nights without any sleep which made me feel about [as] a citizen in Washington told me I looked, viz. drooping in spirits.

I am now in the above named Hospital near Alexandria, Va. I hope I'll not remain here long, but as I am traveling under orders, I shall wait until I get an order to move which may be to-day and may not be for one month yet. I am unable to say—the sooner the better.

In answer to some of your questions of Nov. 28th firstly I can say, I cannot tell you what it means. 2nd I am not sick. 3rd the opperation has been successfully performed. 4th No, I am not angry. How could I

A U.S. Sanitary Commission building near Alexandria, Virginia, where wounded soldiers could recuperate. (Maryland Historical Society.)

be angry with one whom I love as dearly as I love you? 5th You have not displeased me. 6th the matter is I suppose that you have not received my letter of the 19th inst. 7th I read the letter you mailed me on Wednesday and replied as soon after as I could. 8th I can write and have written but you have not received. 9th I am not too sick but I'll confess I am nearly played out. 10th I will consider you very thankfull for those copies of the "Waverly" and only wish I could send you a copy this week, if I remain here I fear I cannot, accept the "will for the deed." 11th I spent Thanksgiving day as well as could be expected under the circumstances. 12th I believe that is all, is it not? I had not before heard that Will Van Winkle was married, I can only say that, there is where I admire his judgment, don't you?

I wrote you a letter at Haddington Hosptl. stating that the ball had been extracted. When I have a good opportunity, I will give you more detailed accounts of it. The wound is still very painfull. It has been dressed but twice since Monday morning and I can assure you that it feels very bad. I am not discouraged. I saw Martin T.[28] yesterday. I will write you more. Do not write until you hear from me again, I will write soon.

Accept my love and Dear Emma, believe me to be yours sincerely

Walter G. Dunn

Jarvis U.S.A. Genl. Hospital
Baltimore, Md.
Dec. 21, 1864

Dear Emma

You will perceive by the above that I am again in Baltimore. I returned on the evening of the 17th inst.

For the past three weeks I have been traveling from place to place without rest or sleep and I can assure you that I am about worn out. You would think so could you see me. My feelings will not permit me to write much this time but soon I will give you a detailed account of it all.

I was made the recipient of your favor of the 5th inst. last Sabbath evening, this is my first opportunity to reply. I wrote you a letter while at Augur Hospital, I presume you have received it ere this, have you not?

I have received four of your letters since I was home, is that all you have written?

I regret to learn that you are ill and sincerely hope and pray that you are entirely recovered by this time. When you write, please state the nature of your illness.

For the lack of proper care since I left this Hospital, my wound is worse than it was three weeks ago. I have just had it dressed, at present it feels quite easy and I hope with proper care (which I have here) it will soon heal.

I beg to be excused for sending such a letter as this is. I know that you would not ask me to write more if you knew my feelings. Don't

---

[28]Martin D. Titsworth joined the 11th New Jersey Infantry in August 1862. He became a corporal and was discharged from Augur U.S. Army General Hospital in Alexandria, Virginia. He died in 1914.

think me cool. That you may be in the enjoyment of good health is the sincere wish of one who loves you dearly and will never cease loving you.

Ever Yours
W. G. Dunn

P.S. Address me — Jarvis U.S.A. Genl. Hospital, Baltimore, Md. Write immediately.

Walter
Merry Christmas

Plainfield Union N.J.
Dec. 27, 1864

Dear Walter

Yours of the 21st was received in due time and "right glad" was I to hear that you had arrived at Baltimore. I should have answered immediatly but was verry busy fixing for Christmas. What happened then you shall know more of presently.

The weather is what I call horrible. We have had as hansome sleighing as I ever see. From last thursday morning untill yesterday morning (26th) it has rained almost constantly for two days. I do hope it will clear off.

Yes I received a letter from Augur Hospt. and I believe I have not sent but four letters to you since you went back. If my memory serves me right. I thought I was never going to hear from you again, it did seem so long. I did begin to look for you home and of course was disapointed. Thank you and may you have many verry many "Merry Christmas"es and "Happy New Years." I shall look forward to next Hollidays, with pleasant thoughts, to what I have now I think. You will too, I hope dont you?

I guess you think I've been spending Christmas by the looks of my letter. Well I guess I have. If you could only see me I think you would say I look as if I had been up a week of nights. Well I have. Perhaps you think you know how sombody looks after sitting up four or five nights and runing. I will try and give you a short discription of how and where I spent my Holliday, or rather I will give you or tell you from thursday.

About four O'clock on said day, Harrie and Lew came up to our house and took tea. Afterwards we came up to Aunt Ems to spend the evening. The sleighing was so nice, we changed our minds. Harrie got

Nan, who is helping Aunt and we went down to New Market not to Uncle Abes, but to see cousin Aurelia. Had a nice time and got home early. Friday afternoon Lew stoped and got Real in your fathers two seat Sleigh left her at Aunt Ems, came down to our house. Ollie hitched Charlie and Patriotic up to our large "caboose" and Lew, Ollie, Real, Kizzie, Nan, Miss Morgan, Jennie, and I, went sleigh riding down to Uncle States Randolph.[29] He sent one over for Harrie and the rest of their young folks, but none of came but Mont and Cal. We had a verry nice time indeed. Got home about ten P.M., good reason wasn't it? Sit up untill twelve to finish Pa's Christmas present. Went to sleep about one.

Sabbath morning was up by times. Went to Church. Aunt Em, Cousin Nan and I went to Uncle Jims. They had a house full of company. Ellis Dunn one of the many, his broken limb is gaining strength slowly. He is not able to get along without crutches. He is looking verry well. In the evening, or about five o'clock, a party of us went to Rahway. Arrived there at 7 o'clock, got supper at Crowels. The party seemed to enjoy themselves hugely. I expect I should but Em had such an awfull headache but it got better and we had lots of fun. Had Christmas Eve in earnest, and do you believe it, I was the smartest one, for when the Clock struck twelve, I caught them all. Sunday Oh! my the company there was to Uncle Jims. While we was to Rahway there was a load from Newark come to our house, and then down to New Market and when we came in there they were siting around the stove. Sunday morning our folks all came and spent the day. We went on the pond, the first time I have been near it this winter, but I hope it wont be the last. Went to the Church (a jolly big load of us from Aunt Ann) to sing for the Christmas tree. In the evening Cousin Aurelia and I had company from Plainfield and of course did not retire verry early. Monday morning I got down stairs about ten A.M. None of the rest of the cousins would go so Real and me had to go, and a nice time we had. There was none of the ladies there, that was on the commitee but Cous and I untill nearly 4 oclock. The church was all to be trimed, the presents marked and the tree to arrange. It was hurry and bustle. When it was verry late, we had to[o] much help. The Christmas Tree

---

[29]States Randolph was born in 1818 and died in 1891. He is buried in New Market.

was verry nice indeed, the present much hansomer, but the arrangements were not as good as last year. The exercises began with the
Sabbath School scholars singing, then Prayer by Eld Rogers. The
waiters was called. Miss Mate Davis and Mr. Clauson, on one side A. J.
Titsworth and your humble servant on the other. There was verry nice
and verry many gifts. I am Cristening one now while writing to you. A
verry hansome Portfolio who it come from I dont know, nor my album
either. It is a verry good one, and holds thirty cards. I have enough to
fill it, and some left. My cousins are quite jealous of me. Jennies to[o].
She has a plain gold ring. I think she does not like the way from which
she thinks the ring came. I would like verry much to know where my
Album and Portfolio came from. Ma said, Sabbath evening there was a
young gentleman called and left the Port[folio] and presently another
come and left the Album, but I cannot sway them to tell me. I have
some idea they come through the P.O.

Say my dear do you know any thing about them? I'm sure I'm verry
thankful for them but I would much rather know from whence it
came.

Eld Rogers had a very hansome album with a number of familiar
faces. Prof. Rogers from the navy made a short speech and presented it
for the members of the congregation, many of whom he had had the
pleasure of burying in the Baptismal waters, and some whose faces
seemed familiar, but who had gone never to return. It was a complete
surprise and he seemed pleased with it and spoke beautiful in return.
They had a live Turkey in a coop for Eld R. and you would laughed
had you been there. He tried to make it play with his pocket handker-
chief, but failed in doing so. I. S. Titsworth received a corn stalk fiddle,
but it would not go much. Eld Rogers said probaly because it was in
church. Mate Davis read an Essay and Judson made a short address. I
think every thing passed off pleasantly.

I think this is getting rather lenghtly feeling as I do for this morning. We Aunt Em, Cous Nan, Jule, and me come up on the first train
from New Market this morning, and I feel rather inclined to go and lie
down on the longe. I reckon I sympathize with you deeply Dear Walt
and I wish I could be with you, if it would help you any. If you was only
on North I would have you transfered to "Randolph Hos." and be the
best nurse you ever had. I'll bet you, I would laugh and sing and read

to you and if we both felt like it I could cry to — and not half try. I think you would improve rapidly. Do not you agree with me there. It is nearly mail time and I must close. Please write me just how you feel and let me know if your wound is verry bad will you? Please write me a good long letter if your arm will permit. Do not get discouraged, but keep a good heart, for one who loves you so verry dearly. "Hope on hope Ever" you know is the rule for some. Remember me Dear Walt as you wish to be remembered and write soon if not sooner to one who is

Ever yours
M. Emma Randolph

Baltimore, Md.
January 6, 1865

My Dear Emma

Yours of Dec. 27th was duly and gladly received. I regret that my circumstances would not permit me to answer before, but I trust you will consider the matter and forgive my tardiness as you wish to be forgiven. [I'll] endeavor to be more prompt in the future.

I am glad to learn that you enjoyed yourself so well, as the tenor of your letter indicated, on Christmas and hope that your enjoyment was increased ten fold on New Years, was it thus?

I enjoyed myself hugely on Christmas, making calls, drinking Egg Nog. On New Years I enjoyed myself quite well under the circumstances.

Lew reached here one week from today. He says that he is enjoying himself quite well. He has exhibited no signs of homesickness yet. We called on Mr. Stevens this morning. I returned to attend to my biz and he remained. Mr. Stevens, Lew, and self intended visiting Washington Monument[30] this P.M. but I fear that the inclemency of the weather will disappoint us.

I have lately returned from witnessing a very sad scene which happened by a building on H[o]lliday St. falling and burying in its ruin, seven men. The latest report is that four of them have already

---

[30]The monument to George Washington referred to here is in Mt. Vernon Square, a mile or so north of Baltimore Harbor in the center of the city. It was an affluent neighborhood, with some Southern leanings, and at the war's outbreak Union gunners on Federal Hill trained their cannon on it as a registration point and barely veiled threat.

died, and the remaining three, seriously wounded. It was a very sad affair indeed.

No my Dear I know nothing about your presents. I am the wrong one to thank for them. I rejoice to learn that you have been so highly honored. Will you be kind enough to inform me, (when you learn) who the donors were.

I should very much liked to have been to your "Hospital" and I doubt not but you would be an excelent nurse. You would have to be extraordinary to be superior to the one I had. I am thankfull now that I need no nursing. My wound has entirely healed and I can assure you that my shoulder feels much better. I was weighed yesterday. I was two and 1/2 lbs. lighter, than [before] I had the opperation performed. I am improving rapidly and in a very short time will weigh more than I ever did. I never enjoyed better health than at present. I hope and pray that you may be able to say the same when you receive this. I request an immediate reply with a true statement of the state of your health. Will you please pardon me for delay and grant my request? I am so anxious to hear from you. Please excuse this brief letter and if your time will permit, reply with a lengthy one.

That you may be in the enjoyment of perfect health is the sincer wish of one who loves you dearly and is ever yours,

W. G. Dunn

P.S. Address, Box 1203. Balto. Md.
Care of Maj. Wharton

Walter

M and D. O. 8th A.C.
Baltimore, Md.
Jan. 17, 1865

Dear Emma

I was made the happy recipient of your last though tardy favor this day about M. after many long and weary days of disappointment. You requested that I set you an example, which I will now endeavor to do and earnestly request that you follow it in one respect "vis" answering promptly, will you not? My time is limited and it will be impossible for me to write you a lengthy letter, which I would do if it were otherwise. I regret that we have been so tardy of late in answering each others letters, I sometimes fear that we are growing cold and indifferent but I sincerely hope that such is not the case, for my part I am sure its not, my affection to night for you is stronger than ever and how very sad I feel when I think it is not returned. Should a cold feeling exist between us and if I have said or done anything to cause it I ask your full pardon and beg of you to fully express your feelings in the matter, in your next.

I have just returned from a very sociable evening visit. Lew, Mr. Ernest and myself called our Oregon St. friends and enjoyed a very pleasant evening indeed. Mr. Ernest is a very intimate friend of mine, clerk in the Med. Directors Office of this Dept.

I regret very much that you feel so ill. Would it ere in my power to relieve you, but such is not. It is directed by an All Wise Providence and certainly will be for the best. I pray for you not to be discouraged dearest; live in hopes and all will yet be well. No never will I forget you in my prayers, you are always thought of first, and ever will be as long as I am permitted to utter a prayer. Pray for me.

Allow me to differ with you in refference to my being among strangers and no one to care for me when suffering from my wound. There were five ladies who did more for me than I could ask a mother to do. You are mistaken if you think I am among heartless strangers here, I have several very warm friends in Baltimore. Those unfortunates that you referred to are improving.

I have as yet heard but little concerning Eld. Rogers Donation.[31] Please inform me in your next.

I have not the least idea who of my Alfred friends has went and got married, please tell me.

With the exception of a bad cold and a corresponding bark, I am enjoying good health, never enjoyed better. Since I returned to Balto. I have improved rapidly and now weigh heavier than ever before. I hope and pray that this will find you much better than when you wrote me.

---

[31]At a donation giving visit, church members donated goods and money for the use of the pastor and his family. A church publication, the *Seventh Day Baptist Recorder,* reported that at a surprise donation visit for Elder James Bailey in 1864, members contributed articles worth seventy-five dollars, and twenty-five dollars in cash. In January 1865, when I. D. Titsworth had a donation visit for Pastor L. C. Rogers, members contributed five hundred dollars.

Please accept this hastily written letter and reply as soon as you possibly can and greatly oblige one who loves you devotedly and ever regards you as the object of his affection and life.

Farewell, Dearest Emma

Your promised companion

W. G. Dunn

I will send you another "Waverly" tomorrow. Walter

Write me a long letter as usual and address as before. I wish you knew how anxious I am to hear from you. If you did I am sure you would write very soon. W. D.

I'll write more next time.

P.S. Excuse all imperfections, write immediately. I am very anxious to here from you. Walter

Baltimore, Md.

January 22nd 1865

My Dear Friend

In a previous letter I promised to give you the detailed accounts of my Military Excursion as I term it, firstly, about one week after having the ball extracted, I was transfered to Philadelphia, at my own request, and assigned to Haddington U.S.A. Hospital, situated near a small vilage of the same name, about four miles from Phila. in a westerly direction. I think I gave you a brief description of said place and therefore merely say now that I was very much dissatisfied. I applied to be returned to Balto. soon after arriving there and on Monday following I was sent to the Provost Marshals Office, and forwarded to Washington D.C., from there to Camp Distribution, where I was put in Augur Genl. Hospital remaining there five days and again sent to D. to await transportation to Balto. which I received four days afterward and on my way to this City, through some misunderstanding put in the [s]lav[e] pen [?][32] which place cannot be de-

---

[32]During the war, Maryland sheriffs housed slaves in jails and slave pens against the possibility of their being freed or running away. By November 1864, Maryland had emancipated its slaves, and those places would have been largely clear of occupants. Given the expediential nature of some army logistical moves, it is possible that wounded soldiers were briefly housed in slave pens, but unlikely.

Fort Federal Hill overlooking Baltimore harbor as it appeared in 1862. (Maryland Historical Society.)

scribed with words better than the following. If there is such a thing as Hell on Earth, that is a branch of it, sure. I was then placed under a strong guard and sent to Fort Federal Hill,[33] and through the influence of a friend there, I was released it being three weeks from the time I left Baltimore and I can assure you that I both felt and looked rough as I lived mostly on Hard Tack and salt meat.

W. G. Dunn

V.R.Corps

---

[33]An eminence overlooking Baltimore's harbor and fortified from the beginning of the war by Federal troops. At the time of Walter's stay there, it was occupied by the 8th New York Heavy Artillery. For a description of life there at the time of Walter's visit, see Kathryn W. Lerch, "The 8th New York Heavy Artillery in Baltimore, 1862–1864," *Maryland Historical Magazine*, 92 (1997): 93–118.

Newark New Jersey
Jan. 25th 1865

Dearest Walt

As you perceive, I'm at Newark. I should have writen to you and informed you of the fact, but did not know certain myself untill about twenty minutes before I started, for I did not want to come when I did. But Ma wanted me to come down and consult a Homepatha Dr. so here I am, and have been here since last friday noon.

Jennie was coming down last Sunday, with a young gentleman sleigh riding, and as I expected your letter Sabbath, she was to bring it to me. But the sleighing went so fast they did not come. I wrote to have them remail all my letters, that had come since I left. But not thinking to give them the directions, they would not trust it to the mail with directions they guessed was right. Jennie wrote that there was a letter for me and wanted to know how to send it me. You better believe she will find out when she gets my answer, for if I did not scold Jen, you would not think I could. I'm expecting the precious missive every time the door bell rings for the letter man bring them to the door.

I am in great haste this morning for Aunt Mary has a letter she wants to go in the next mail. And I must be verry brief, but when I get yours I will try and write a long letter but you must not expect a good one for that is impossible. Cousin Emma is talking to me so much.

I do not know how long I shall stay here, just as long a time as the Dr. requires. By the way, Walt! Do you believe in "Homepatha" treatment? I believe I never have heard your opinion, what is it? Please tell me my Dear! will you? I will tell you when I answer yours (which I will do immediately on receipt) how I like my new Physician. I do not think I could give it a good recommend just now, but I must close. Oh! How I wish you could step in and give me a good ___well, never mind. If I cannot spell it you can guess what I mean, can you? But this is not what I must do, so I must bid you Good bye for the present. Remember me as ever your

True and still Loving
Emma R.

P.S. Write soon and Direct—41 William street, Newark N.J.

Newark N. J.
Jan. 30th 1865

Dear Walter

Your last kind prompt and more than ever welcome letter I have received after some scolding and considerable of impatient waiting on my part and now I hasten to answer with right good will.

Thank you for your promptness and I hope that in the future we shall be more prompt in responding. Most sincerely have I regreted our seeming coldness, and have endevered to think of the cause, and of course it is quite natural that we should try to find some place to throw all the blame, where it would not rest on ourselves, or rather I'm inclined to think that way. Its my nature and now Walt, I want you to put away all your sad thoughts. Believe me the language you use just suits my feelings exactly expressing my mind on the subject. And it makes me feel doubly sad to know that you sometimes think the Love you have for me is not returned Oh! I should feel so happy did I think I could write anything that would assure you without the doubt remaining that my Love for you Dearest is the full heartfelt, and as I believe it to be the only and everlasting true love such as I think is necesary to make married life happy. Your beging my pardon is not required for I have nothing to forgive and now Dear will you please take my word for it untill I can give you some better proof? It has lifted the cloud, (this explanation on both sides) from of the spell, and now let us be more prompt in the future. I will endeavor to make my letters more as they should be. You will see how I succeed. Do you understand me?

I am very glad to know that you have friends in Balto. with whom you can spend some pleasant time with, more especially evenings, for I know you would get lonsome, did you not have something to while away the long evenings. You mistook my meaning when speaking of you being among strangers. I meant when you was at Phila.! Yes! of course I will allow you to differ with me, but if you was where I could get hold of that moustache would not I pull it? I reckon I would just because you was dull of comprehension. No I believe the ladies of Balto. have hearts, and Walt you better look out as to the lock on that verry important part of your body, lest some of those kind ladies (that have done more for you than you would ask a mother) daughters runs away with said member, but enough.

I guess you think how I am feeling better, dont you? Well I'm getting better fast, and you do not know how thankful I am. If I had only tried this before. I'm improving rapidly under Dr. Safons treatment allthough it is rather unpleasant to be compelled to live on such simple diet, when one has as good an appetite as I have but I can get along verry well with that now. They tell me I am looking better than I have in some time. Do you think the same? I guess your and my opinion will agree that there is much to much of a grin. Think so, dont you Walt?

As you perceive I'm still at the City. I did not intend to remain here but three days when I came, Jennie had been here a week. I came with her Henry Runyon or was to come with him and show him the way, but he missed the train, and so Pa said I must come and get Jennie. So come I did, and when I got here Henry had been here and cousin Em and Jen had taken him sleighing for it snowed thursday night as I came friday morn. I should have been here in time to have gone with them, But – I – did – not. I will tell you why. Its a secret. I bought a paper shortly after I left Plainfield and I got so interested in the contents, that when the cars stoped at Elizabeth, I did not think what I was doing. Sit still, and when it was to late to jump off, I noticed where I was. Then I laughed, you may believe so did the ticket man. I had the pleasure of riding over the bridge across New York bay, oh how the ice did crack. There was lots of Plainfield gentlemen on the boat, and I knew two or three of them would speak to Pa that they see me on the road to N.Y. so I just told them why I was there alone. They enjoyed a good laugh at my expense and then a gentleman acquaintance asked permit to see me across the City to Jersey City Ferry and see me safely aboard a train for Newark, which kind offer I was verry glad to accept, as I had never been in N.Y. alone. I left Plainfield half past eight A.M. and did not get to Newark untill twelve noon, tired to Death and nearly frozen. I know my folks at home would feel worried about me did they know my extra tramp so Jennie is none the wiser. I had to inform Aunt Mary for she knew there was no train due at that time from Plainfield. Keep mum.

I will endeavor never to get discouraged again. And Dear do not think I doubt, but that it is all for the best. I feel verry well this morning with the exception of a slight headache caused by keeping rather late hours or early for Walt. They have got a sofa here and we had to hurry to get in bed before the clock struck 3. It was Sunday evening and we had company. I have not been up so late in a long time.

I am very glad to know that you are enjoying such good health and do sincerly hope you may be blessed with a continuance. For I consider health so desirable to our happiness, I feel confident that our prayers will be heard and granted, as far as consistent to Divine will. Oh that we may gain faith grow in grace and fully rely on the decrees of an All wise Providence that does not permit anything to happen to us, but that it is for our good.

Your friend that has gone and got married is Miss S. Emma Brimmer. Judson T[itsworth] was my informant. By the way he thinks there will be two or three or half a dozen weddings when all the boy's come home from the war. What is your opinion?

Vermont was here Friday afternoon. He thought that I was going home with him. Perhaps I will next Friday. I think not for Dr requests me to remain where he can see how I get along so it is undesided wether I go or stay. So please answer soon and I will get it before I leave. I must draw this rather lengthly letter to a close for I have several others I ought to write but I think I shall have to postpone them a day.

I wish you where here to stay a short time. I think you would like my relatives. But wait untill you come home there to remain and then I want you to come to Newark with me. Will you? Oh how I long for this war to cease. I should feel contented to lay down and die. I should feel so happy. It is not quite six (6) months before your term of enlistment expires. Is it? I must close so please excuse all the imperfections and tell me is this to long? Please write soon and write me as long a letter as possible. I must bid you Good Bye Think of me still and allways as your own and one who Loves you better than her life.

Your Emma

N.B. I have had my picture taken and I will send you one.[34] How do you like them?

M.E.R.

---

[34]Unfortunately, Emma's photograph has not been found.

Newark N.J.
Feb. 2nd 1865

My Dear Walter

I am still at Newark as you perceive, and have during the past half hour, been as happy as a lark for I have been the possessor of another dear missive dated Jan. 30th. The door bell rang. I knew there was a letter for me, consequently I ran to the door in something of a hurry and was verry much pleased to see the well known hand writing. I was going out to do an errand for Aunt Mary and of course I must do something awkward to make me apear natural, so I asked if Aunt wanted two (2) quarts of fresh pork instead of lbs. How they laughed.

It is a beautiful morning—the air is rather on the inclination to bite—but the sun shines brightly making it verry pleasant to take a walk providing you step briskly.

I'm verry verry sorry to hear that you have such a heavy cold. I fear that you will not yet clear of that cough verry soon. Now I feel as though I ought to caution and give you a little advice, for I am anxious about you. Be verry careful of your self Dear Walt, for remember there is a mortgage on you. Will you? Do not expose your self more than is necessary for if you have got such a strong constitution, nothing will help to restore it after its once gone. Your opinion in reference to the treatment I am now trying is just what I thought it would be. Yes I agree with you that diferent constitutions require diferent treatment, eating without drinking, I have tryed, and find it helps me considerably. I am verry thankful that I can say that I'm still improving fast—so regards my health.

It is two weeks to morrow since I left home, and the letters begin to come wishing I would come. They hear I'm much better than when I left them. They are getting anxious to see me, probably. Although I've enjoyed myself verry well since I have been here, I'm longing to be at home again. I wonder if I shall long for home, when—well you know, when I mean do you not? We shall see.

I am verry poor at guessing, so please tell me who informed you of the persons who went with us to Morristown. Do you know who was to go but did not?

Yes indeed I remember the engagement next August, with Little Dave. But I do not understand why you wished that you had known that it was on your birthday before. Why is it that you regret not knowing it, please tell me won't you?

I am just as willing as you are to keep up a compound correspondence, for it will make up for lost time. I can not write you more this time, for I am in a hurry. But that does not hinder me from boring you just the same, so believe dearest beloved to be as ever your loving

E. Randolph

Please write soon and you will greatly oblige me for I am verry anxious to hear from you. Address to Plainfield for I am going home to morrow or Monday morning. I have some "Waverlys" to read. How I wish you was there. But tis only six long months and then Good Bye to war for you.

Vermont was telling me that Lew had come home and looks as though he might have been sick ever since he had been gone. I guess you must have kept late hours. And your Father has been down to see you. Now would not you like to see me?

Aunt, Uncle have gone to Scotch Plains to attend the funeral of their sister in law. We were planing fine times for to day when they come for us. We are again reminded, That in Life we are still in the midst of Death. I'm sitting by the front parlor window waiting for Mont. Em wants to see him when he passes to go to dinner. Please excuse the writing for I have to look out the window. No other word,

Emma

Plainfield Union Co. N.J.
Feb. 13, 1865

Dearest Walter

I suppose while I'm writing you are expecting my letter. I'm verry sorry that you will have to wait in vain for I hate to be the cause of your being disapointed. But it has been impossible for me to answer before although I have made an effort several times.

I came home last friday week and have received two letters and three "Waverlys," which helped me verry much because I knew that as it happened that I could not write to you I was not forgotten. I will not tell you the cause of my delay for it would be like "oft told tale" so I will try to interest you with something new.

Well what comes first, is the verry tedious storm we have had, a genuine old fashioned drifting snow storm. Pa says it has drifted nicly

for upsets. This morning it is as clear as a bell as the saying is. I have
had plenty sleigh riding — thank you!

Last Sabbath day, 11th of Feb., was the 25th anniversary of [when]
my Dear Parents was married. We went to church at New Market and
on our way home we stoped at Eugenes and got Jersey and the little
one, and all of us was home to spend the 25th anniversary, an unbroken family circle. I lay upon the sofa and watched them all seeming to
enjoy themselves, and many times I found myself wondering wether by
the time another year rolls round if it will be the same. Or if there will
be a vacant chair. God only knows. My thoughts were both pleasant
and sad, for I thought there is soon another here by me but we can not
spare any of them, and again Our Heavenly Father may think it best to
remove one from among us, to draw our afections away from earthly
things that we may think more of Heaven. If so, tis all for the best. I
have resolved to do more as I ought to try and be more patient with
the little ones. Do not forget to pray for me Dear Walter.

I wish that I could write and express my feelings but it is impossible. I will answer both of yours now and then I will write again in a
day or two. If I am well enough for I like the compound correspondence, are you getting tired of it? I have read and reread your kind
and loving missives and wish I could express my sentiments half as well
as you do. You are perfectly welcome for that "grining Picture" and as
to what you said about it, I will say, "all do not see alike", and I suppose
you don't care if they don't. And now my Dear aren't you going to let
that moustache grow? I fear I shall hardly know you without it. There
will be fun for you when I vote that claim out. You will wait untill I do.
I'm happy to know that you trust me so fully and believe me Walt, you
shall never have cause to regret it. Yes indeed I look forward to many
verry many pleasant chats and hope that our anticipation may all be
fully realized. It seems a long time to wait. But Dear you know "the
longest day will have an end."

I do not know what we shall do with you when you come home to
make you contented. Your Father and Lew was at Dominer Bailey
donation, and I suppose you have heard all the particulars. We had a
verry pleasant time. Your Father was the means of Eld. Rogers enjoying
a good laugh with several others, at my expense. I had promised Eld.
R. one of my "Pics" and I had them in my pocket. When he asked me

for it I gave him three to select one of them to suit himself. Your Pa he stepped up took the remaining two, looked at them, sliped one in his pocket and to help it along asked me if I was most ready to go home. Oh how they did laugh quite a number, soon Lew came in with me and Cousin Joel could not go home untill Lew went. They enjoyed it muchly. It poped in my head would he be so willing to take the original for a Daughter. We shall see.

I ought not write you any more—my head warns me to stop—but I have not written half what I want to, so please bear with me a little longer. Jennie has just come up and is in high glee over a "valentine" that is fresh from her Dear Henry from Trenton. We know that it is from him because we have seen his hand writing before this. I promised Jennie I would show her all the letters I received from Henry R. if she would return the compliment. Oh Walt, his love letters is genuine. How you would laugh. I tell Jen, he's to young to marry yet. A rumor is afloat that Mr. Runyon, Henrys father was out looking for him the night he stayed to our house. Did your folks ever look for you when you stayed all night?

I supposed your father informed you about Morristown the way he spoke of it when I was at your home last Sabbath day. We all of your folks and I got in a discussion about long courtships and short engagements. A rather odd subject for us, you will say we had free opinions expressed all around, me excepted. I did not agree with Cousins Joel and Joanna.[35] That visit to your home was unexpected nevertheless I had a verry pleasant visit. But I missed one who I would dearly loved to have seen come in the door, even if you had been a little late to dinner. But of course that was impossible. I see his picture as Asa took particular pains that I should see the Dear [fuz?] Lew showed me Mr. Ernests picture. I like his looks verry much. What is his first name? He is full of fun, I should judge by his face. I should like to comb his curls and part them a little more on the side.

Now, I want to know how that cold and cough is. I hope it is much better. I wish I could "follow suite" and come and scare that cough away. I so much dislike any one to get a cold with a hard cough, so late

---

[35]Emma is referring to Walter's parents, both of whom were Emma's cousins. Joanna Fitz Randolph Dunn was born on February 18, 1824, in Plainfield. She died on April 8, 1904.

in the winter, and yours must be verry severe, to keep you to your bed. Be verry carful Dear Walt and do nothing to renew it. Please tell me just how you are getting along when you write to me, will you?

I'm verry thankful for your kind wishes and Prayers, for my release from disease. And remember Dear Walt you have mine in return.

No mystery if you please—so what is ["Prve Pale"?] I do not understand. Is it something concerning Substitutes?

I must close, please write soon and write a good long letter. I shall not be able to write so much nonsense next time, to show that you apreciate this, answer with as long a letter as your time will permit.

I shall look for an early reply. I must now say "Au revoir" for a little while, and believe me to be as of yours, truly and ever your own loving companion to be.

M. Emma R.

Plainfield Union Co. N.J.
Feb. 20th 1865

Dearest Walter

I to was just upon the point of writing you the second time when Gracie came in from the Office with a missive for Em and from Walter, she knew because it was from Baltimore.

I began to think you was sick. Now I feel like scolding so you had better not tempt me by a tardy answer to this. Do you hear? I'm verry sorry indeed that you was so verry often disappointed. I'll be good now, you see if I'm not. I wish you would give me a good talking to. I will let you stay one week and you may talk all the time if you'll [do] as well as you did when you were home last. Remember one subject to talk about would be Substitutes. Will you now?

I'm verry glad to hear that your cold is better. And I hope when this reaches you, that you will be able to say it has left you entirely. I'm happy to inform you that I'm verry well, thank you.

Last Sabbath Eld. J. Bailey[36] and Eld. Rogers changed pulpits. Eld. B. went down with us. He sit on the back seat with me and we had a verry pleasant chat. He is verry much pleased with his donation, which

---

[36]Elder James Bailey (1813–92) was the pastor of the Plainfield Seventh Day Baptist Church from 1853 to 1864. In the latter year he moved to Alfred Center with his wife and two children, then moved again, this time to Walworth, Wisconsin.

amounted to considerable—$300 cash, a silver cake basket presented by the Sabbath school scholars, a verry hansome album, nearly filled with cards. Hattie D. gave Mary a verry hansome picture of her own printing, and other presents for diferent members of his family, to numerous to mention. Abe Titsworth gave Eld. Bailey and his Mother the hansomest floral offering I ever see—to large baskets that he bought at Newark filled with a beautiful variety of Hot-house flowers. Eld. Bailey has had these pictures taken of his basket, and as he has preserved them by simply placing a linen handkerchief dampened over them, Mrs. Spooner is going to paint the pictures and each flower its natural tint. I think it will be verry nice.

My opinion on said subject I thought you knew already, but it seems not. Your folks views were that long courtships and short engagements was best, for then there was not so much danger of a disturbance or quarel, as your Father said. I think that it would be better, should there be anything upon which a couple that are engaged does not agree, to have it settled, if it can be. And if it is of a nature to cause unhappy feelings to exist after marriage, they had better not marry, that is my present view of the subject. I do not know that they are right. Do they agree with yours? Do you think I am right or wrong? Please tell me what your opinion is, in your next, will you not?

My Dear, which did you mean, that I dare not send you one of Henry Rs genuine love letters or one of my own writing, to your own dear self? I guess you mean one of his, for I think I give you enough in my poor attempts that you do not wish for more. I feel just like — well just like smacking you in the mouth to think you would allow your self to think yours were laughed at. The reason I spoke of his as I did, I thought they was verry affectionate or loving for so short an acquaintance. You are mistaken if you understood that I received them. My letters number two from him and are of a business nature, as I had to mail him some "Carte de visites" from Newark. He enquired of you and sent his best regards.

I can not write much more for my time will not permit. This after noon Mrs. Asa Randolph has a vendue.[37] It is a verry pleasant day for

---

[37]Probably the family of Asa F. Randolph (b. 1795) who moved to Piscataway about 1820. On May 4, 1816, he married Rachel Vail, daughter of William Vail, and they had seven children. A farmer and, briefly, a miller, Asa

it. Last Sabbath Jennie and I went home with Lib. R. and we had a nice visit. Aunt Clansy called me "her poor Daughter" and I called her my "Fat Mother". I now hear her call me mother when she is going across the brook to live, that what Mrs. R. said it pleased Mont and Harrie, especialy. Harrie says he is sure of the Oysters. I must stop this scribbling. Please excuse all imperfections and write soon to yours Forever

Emma

N.B. Please answer this so I can get it Friday as I expect to go home with Gertrude Dunham[38] next Sabbath after meeting to stay a few days, and oblige your Mate

I must tell you how holy it is in Plainfield this week. Last evening a young miss just sixteen years old lectured at the first baptist church. Subject — temperance. It is said that she is verry eloquent, and has a splendid education. I did not go to hear her. I would have liked to verry much. To night is the Fire mens ball. They genrly hold it on the anniversary of Washingtons birthday. But young Jackson Pounds wedding is to be the evening of the 22nd and several of the fire company have invitations to said wedding. They have their ball to night. I hope it will not end as the one did a year ago, with a fight. Tomorrow evening the Ladies Patriotic society have sort of a concert at one of the Churches for the benefit of the "Soldiers widows and Orphans." Every evening this week there is something going on. I do not expect to go out in the evening this week, unless I go to the Oak Tree to singing school next thursday evening. I was there last week, the first time this winter. I had a verry pleasant time. Harris and Calvin went in their Grocery with their two fractious poneys — the consequences was a bill of about twelve dollars. Harrie run into a buggy, smashing the wheel to splinters broke the tongue to his wagon, like to upset and have bad luck in general. Others went in our sleigh and took a load of us. I wish you was home so that you could go. But hope on hope ever for there must certainly be some pleasure in place for my Dear Walt and his Emma.

---

was a member of Plainfield's Seventh Day Baptist Church. He and his wife are here holding a public auction of their property before moving west with several other Seventh Day Baptist families.

[38]Gertrude Dunham, b. February 28, 1843, had lost her father, Jeremiah Dunham, at the battle of Locust Grove, Virginia, in November 1863.

P.S. I will endeavor to write to you again this week, for I'm not tired of the "compound." M.E.R.

Plainfield Union Co. N.J.
Feb. 28, 1865

My Own Dear Walt

Agreeable to promise, I have seated myself, pen in hand, to have a short chat with my absent loved one. Tis useless to inform you of the fact that I would Oh so much rather throw down my pen, jump up, hop skip or any way to get the front door open, put my arms around your neck and give you — well a good earnest welcome. But, no doubt, I would frighten you. As you're not used to receiving such greetings, I guess you would come to your senses, when you see what a cheerful fire light I would make, that old stove throws around the room, with the Sofa drawn up to the old place. We would need no company to enjoy ourselves. Dost agree with me? After sweet thoughts of the Past, never to be forgot by me, a sigh for the Present and a hope for the Future. Which seems so uncertain. I will pass on and tell you what little news there is.

Walt I've been trying to think of somthing new. I guess I told you all my news in my last. I'm at a loss how to fill this sheet. Unless I give you a real genuine love missive. No! I won't, for I do not know yet wether it is one of Henrys or one from Emmas you want. My Dear, which is it?

Let me tell you about one of the Jersey boys. His sister, Cousin Keziah as they call her, Randolph Dunhams[39] wife, Lew Clausons[40] sister, she was here yesterday after noon and spent the evening. We spoke about Alfred Center and she turned to me, says "Em have you ever heard that Lew had a young lady at Alfred, he intended to make my sister in law?" I told her I supposed so of course, for the verry reason, "That all the young people that went from our Churches left their Hearts at 'Alfred University'" or with some one that left for their homes, with one exception. She wanted to know who that was, and I

---

[39]Randolph Dunham was a town father of Plainfield, the man who had apprenticed I. D. Titsworth. He died in November 1865, in his seventy-ninth year.

[40]Lewis T. Clauson (Clawson?) enlisted in the 11th New Jersey Infantry August 1, 1862, at the age of eighteen.

told her Miss Ernnis. She laughed and said I better not go, if I had that presentiment. Her husband went to A[lfred] C[enter] to see their son, and he visited Mrs Langsworthy (she used to live with them). It was after Lew had been home on furlough. He spoke of Lew. And Mrs. Langsworthys step Father said "Oh we know all about Lew Clauson. We know more than you can tell us. We get more letters than you do. I'll guarantee." He came home told his wife about it. Its being the first she had heard, went right to her mother. And it was about the time Mrs L. was here. His mother wrote to Lew stating that she was on, and that she would like to get acquainted with her. Lew wrote back to his mother that she ought to get an introduction he wanted her to know her. "But never mind wait untill next fall and then you will have a chance to know how you like her." Mrs. Clauson wrote Lew that is all I want to know I know I shall like her.

Tis thursday evening, and knowing that I should not have another opertunity to write to you this week, I've declined my invitation to go to singing school and remained at home to write to you. I wish I could express my feelings half as well I would like to. I could talk to you untill the "wee small hours of morn" but can not write to you. It does seem impossible that we have been engaged nearly a year. But as it is, I wonder if time will always seem to fly so fast. I hope by another year I shall be more worthy of the love that is given to me. For I do not doubt you dear, but what you say you mean and you do not know how happy I am at times, when I think of you. And when I feel quite well, I have reared many castles in the air. And then when I do not feel well Ma say Emmas got the blues and she often says she will be glad when Pa brings Em a letter from Baltimore for then I must allways have to smile. If I feel ever so bad, I do not know what I should do. If you should go away where I could not hear from you often, I guess I shall have to go with you. Cousin Joel has gone to Washington to buy land. And I have heard it rumored that it is for "Walter." What a grand idea, and how I wanted to laugh when I heard it. But I managed to keep mum.

Harrie took Nan down to New Brunswick sunday to stay two or three weeks. Some say they would not be surprised if she went to purchase her wedding things. I should, would not you? We would gain the Oysters. Harrie said he wanted to come see me while Nan was gone. He guessed Walt wouldn't mind it, being as how he was a particular friend. I told him if he felt shure of it he could come and see his cousin Em to be. He will have to come to Piscataway for I intend to go home with Gurtrude. So do not be worried Dear if you do not hear from me next week. I do not expect to stay but a day or two, but it may storm. I must close this nonsense for it is getting late. Please write soon. I'm looking for one to morrow. Pleasant dreams my Dearest and also Good night. Remember me as ever yours with much love.

Emma

The Front Street Theater, Baltimore. (Maryland Historical Society.)

Part IV: "Until My Enlistment Expires"

By March 1865 the war was clearly winding down, and men and women so long separated could seriously begin to think of peace and what it would bring to them. For Walter and Emma, that meant the prospect of marriage, which he seemed to view a little uneasily. His days of youthful freedom—of visits to his "Oregon St. friends" and to a particular Baltimore belle, Miss Imes, who regularly sent him flowers— were numbered by the days of his enlistment.

Six weeks passed, and suddenly the war ended with the capture of Richmond and Lee's surrender at Appomattox Court House. In Baltimore, those who had supported the Union exploded in noisy celebration, and in Plainfield young women rejoiced in tears and waited to hear when the men would return home. John Wilkes Booth's dark shadow wrenched the nation away from celebration, and in New Market, Plainfield, and Baltimore ministers tried to explain the nature of martyrdom once more to men and women who had known it in their families and in their towns for four long years.

Another month passed, and Walter dallied. Knowing that some soldiers would have to remain at their posts while the rest of the army mustered out, he assured Emma he would return only in August, when his term of enlistment expired. Emma responded with growing impatience and frustration as the armies gathered for a last Grand Review in Washington, then returned home. All about her, friends and lovers joyfully reunited, while her betrothed lingered in Baltimore.

"My Dear"

New Market New Jersey
March 1, 1865

Dearest Walter

As I have arrived in the land of the living again, I thought perhaps you would like to have that verry short note answered. I suppose you have received my last, or second letter. I shall look for a letter (not a note) from you when I get home. You can not imagen how disapointed I was. When I read that verry short missive, I was tempted to sit down and send one back to match it, but did not.

You must excuse all the flourishes as the above for Cousin Emma Ayers[1] seems determined to be around "Dear Cousin Em," as she verry lovingly calls me, about 50 times during the morning. Do you ever have any little ones to come in and hinder you when writing? If so you can sympathise with me. I verrily believe Em has kissed me two dozen times. "Aunt Em" "Aunt Em." Kizzie, Jule and little Bertie has gone down to Cousin Joel Dunns to spend the day, left Rele and I home to keep house. We are having a gay time. And we should be verry happy to have your company to dinner. Do not fail to comply with my request. If you can possible avoid it. I won't say we shall look for you.

To day is the first day of spring. It is a beautiful day over head. But verry damp and unpleasant underfoot as the saying is.

---

[1]Probably a daughter of Hannah Ann and Jim Ayres.

Last Sabbath evening Cousin Thomas R.[2] took Aunt Sally
Rhiben[?] and myself down to Cousin Libbie D. where I staid untill
yesterday when Cousin Mary Jane[3] and her husband came down to
pack up the things that were to go west, of Aunt Sallies.[4] Oh what an
undertaking it seems to be for her to break up and go west.

It is bad enough for the younger ones to go and she is getting so
old. Grandfather feels bad, having only two left so far apart. Indeed
they all are feeling verry sad. Cousin Mary Jane especialy as she is to
remain behind. But Jonty promises me to take me out to see Mother
next fall. And that is one drop of consolation. We had a verry busy
time packing, but succeeded in finishing. Thomas has his vendue the
12th of this month and starts for the west on the 20th or 21st. Aunt
Sallie and Alfred goes with them, Cousin Thomas's family.

March 15 Cousin Libbie has her sale, and Getrude and her ma
does not go untill the first of May. I have been with them so much and
they have talked so much about the west, I realy have got the "west
fever." I shall not promise you Em will be here to welcome you home
next fall when you come home from the war, because they think it
would be good for my health to take a trip. Cousin Jonathan and Mary
want me to go when they go. I will let you know, however, before I go.

----

[2]Thomas Fitz Randolph was born on August 17, 1833. On December 1,
1859, he married Sarah Ann Dunn (b. 1831). They moved to Wisconsin in
1865 with their two children, Minnie and Edward James. Thomas died in
1896.

[3]Emma's Cousin, Mary Jane Randolph, was born on April 4, 1837, the
daughter of Reuben and Sarah Fitz Randolph, and was a member of the New
Market Seventh Day Baptist Church. Her brother-in-law, Jeremiah Dunham,
was in Walter's company in the 11th New Jersey and was killed at Locust
Grove, Virginia, on November 27, 1863.

[4]Several Seventh Day Baptists lived in or near Milton, Wisconsin. In the
Sabbath Recorder of July 19, 1860, one of them, A. C. Burdick wrote, "The
prospect for a bountiful harvest in this vicinity was probably never better. . . .
Barley, corn, potatoes, etc. look equally well and promising." Although there
was no formal church plan for members of the New Market and Plainfield
churches to move, several did move west to Wisconsin and other states. Many
took advantage of the new homesteading laws. In addition to the people
mentioned in the letters, Deacon Barzillai Fitz Randolph, son of Rubin and
Sarah Randolph, moved from New Market to Albion, Wisconsin. When Pastor
James Bailey of Plainfield moved west, his description of the trip was included
in the July 27, 1865, *Sabbath Recorder.*

By the by, we had quite a controversy here this morning, about when our New Market soldiers are to return. Aunts say that you will not be home untill just six (6) months have passed away, while I say you come the last of July or the first of August, now who is right? I sincerly hope that I am. For that is plenty long enough.

I have just heard the news that two of my cousins Ed and Alfred Dunn of Newark are drafted, also a particular friend of mine Mr. Charlie Brown.[5] He is a very nice young man. I have know him several years. I like him verry much. He is one of the five. I hope you will have a chance to know him one of these days. I'm sure you will like him, for I do, as a friend.

I hope you are over your hurry my Dear by this time, for I want one of those "Dear old fashioned letters" again. I do not like the new kind. I feared I had writen something that offended you, perhaps I have. If so please name it, and I will endeavor to rectify, as I'm sure it was not intentional. I write so much that I ought not to. You must excuse me if I forget what I'm writing. I must close. Please write soon for I'm verry anxious to know if I have offended you. Believe me it was not meant. I do not wish to let that seeming coldness come between us again. For I am still the same in Heart to you and trust you as faithful. Remember me as Yours till Death.

M. Emma Randolph

Plainfield Union Co. N. J.
March 5th 1865

Dear Walter

Your last of the 2nd arrived yesterday, and "right glad" was I to hear from you. Although you did not inform me as to wether you was displeased, I take it for granted that such is not the case from the tone of your last.

I'm once again at home where I think I shall remain for one while. I'm tired of visiting. And should you find it in your power to call on me, you will find me Home most any time, between now and the time I start "west." No I shall not forget to leave my address when I go. So you are going way down Maine, to live when this war is over. Well I suppose

---

[5]A Charles Brown was one of five men who had proposed to Emma.

that will be next fall. For I do not think that the war will be continued after you leave. They could do nothing without "Walter": I should judge by what Lew sayes they think of you. Do not think I'm jealous.

Sargt. Andrew Webster called Lew this after noon. He is from the front and is looking verry well. I did not think he would ever get higher than a private.[6] He returns thursday. Oh what a stormy week we have had, and the mud is awfull. And I have been where there is plenty of it. Yesterday it rained verry hard. The bells rang merrily about a quarter of an hour before the inauguration prayer meeting. Ollie attended. He said there was about 30 or 40 persons there. Now do you not think that was small for Plainfield? I do.

How are you? "Hero" in imagination? You think perhaps I would execute my threats when you return. I will remember you can use two arms. But shall not own your "superior strength" will not give way before something els untill the contest decides we shall see. As to "living across the brook." Yes! that would appear verry cold and quite a change for me. Some say "variety is the spice of life," you know. I can tell better when I have seen a little more of this world. If I'm to be permited to live. If not, I shall not care.

Thank you Dear for the effort it must cost you when so tired and nervous to write to me. Your last letter gave me a great deal of pleasure. I should feel satisfied could I think my letters were half as much pleasure to you as yours are to me. Believe me to be sincere, will you dear! I must stop writing to you now for this time. I have two letters to write yet to night. I have much I would like to tell you. But take the will for the deed and remember "still waters run deep." And when you get home, also remem[ber] I'm going to talk a blue streak. Good night and pleasant be your dreams. Write soon, think often and ever of one who loves you dearly and is yours forever

Emma

Baltimore, Md.
March 8, 1865

My Dear Emma

It is with much pleasure that I acknowledge the receipt of another

---

[6]Andrew Webster had enlisted in the 11th New Jersey at age eighteen on July 28, 1862.

The Eighth Corps Office of Commissary and Musters on Monument Square in Baltimore. Walter lived on an upper floor. (Maryland Historical Society.)

of your letters, which are the source of many pleasant thoughts. Your last, I received about noon today. I attempted to write you, last night but was compelled to give it up, ere I finished, by a severe head-ache, caused by attending a ball, too hard, the night previous.

You undoubtedly think that I disaprove of the compound correspondence, by not writing, but allow me to undeceive you, as lack of time alone prevented me. I shall not give it up yet, and shall endeavor, ere this reaches you to write another.

You have done nothing to displease me, had you I should have written to that effect. I will conceal no displeasure, and should I take offence at anything you write, I will immidiatly inform you, until then drive away all doubts and fears concerning the above subject. I trust you will do the same if I, at any time, ignorantly offend you, will you not?

Monday evening, I attended the Grand Sixth Ward Inauguration Ball held in the Maryland Institute the largest hall in the City.[7] The

[7]Marking the second inauguration of Abraham Lincoln as president.

evening was very pleasant and the attendance large. It is estimated that there were over two (2) thousand present. I never saw so many homely ladies togarher before. They were not all so however, for in such large crowds, you will always find the good with the poor. They all appeared to enjoy it. I did hugely. I wish that you would have been present, you would have seen some of the "Baltimore styles."

I expected to attend another Grand Ball given by my Company (72d V. R. Corps) to night but the rain which is falling fast, prevented. I feel quite much disappointed, as I anticipated a very pleasant time, and would have it, without doubt, if it did not rain like a blue streak. This morning, it had the appearance of a clear day and gave promise of a pleasant night. I wished you here, for I would much rather take you this evening than ——, but under the existing circumstances I will be content, knowing that the time is not far distant, when I can enjoy the society of one I so dearly love, and in whom I fully trust.

To day, I witnessed the remains of Senator Hicks of Maryland, (known as her "redeemer") who died recently at Washington.[8] He was sixty-six years of age. His loss is mourned by all who knew him.

In a previous letter you spoke of a young "Miss" lecturing in Plainfield. A few evenings since a Miss Anna Dickinson lectured in the Maryland Institute. Is she the same one that was in Plainfield? I will enclose, to you, the opinion of her as expressed by a Baltimorian,[9] does it agree with the opinions of those in Plainfield. I did not go to hear her and I am quite sure I did not loose much by not going.

---

[8]Thomas Holliday Hicks was governor of Maryland when the secession crisis erupted. Largely through inaction, he kept the state in the Union. In December 1862 Unionist governor Augustus Bradford appointed him to fill a vacancy in the U.S. Senate, where his record was undistinguished. Long suffering from ill health, he died in Washington on February 13, 1865, and was buried in the Congressional cemetery. On March 3 he was disinterred and brought to Baltimore, where his remains lay in state at the Maryland Institute before being conveyed to a final resting place in Cambridge, Maryland. George L. Radcliffe, *Governor Thomas H. Hicks of Maryland and the Civil War* (Baltimore: Johns Hopkins University Press, 1901), 124–28.

[9]The newspaper clipping, evidently written by a Baltimorean sympathetic to the South, was highly critical of the patriotic Dickinson, a popular speaker. "Having flitted throughout the North, insulting its intelligences and invading its proprieties, Miss Dickinson, a second-rate champion in the fraternity of free-lovers, Fourierites, &c., came to try her fortune in Baltimore, and by a repetition of the cry for blood and slaughter, a fierce exhortation to ruin and

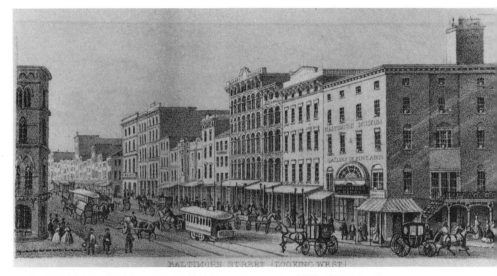

View of Baltimore looking west on Baltimore Street, ca. 1860. (Maryland Historical Society.)

Has Nan returned from N[ew] Brunswick, if so are there any prospects of a union? We are sure of the oysters.

How long since, was Andrew Webster elevated to the position of Sergt. I had not heard of it before I received you letter. I was told by a member of my company (D 11th N. J. V.) originally, who I met at Convalescent Camp Va. shortly after having the ball extracted, that I would have been a Lieutenant before this time if I had remained with the Regt. I do not admire his judgement in that respect. After being disabled, I was transferred to the V.R.C. [Veteran Reserve Corps] in which there is no promotion, unless special cases where it is obtained by many and very influential friends, consequently I am just as high a private now as when I entered the service, never having a chance to distinguish myself, but being gradually extinguished until I go out

---

death, to display the cruel passions of a vindictive woman's diseased and perverted imagination. With brazen effrontery she paraded her stale, second-hand, putrid thoughts, and when some coarse invective or fanatical sentiment failed to elicit applause, she rebuked their lack of patriotism and threatened her derelict audience with further insult."

entirely. A young man, formerly a clerk in the office and recently from the front, said if he was back here again he would not give his position, for a Captains Commission at the front. I am very well satisfied. I could not ask to be better situated. I think very much of Major Wharton and have abundant reason to think that I am well thought of by him. He has done a great deal for me and has never refused to grant me any favor I might ask of him. He places a great deal of confidence in me and is determined to keep me here as long as I am in the service, if he can. He complimented me highly, when father was here. Do not understand me to be boasting. I wish merely to convey the idea that as I have not gained promotion, I have won the confidence of my superiors, which I consider just as good.

The 4th was celebrated here by firing salutes, ringing bells and displaying flags.[10] We had over two (2) thousand square feet of the "Stars and stripes" flying from our office, more than any other building in the City. It was a splendid sight and attracted much attention. I read the Inaugural Address in less than one hour and thirty minutes after it was delivered.

How are Dave and Sallie Johnson?[11] Are they as constant as ever? I think them a very affectionate couple, do you agree with me in this respect? I suppose, ere long they will go into a matrimonial contract.

We are still quite busy and will be for some time. The approaching draft adds a considerable to our duties. Is Plainfield out of the draft?

In your late letters, you have said nothing concerning your health, are you improving? I hope and pray to that effect.

I saw Abram Dunham Sunday night. His company staid over Sunday at Jarvis Hospital. He looks well. Is in Wilmington Del. where a detachment of his Co. is stationed.

You will perceive by the many mistakes that I have made, that I have written this in great haste. Please excuse all imperfections, accept and reply early. I will write you again in a short time.

Remember me as
Yours forever, Walter

---

[10]The presidential inauguration took place on March 4, 1865.

[11]David L. Randolph of New Brooklyn, New Jersey, married Sarah "Sallie" Johnson of Plainfield on September 19, 1865, at the New Market Seventh Day Baptist Church. They were the friends with whom Walter and Emma wagered the "oysters."

Baltimore, March 13, 1865

I mailed you a copy of the Waverly this morning.

Baltimore, Md.
March 13th /65

Dear Emma

Pursuant to promise and in accordance with the dictates of my heart, I will devote a few minutes in communicating with you by means of the pen which has been our only means of communication for a long time past and will be for some time to come. But I rejoice to know that the time is not far distant when we can lay the pen aside, and express to each other by mouth what we are now compelled to do in the above named maner, then only, can we fully understand each other.

We are having very pleasant weather indeed, such as you have in New Jersey in the month of May. To night is beautifull, the moon is shining in all its splendor. I have thought, several times this evening, that I could fully appreciate a good buggy ride now (even in a Grocery wagon), but wait until the 12th of August,[12] and then if nothing happens to prevent, I will enjoy what I now anticipate. You may consider yourself engaged for that evening, will you?

Last evening I attended Union Square Methodist Church. The discourse which was very good indeed, was preached from the text, "I am not ashamed of the Gospel of Christ." It has been a long time, before since I told you I attended church, you will probbably infer, from that that I do not attend very often. I regret to say that such is the fact. I have had such a bad cold this Winter that I disliked to go to church, or any other place, where my continual coughing would be an annoyance. I shall do better hereafter.

I have since seen some of the boys who attended the ball, on last Wednesday evening and they said, considering the unfavorableness of the weather, they spent a very pleasant evening. I wish now that I had gone. We are going to give another, soon. We will show Baltimore that the 72nd Co. V.R.C. [Veteran Reserve Corps] is the best company in the City, but not because I belong to it.

---

[12]The date set for Walter and Emma to share a buggy ride with Dave Randolph and Sallie Johnson.

I shall look tomorrow for a letter from you. I hope I will not be disappointed.

Mrs. D. P. Bowers commences an engagement at Holliday St. Theatre to night. I would like for you to hear her. I think I shall go tomorrow night.

In your late letters you have said nothing about Jennie, how and where is she?

I judge from your silence regarding your health, that you are improving, are you not? I would advise you to take all the out of door exercise possible. I think you will find it beneficial. Please tell me in your next, just how you feel, will you?

With exelent health and the hope that you are equally blessed. I will subscribe my self as,

Yours devotedly

W.

P.S. Please reply as early as convenient and oblige one who loves you dearly. W.

Plainfield, N.J.
March 15, 1865

Dear Walter

To oblige one who is dearly loved in return, and to enjoy the only means by which we can now communicate, I seat myself pen in hand "for my thoughts do roam to a loved one that's far from Home."

It is now quite late in the evening. I intended to have writen to you immediately after supper, but Pa wished me to play and sing for him. And not untill I had completly sung out my list (which is small) and seen Maggie, snug in bed could I get a chance to write to you unmolested. Now the folks have gone to bed, where I ought to be Ma said, as she spied my Portfolio. Ma thinks my head aches.

Oh! Walt, you do not know how glad I am that spring is coming. I'm in hopes I shall escape my usual time of inflamation on the Lungs. I'm taking unusual pains to avoid catching any cold. I shall be discouraged if I do have another severe time with my Lungs. We have had three or four verry pleasant days of spring weather. But have not been out-side the gate for the walking is verry bad. To night it is raining quite smart just for a change. But enough of that.

I suppose Cousin Libbie to-day has broken up housekeeping, and has sold nearly all of her furniture. I[t] must have been a hard matter for her to do so. Pa, Ma, Jennie, had intended to have gone to the Vendue this after noon, but could not. My Dear Mother is not well at all to night. I dislike to have Ma sick for I allways think what would we do without her. My prayer is spare her, my mother, and take me in her place, not that I feel I should not be missed. But I'm not needed as much and I could not fill her place here in our home. I hope a long life will be the happy lot of my Parents. But whosoever is to be called, I hope and Pray will be ready, for the sumons. Do not forget me in you prayers. You are allways remembered by me in my poor suplications at the "throne of Grace."

You want me to consider myself engaged for the evening of the 12th of August. I can tell you I expect to be "engaged" all that month, and I hope and trust I shall be many more, so of course I shall consider my self engaged. If I get home from the distant prairie.

My head pains me so severly, I must lay this aside for to night. I wish I could lay my poor head on sombodies shoulder as easily. But a brighter day in the future. Good night and sweet be your dreams tis the wish of your

Emma

8 A.M.
Second Edition Morning

Dear Walt

It has stoped raining and is clearing off. But it is March and we may have half a dozen kinds of weather before night. I hope not for it is disagreeable when it is so damp.

Please tell me the exact time as near as you can when you received my letter of the 12th and oblige me will you?

Yesterday when Ollie came in from the office, Cousin Nan was here, And Jennie & Nan was on one of their teasing tantrums and it was sometime before I had an opertunity to read said missive, and when I did I had somthing less than a hundred questions asked me. Cousin Nan asked, "Did he say anything about me?" She told me to inform you that if you did not say somthing about her in your next, Nan would write to you herself. I told her I would tell Harrie, "twas non of his business." I told Nan I was asked the question, not long ago. Was there any signs of a "Union" between Harrie and Nan verry soon?

And guessed she could inform me as correct as any one. She is going to give me an answer next time she sees me.

Jennie is alive and well. As fat an[d] sassy as ever. I would give most anything but the mortgage, if I had as good health as she has. Jennie wished me to ask you if you had found any girl in Balto.? If not, you need not look for she would wait untill you come back. How are you? "Miss Than—"

I shall look tomorrow or Sabbath day sure for a letter from you. I trust I will not be disapointed. I'm verry glad you enjoy such good health. I am verry well, for me thank you. My time will not permit me to write more at present, so "au revior," for a short time. Please excuse all blunders, and remember me as your "Engaged" and devoted future.
. . .

                                            Emma R.

    P.S.

We shall see how the 72nd Co. V.R.C. prospers after you leave. I shall not be surprised if the War should end then, if not before, what is your opinion. Oh what a happy time there will be then.

    I'll bet you. M.

                                    Baltimore, Md.
                                    March 16 1865

Dear Emma,

    Now for a brief chat with you. To begin with, the acknowledgment of the receipt of your last kind favor, which arrived in due time, having the powerfull effect of driving away the "blues", as you term them, something very rare for me, but nevertheless oaccasional visitors. I had finished my labors for the day and in order to kill time seated myself by my desk and was reading a lengthy editorial of the "American"[13] when the clerk (who carries the mail) came in unnoticed and reaching over my shoulder, droped your letter before me. The paper was immediatly laid aside, your letter, eagerly torn open and its contents speedily devoured. I would have answered immediatly had I not written to you the day previous, which letter, I presume you have received ere this.

    I contemplated visiting a friend at Fort Federal Hill this P.M. but

---

[13]Probably the *Baltimore American and Commercial Advertiser*, a newspaper that supported the Union. Pro-Southern papers in Baltimore were closed down.

business deprived me of that pleasure. I am determined it shall not prevent me from writing to you, so here goes, (all in three years) with any amount of work unfinished.

You expressed a preference for long letters. I must confess that I like them as far as receiving is concerned but I cannot say that I like to write them. Would it not suit you as well to receive short ones and more of them? Two letters a week, of one sheet each, are equivalent to one of two sheets. I hope you will continue to write good long ones, knowing I like to receive such, and accept of mine, brief as they frequently are, as I cannot always write lengthy ones. You must consider that my time is not all my own, and when I would write you, I am frequently called upon to do something else. About next August, I will be a white and free man if I live.

You stated, at the reception of my letter, that you were "longing for that which can not be, just now." Will you please inform what that was? The grounds for imagination are so large that I cannot form an idea of what you so much long for: and also what is that which you so much dread and causes you sorrow when you think of the future? Please be sincere in answering these questions and retain nothing. Be not afraid to tell me all, for I should be more to you than a bosom friend. You will cause me to feel very unpleasant unless you fully explain yourself.

Tis true, there are some very odd names in Baltimore, tis an odd place. Miss Imes was the name of my intended partner to the ball, if you wish to know.

Yes a year has nearly expired since our engagement. Time is indeed, passing away very fast. I hope the second year may be one of more pleasure and happiness to you than the first. How old is your nephew? Please give me his name in full. Not much, he is my name sake. I hope you are not troubled with the headache and not in need of a "sure cure." Should you be, I fear the one would be as bad as the disease, if you take this lot of scribbling for a remedy. With a special request, that you reply immediatly if possible and answer all my questions in full. I close. I am,

Dearest Emma,
Yours in true love, forever, Walter

P.S. I will mail you another copy of the "Waverly" tomorrow.

W. G. Dunn VRC

Plainfield, N.J.
March 21st/65

Dearest Walt

Yours of the 16th is here. Let me tell you firstly— I did not find it so bad as the headache, as you imagined I would. My naughty boy I do not know what I shall have to say to you, to prevent your runing Walt's letters down. I shall threaten a severe penalty, to be paid when you get home, if I hear any more of it. For I think your letters can't be beat, none could suit me as well. I prize them verry dearly, and I have quite a pile of them. No. 59, counting the last missive.

I'm partial to long letters, But I think I would rather receive two a week containing one sheet than one, containing two sheets. This one will be short, but I shall not promise you it will be sweet, because I do not feel that way inclined to night, and it is not natural.

How are you? White and free man next August? Walt, I enjoyed a good loud smile when I perused that item, for I accidently thought of the Mortgage. Just remember I'm going to be "the plague of your life" when the war is out of the way unless I go West and Eld. Bailey told me if I come out there he would marry me right off, and you way "down east" would not be there to put in your claim.

My little Nephew is, or was, three months old the 19th of this month. He is a sweet little one. I believe he knows his aunty. His name is Walter Grant Runyon[14] he certainly is named after you, pretty isn't it. Dannie says "heavy."

To day we had quite a stranger here. Aunt Eliza. She said she is preparing to leave R.I. She wants Jennie and I to come and see her when she gets married, think I will. Will you go with me?

To morrow evening, there is to be a grand ball at Laigns from Elizabeth & Rahan [Rahway?] most of them and thursday evening the Dancing Class of young men hold a "sociable" they call it, at the same place. I hope they will have a good time. I suppose you have heard something about this before.

To night Cousin Thomas R's family, Aunt Sallie and Alfred was to have started west, but owing to an accident on the road, they remain

---

[14]Walter Grant Runyon was Emma's nephew, son of her sister, Jersey Ann and Eugene Runyon. For many years he was the director of Runyon's Funeral Home and Livery in Dunellen, New Jersey. He died in Lake Helen, Florida, on December 22, 1953.

Laign's Hotel in Plainfield. (Courtesy, Plainfield Public Library.)

over another day. I intend going with several others to see them off, to morrow evening half past nine.

About the time you receive this if nothing happens, Jennie, Gertrude D., and me will be at Hatties spending the evening. I called them this evening, they are all well. I have been out transacting some business for Pa while he went fishing. I'm verry tired. I cannot write any more, this time. Please except and reply immediatly, and you will greatly oblige one who loves you verry dearly, and allways will. Good night Dear.

M. Emma R.

O.C.M. 8th A.C.
Baltimore, Md.
March 24th/65

Dear Emma,

As this is my first and I fear the only letter that I can write this week, you will undoubtedly expect a long one, of two or more sheets. It is with regret that I disappoint you, nothing gives me more pleasure than to receive one of your good long letters and as you have expressed a preference for long letters, I take pleasure in writing such but you are aware, in my situation, that it is not always convenient for me to write when or as much as I would like. I will endeavor to do the best I can.

It is useless for me to apologise for my tardiness in writing this, as you know that no small obstacle prevents me from writing to you. Tomorrow night will be just one month since I wrote home with the exception of one very brief letter to Lew about two weeks since. I expect a blessing in the next one I receive.

Major Wharton asked me, yesterday, if I did not want a leave of absence to go home. I told him, I had no desire to go home until August. Since he carried your letter so long, in his pocket, he has frequently tried to tease me about my sweetheart. He is quite lively for an old man and is running some of his clerks most all of the time when not too busy. A few days since he had some young lady visitors in the office, and he told them that his "clerks all had sweethearts," "Dunn's was in New Jersey." How are you, s———? Enough of that.

In your letter of the 15th you requested that I tell you the exact time as near as possible, that I received your letter preceding it. If I mistake not, it was about 3-30 P.M. Allow me to ask your reason for knowing so exactly?

Tell Nancy I like to talk about those who are better looking.

I hope you had a pleasant visit, at Hatties, did you not. I would like to have steped in and supprised you. Did Hattie speak of going back to Alfred next year? Did the folks go West as they expected? When you go West I will give up all claims.

Mr. Stevens called here yesterday P.M. We had a very pleasant chat over the past. Mr. Ernest and I attended the Theatre togather a few nights since. He is quite well.

It is quite dull here at present. I scarcely know what to write to interest you. There is but little additional in the news line to-day.

You used to speak occasionally of being in the shop, but of late you have said nothing about it, don't you attend to your father's books anymore? I am going to appoint you, my "private secretary" and "Treasuress" when I go into business. How would you like that, when I get to be a "Conductor" on the Baltimore City, Passenger Railway? Such, may happen. I will enclose one of my poor "Contrabands,"[15] please accept in return for your picture. With a request that you be particular in answering all those questions in a previous letter, I will close. Please reply soon and oblige yours truly.

P.S. I will mail you a copy of the "Waverly" tomorrow. Walter.

N.B. Do not consider me cool and indiferent. This may seem so, but it is not meant. "Still waters run deep." I will tell you next August, when a better opportunity will be afforded, how dearly I love you. Until then consider me as your truly in much and abiding love.

W. Dunn

Plainfield Union Co. N.J.
March 27th 1865

Dear Walter

Agreeable to request, I hasten to answer immediatly yours of the 24th. inst. I had made up my mind, I would [write] to you this evening if I did not hear from you before then. I was getting real worried about the soon appearance of a missive from Balto. I'm sorry you could not write to me sooner, but I shall not scold you half as much as those who have only had one letter in one month, from you. It's well a certain person I know is not in their place. How you would catch it. I bet you.

To night I'm going to write such nonsense you will have to be wide awake if you can keep up with me, for "Emma's in a hurry" and have been ever since the time was set for the marriage.[16] But I'm going to answer your questions first.

---

[15]The term "contraband" applied to slaves who came into Union lines. Walter was referring to a photograph of himself.

[16]Emma was probably not referring to her own marriage but to someone else's.

Certainly you may know my reasons for wishing to know the exact time. It was about the time I imagined you would receive it. I was thinking of you, Walt. I was foolish enough to think you was thinking of me, my cheeks burned almost as bad as they did one night when I had such a fever. But I did not hear you talk in your sleep and tell me the fact. You just gratified a whimsical old maid as a young gentleman, politely called your humble servant to-day (the reason, I suppose). I told him "I guessed he could catch a weasel asleep" when I got married. He is to be married to-morrow. He says if report is true, I'm to be married next fall to that little "slowger" down at "Baltimore." How are you, "next fall"? The last item, is an old old story with me.

Your hopes may be realised, for we had a verry pleasant visit to Hatties. The same wish was made by two or three of them, Hattie included, vis. that you would step in and surprise us. But I shall not look for you when you say you have no desire to come untill August. Major Wharton won't laugh at you quite as often as formerly, if he sees your not anxious to visit your S————, when a leave of absence is profered. I shall not look for you, but would dearly love to have you hear a few days while the weather, and roads are so good. I'm enjoying the beautifull spring weather verry much. I guess I will have to get another picture taken of Yours truly so that you can see how much better I look, for I'm verry well and have been some time back, on the improving list, untill I weigh heavier than ever. Just let me come and sit on your knee, and you guess at my weight, may I? I never asked to sit there before, have I?

Yes, Cousin Thomas, his wife, two little ones, Aunt Sallie and Alfred started for the west last wednesday night, half past nine o'clock. The depot was full of friends to see them off. I was there among the rest. Aunt Sallie was the liveliest one of the lot, although she had been quite complaining and was quite feeble. They went from here, when the friends was biding them good bye, Uncle Randolph Dunham steped up to Aunt S. chair and put out his hand. "He would bid her good bye now for the last time on earth, for we are both fast passing away." Yes, she told him I never expect to see you again, and jumping up out of the chair she said, "And I want to kiss you good bye. I have all the rest, may I?" He said Oh yes! and bent his head and kissed her. All had to smile and some hurraed for Aunt Sallie, not only that but several other things she said that helped verry much to enliven them.

Walt, it was comical to see them two old folks kiss each other, not only see but hear it too, for it was an "old fashioned smack." I do not understand what you mean when you say you will give up all claims when I go west. I guess I will have to go and try you. Perhaps you think I do not want to. Pa talks of it strong. I must quit this and tell you some of the news for there is considerable.

Firstly, Eld. Bailey had his vendue this morning. Some of our folks attended, and I think they must have enjoyed themselves considerably. They leave here in the course of two or three weeks. He is to preach his farwell sermon next Sabbath day. I think I shall hear it. I wish you could be here to go.

I suppose you have heard of the death of Mrs. Rachel Clauson[17] (I believe that is her name) the one that was married to a member of your company that went with you. She was buried one day last week. Aunt Ann Ayers[18] was telling me that he was verry disappointed [?] — had lost considerable money gambling. His mother was verry much worried about him and told Aunt Ann, no doubt it worried his wife. But now she is better off. I suppose your Mother has informed you ere this of the death of her cousin Samuel Randolph of Temptown. He was buried last Sabbath day. I went to meeting at our Church N.M. Eld. Rogers preached an excelent discourse from 2nd Kings, 2nd Chap— and well the words were "Let a double portion of thy spirit rest on me." We came home immediately after meeting, and Uncle Theo Dunns folks was here to dinner. You must know we have been expecting Cousin Lew home since before the Hollidays, to get married. But it was impossible for him to come until last—surprised them all. They had given up his coming. Susie Force was feeling verry badly, she has been ready since before the Holidays and her wedding clothes were for winter. And all was disapointed, wednesday morning when he steped in verry quietly . . . but now he is here and is to be married to morrow after noon at 2 o'clock, by Mr. Brown at the Second Presbyterian Church, when they will take a carriage and several buggies and carriages loaded with us young cousins are going to Rahway to see them off for Trenton, where they are to remain a couple of days, and then to New York, where Susies sister is going to give them a weding super. We

---

[17]She was married to Lewis T. Clawson, a member of the 11th New Jersey.

[18]Hannah Ann (Randolph) Ayres, Emma's father's sister, married James Ayres.

have been verry busy helping them prepare and every thing to hurry and bustle. We are to come back to Lew's and have supper. I presume we will have a lovely time. Oh [I] wish you was here to go. But better times coming, and Ma has just reminded me that I will have verry busy times to morrow morning and I had better lay aside my writing and go to be'd. I think I had better mind my ma.

There, I was not aware I held a Mortgage on a Contraband. I'm very much thankful for that picture of your own dear self. I prize it verry highly. But Oh my how did you happen to look so sober. Really Walt, you look as sober as I should expect to see you look if you hear some dear friend was dead, tell me is that the way you look when you think of one who loves you better than ought on earth? And longs for next August to come. Please write soon and think of me always as your own in life with much love and if promised hereafter

It is about Eleven O'clock. I can imagine Cousin Lew and Cousin Susie to be their posish. It is the last evening of their single lives. If nothing happens, I hope and trust not. Do you think you wish you was to be married to morrow? I hope If you live to marry that you feel diferent to what Cousin Lew does. His gayity is all assumed. He is most of the time verry silent and thoughtful. I hope and pray he may be verry verry happy. As happy as we hope to be at some future day in the distance. Good night

31 North Calvert St.
Baltimore Md.
March 30th/65

My Dear Emma

The hurry and bustle of another days duties are over. I am alone in the office and with no one to disturb me, I will devote these few moments of quiet in writing to you, but I can assure you that I would much rather be seated by your side, on the sofa and express by word of mouth, which the distance between us now compells me express with pen and ink. I rejoice to know that, that time is not far distant, every day makes it less and soon in the onward march of time, the four remaining months will have passed away and then, if nothing happens to prevent, we will fully realize what we now anticipate. Your letter of more than usual interest, made its appearance about 10-30 A.M. yesterday. I have stated the exact time as near as I can, although you did not request it, and would request that you inform me as near as you can, the time that you receive mine, hereafter. Please accept my thanks for your promptness, in replying immediately as you did to my last. I would have answered this earlier, but about the time I thought of writing, last night, there was a large fire broke out, which appeared to be a short distance from here, but upon going, we found it over two miles off. It is estimated that over fourty thousand (40,000) dollars of property was destroyed in less than two hours. It was a large ambulance factory owned by a man named "Casey" and made a splendid illumination. I have had considerable of fun, running to fires of late.

"Sayres" made me quite a visit a few days since. He reached here on Sabbath afternoon and remained until Tuesday morning, when he started for home by the way of Harrisburg. He has recently been discharged from the Navy and was on his way home. During his stay here, he was quite "taken in" with the many beautifull ladies and regreted very much when the time came for him to leave. He said that he had never met with such a "jolly lot of boys and boys who were having as good times as we are having here." He did not wonder that they hated to leave here when their terms expire. I am very much attached to this place and shall certainly regret to leave it.

I had been informed that your Cousin Lewis Dunn was expected home to be married and that he was disappointed in [not] getting his leave of absence. Although their marriage has been delayed, I hope that they may realize as much pleasure and wish them much joy and the blessings of a kind Providence through life. Were they married as expected and did everything pass off pleasantly? Who were the brides maid and groom? No I hardly think I wish to be married tomorrow morning. I may wish so some time, within this and two years from now. When will you be ready to change your name? I presume the next to make the "fatal leap" will be little Dave and Sallie will they not? I don't think Harrie will "Miss" Nan a great while longer, Do you agree with me? What advances is Vermont making at your Uncle Jims?

I have, this day, written home for the first, with one exception, since the 24th of February. The last letter I received from home was written on the tenth inst. I think they have forgotten me. I wrote this P.M. to remind them that they had a son and brother in Baltimore. I have droped nearly all my correspondents, by neglecting to answer their letters. I received a letter from Dave over one month ago and have not answered it. I feel quite ashamed of myself. One year ago I had eleven correspondents, excepting you, (you are something more than a correspondent) and now only two or three. Major Wharton has gone to N. York for a few days and during his absence I will answer some of my many unanswered letters. I wish you could help me.

I am glad to learn you are improving rapidly. Please give me your weight in your next and then I will tell you whether or not you can do, what you have never asked before.

Concerning the claim, I shall not give it up if you go East, West, North, or South — not I. You have said considerable about going West. Have you the least idea that your father will go? Of course, if he went, you would go, but otherwise you will not, will you, I consider you jesting when speaking about going West. Am I right?

It is raining "right smart" tonight.

With a hopefull future, I close. Please answer immediatly — and gratify one who loves you devotedly and is

Ever yours Truly
Walter

N.B. I shall hold you to the promise within.

W. G. Dunn

N.B. I mailed you a copy of the Waverly yesterday morning will mail another tomorrow.

Concerning that picture, I consider it a very poor one, it looks more like a "Contraband" than anything else, or that reason I called it such. I hope to redeem it with a better one sometime. I think yours is a very good one but if you have some more taken, I trust you will not forget me. Please ask Jennie for one of hers for me. I think, she promised me one, a long time since, but has never yet fulfilled that promise. Please give her my compliments. Nancy also.

Walter G. Dunn

31 North Calvert St.
Baltimore, Md.
7 P.M. April 5, 1865

Dear Emma,

I have just received a letter from Mary, who informs me that you are "quite sick." The non appearance of your letter which has been due for two days, more fully convinces me of your illness, in which you have my full heart felt sympathies.

It is useless for me to state that I was very much disappointed, when the mail arrived this morning, that there was no word from you, I shall look, full of hopes, tomorrow morning for it, but if I am again doomed to disappointment, I shall certainly think that you are very ill. I have, this P.M. mailed you a copy of the "Waverly," the reading of which, I hope, may be the means of driving away the dull monotony of the sick chamber and also thinking a few words of sympathy from one who loves you very dearly will cheer you in your hours of suffering, I propose, to devote a short time in endeavoring to promote your happiness, by writing you a few lines. You have my earnest prayers for your speedy recovery and restoration to perfect and permanent health.

This city is very jubilant, (although there [is] a considerable manor of long faces) but as a general thing the news of our recent glorious victories are received "with a jubilee." Words cannot describe the scene on Baltimore St. Monday afternoon and evening. The excitement was intense. Not since the 19th of Apl. 1861 has Baltimore been in so much excitement, one man said it reminds him of that (19th) day, "turned inside out."[19] There were several very eloquent speeches made, in the evening, in front of the American Office,[20] where an immense crowd was gathered. There is to be a general illumination of the City tomorrow evening, all the bells to be rung between the hours of 8 and 9, a salute of one hundred guns to be fired from the defences of the City and several speeches made, in Monu-

[19]On April 2, the Confederate government had evacuated Richmond. The next day, Petersburg and Richmond fell, and on April 4 President Lincoln entered the former Confederate capital. On April 19, 1861, Union troops had been attacked in Baltimore, marking the first bloodshed of the war.

[20]Office of the *Baltimore American and Commercial Advertiser.*

Monument Square, Baltimore. During the Civil War as through much of the city's history, it was the site of political rallies and celebrations. (Maryland Historical Society.)

ment Square.[21] My Company (72nd) is to turn out on a parade, I have received an invitation to join them, but it is rather doubtfull, whether I can or not.

It is quite evident now, that the time of peace, so long prayed for, is not far distant. The morning of an honorable and permanent peace is dawning upon us, a peace won in such a manner, that we, as a Nation will demand the respect of all nations, and one very much unlike the peace proposed by the Chicago platform[22] last Fall, a peace that is a peace and one that will give joy to all.

---

[21]Monument Square, site of Baltimore's monument honoring the city's defenders during the Battle of Baltimore in 1814, is on Calvert Street not far from the harbor. The Office of Commissary Musters in which Walter worked was located on it. The square was frequently the site of political rallies and celebrations.

[22]The Democratic Party had held its convention late in August 1864, at a time when pacifism and defeatism had clearly weakened the North's will to win the war. It proposed the cessation of hostilities and a return to peace "on the basis of the Federal Union of the States."

We have just received by telegraph, the sad inteligence, that the Secretary of State, Wm. H. Seward, was thrown from his carriage, in front of his house, and carried in, insensible. He is mortally wounded. His driver is said, to be killed. These news will be received with much regret. The country will deeply mourn the loss at this time.[23]

With the hopes that this may find you recovering and a prayer to the same effect, I will close my letter, hoping to hear from you tomorrow. With usual good health, I am yours,

Devotedly,
Walter

P.S. If unable to write, get some one to write for you, as I am very anxious concerning your health.

W.

Plainfield Union Co. N.J.
April 5, 1865

Dear Walter

Your verry welcome letter of the 30th I received yesterday at just 4.30 P.M. I was at Granfathers when Ollie came in and tossed it in my lap. But he would not give me time to open it, when we Cousin Nancy Oll and this nuisance was on our way home. I (you might know) could not wait no longer and I soon (and they thought) greedily devoured the contents. It was and is a dear good letter. I can only thank you now with my pen, for the sincere pleasure with which I enjoyed your last. When I do what I never asked you to before, I will thank you by word of mouth (vis. a smack).

Walter Dear, now I wish you to know that I am sincere in what I say on the subject following, in reference to those questions. First, let me say I'm verry sorry if I have caused you one unpleasant thought. I'm not afraid for I consider you more than friend. I should have ex-

---

[23]Secretary of State William Henry Seward had tried to seize the reins of the runaway team that pulled his carriage, caught his foot and fallen heavily onto Vermont Avenue in Washington. He suffered a broken arm and jaw and a dislocated shoulder and was for a time delirious. On the night of Lincoln's assassination, he was attacked by one of the assassins while still on his sickbed but survived. Glyndon G. Van Deusen, *William Henry Seward* (New York: Oxford University Press, 1967), 411.

plained in my previous letter, but thought probably you had forgotten it. As for "longing for that, which can not be just now" "that" was for a certain "poor contrabands" presence, by my side on the sofa for a little while. Do you blame me? Or think I'm foolish! Could not you imagine any thing like that? I did endeavor to explain the to me unacountable dread I have when thinking of the future. I hope and trust that you did not allow yourself (in your thoughts of this) to be the reason why I have sad thoughts. No indeed, for I have pleasant thoughts of the relation we have and do sustain to each other, and the still nearer tie anticipated in the future. I can not acount for it, unless it be ____ (I dislike to wound your feelings Dearest Walt) the impreshion I have allways had that I'm to "part with all I hold dear on Earth (while I'm still young and life has so many charms) to go the journey from which no traveler ever returns. I used, as you well know, wish that such might be the case. But Dear Walt you have learned me to think diferently. I can not think my self more to you than I am now, scarcly and if I do tis only for a short time and then I must be going. (My desire is to live my allotted time in usefullness and in a way to ensure an inheritance in heaven with all my loved ones.) I think you understand fully. Do you not? Please tell me in your next. And remember me in your prayers will you?

No I have not been "Book Keeper" since the last of Dec. Eugene has been with Pa since Jan. 1st. So I'm to be "private Secretary and Tresurer" for the Conductor of the Balto City passenger Railway. I having never seen said place. Do not know how I should like the situation. I think I should like it, if you are so particularly atached to it that you'll regret to leave it when your term of service expires. It is now quite late. I shall have to lay this aside for to night, so good night. I hope your dreams are sweet, only four mounths, and I shall not use my pen so often. Remember me as your own,

Emma to be, E.R.

Afternoon 3.30

Dear Walt

Once again I resume my pen to chat with you a little while.

It has been quite a disagreeable day, untill now it is blowing over and looks as though we would have a "brighter day to morrow." My duties have been quite irksome today and I feel more inclined to delay writing, and instead of sitting here on the Sofa lie down and think of the pleasant times we have enjoyed together. But now my "Pillow" would not have a bullet in its shoulder. I think I hear you say, "I had better try it." Such a move would not benefit you any. I should look in vain for a letter next week. I should have answered the evening I received it, but a severe headache compelled me to lie down immediately after tea. There was quite a livly time here on that evening (4th) "Glorifying" over the news the folks went up to hear the illumination and see the speaking.[24] Did not get home untill quite late, from what they tell me they had a gay time. There was great inquiring for "Em Barzillia" as they call me, that is about as pretty as the name to the "promise within."

Yes they were married as expected, just at two o'clock. The relatives had just got seated when in came Lew and his s[weetheart] soon to be one. They walked diliberatly up the asile and steping in front the pulpit "faced the music" as Lew said and soon had taken the "fatal leap" as you call it. They took carriages and fourteen (14) couples went to the Rahway with them to see them off for Trenton on their weding trip. Not however untill we all went to Crowells [and] saluted the married couple. There was no waiters. Drank their healths then we came back to Uncle Theo's and had supper. Every one seems pleased with the wedding and I have heard several say it made them wish they was married. It did not effect me that way. I may be ready to change my name about two years from next Holidays, will that suit you? Or is it to "short an engagement"? I'm inclined to think Harrie and Nan: well Walt, I know it, that if nothing happens, they "H" and "N" will be married next Thanksgiving. I'm the only person beside Harrie and Nan that know it. It is to be kept dark and "mum."

I do not know wether Dave and Sallie will have the knot tied before then, or perhaps they two will be "thankfull." I presume "H" and "N" will go west on their wedding tour, as it is her wish. She says if I'm not married before then she wants me as bridesmaid. What say you?

Well Walt my Dear, my weight is or was 100.41 lbs.[25] the last time I

---

[24]The celebration was occasioned by the fall of Richmond.
[25]Emma means 141 lbs.

was weighed. Now may I? I will not place you in the situation the fellow was that Pa was telling me about last Sabbath.

Yes certainly I was jesting about my going west. I have had the "fever" this spring. I was not afraid of your giving up the claim.

I have been gasing out the window quite a little while and the last comment I made on the scene that met my view, was that e're the leaves which are coming so thickly to clothe that little weeping willow fall we shall not have to use the pen to communicate to each other. I hope and trust nothing will happen to mar our pleasure then. Jennie returns her compliments, also Cousin Nancy. Jen is singing "When all the boys come home." "Oh won't we have a happy time." Alass one I think she held dearly will never return, and tis so with many that has lost their loved ones, we have cause to be thankfull. I must close. I realy feel ashamed to send this. But hoping it will be better than nothing, I will send it. Please write to me immediatly and tell me where the "Compound" is. I believe it is on your side. I'm not mistaken I guess am I? Write soon, to one who is yours in life with much and ever abiding love.

M.

P.S. Mr. Nelson Blackford and Miss Annie Sletter was married at the Piscataway Church at half after three, on the afternoon of the 5th. Morgan S. called on me Sabbath evening, gave me an invitation to get up a load and go down. But I did not. How do you like getting married in Church?

N.B. Father and Oll has been fishing — and as usual have caught a fine lot. Pa wish me to tell you that it was a good time to come home on furlough and if you come you might "pitch your tent" here. How are you? Fathers House — I dreamed you was home last night and I was just going to — well salute you when — bah — I awoke and found you was not there. I bet I have some thing as good to tell you as your "Substitutes." But shall wait untill I hear about them before I tell you.

Your Loving "Mate"

Baltimore, Md.
Sunday, April 9, 1865

Dear Emma

The ringing of bells and the large crowds passing to and fro indicate that it is about church time. Tis a bright and beautifull morning, I should very much like to attend church, but I prefer this pleasure, for I know that I will be compensated, in a few days by a good long letter in return, and you know how very much I appreciate your missives.

Yours of the 5th inst. was received, while you were at church I presume, about 11 A.M. yesterday, but for the rush of business I did not get a chance to read it until quite late in the day. I think you are mistaken concerning the "compound correspondence," I think that it rests on you, I presume you think the same, now do you not?

I told you in my former letter that an evening had been appointed for a general illumination of the city. It came off according to appointment and was perfectly grand. The citizens of Baltimore never before witnessed such a scene. All the government and public offices and very many private residences displayed a perfect sheet of light, togather with the fire works, gave the city the appearance of 4th of July, only a great deal more so. I appropriated Maj. Wharton's rifle and did some tall firing. Baltimore St. was literally crowded from one end of the city to the other, not only the side walks but the street was so full some of the time that it was impossible to get allong. I saw "Johnny rebs" parrading the streets in their uniforms with their ladies. Although the illumination was general throughout the city, yet there were a great number of dark houses and some of them our next door neighbors. Near Washington's Monument, in the arristocratic part of the city, it was noticed to be quite dark and a little or no display of the "good old flag," this fact being known, one section of a battery was ordered there and one hundred guns fired in their midst, between the hours of 8 and 9 P.M. It would be folly for me to undertake to describe the grandeur of the scene. I only wish that you could have been here to see it for yourself. I know that you would have enjoyed it, but better times are coming.[26]

I expect to go to Druid Hill Park this P.M. in company with several others. I wish that you were here to go allong. The time is fast approaching for our anticipated ride in August next. Over one half of

---

[26]Walter was more perceptive than he knew. In a matter of hours, early in the afternoon of this Palm Sunday, the Army of Northern Virginia would surrender at Appomattox Court House.

the time since the engagement was made has already expired. I was in favor of getting all to go that I could, thinking the more the merrier but Dave thought that four of us (viz.) you and Sallie, himself, and I would be sufficient for us to have a happy time. What is your opinion on the number? You will probably think that there is ample time yet to talk about that. I hope that our anticipations will more than be realised.

A few days since, I had a beautifull rose shoot ("house plant") presented to me with two full bloom roses and three that will bloom very soon. It is splendid and I prize it highly. I have not yet learned who was the generous creature. I think that I can ascertain soon. I think I have heard you say that you took a great deal of pleasure in cultivating flowers, do you not? I would like to place this under your care and protection. Will you please tell me the language of the rose, in your next? I have the one that you sent me when you were sick last Summer.

I will lead you into the "Substitute" secret if you will promise to reveal to me your secret. It is nothing, at the greatest, which you will perceive. Tis this, while at Sallies with Dave on a call, when on furlough, a picture was observed on the mantle, of a young gentleman, who, Dave said was her beau and that he was only a substitute. I am candid, that is all. I probbably represented it to you as a great deal more than the above, it was because you refused to tell me something concerning Harrie but a short time before and I wished to be even with you. You know all now and I will trust to your kindness to tell me that which you have been holding back until I told you the above.

Yes you, (and you only) may do what you never asked to before. When you do, you must remember that according to promise, you have a debt, that must be paid in full, do you understand?

As for your being Nan's Bridesmaid, you are (of course) at liberty to act your own pleasure, regarding it. I shall keep shady.

My weight is one hundred and fifty one (151) lbs. ten (10) heavier than you.[27]

I do not blame you, or think you foolish, for thinking as you

---

[27]The average Civil War soldier weighed 158 lbs. and stood five feet eight inches tall, with blue eyes and light brown hair. Although we have no photograph of Walter we know that his weight at least was about average.

expressed yourself in answer to my questions, I can assure you that those feelings are mutual. I long for an interview with you, but the time will soon come and then we will make up for lost time, will we not?

As to when we shall be joined in the "bonds of matrimony," I beg your permission to delay the answer of your question until an interview is granted us, then I can more fully express myself. I trust that this will meet with your approval.

While I have been writing, about fifteen hundred (1500) rebel prisoners, (officers and men) have passed our door on their way North. They looked very rough and receive a great deal of sympathy in this city. I have been talking, watching the prisoners and writing a little now and then, until the hour has passed and the bell rung for dinner. The cook by brevet told me this morning that he was going to have a delicate dinner, so I must rush. I hardly think we will have fish. Dearest Emma, please oblige one who loves you beyond expression, by an immediate answer to this. I remain yours fondly and sincerely

Walter

P.S. I dreamed last night that I gave you an introduction to one of my young lady acquaintances in this City. You appeared very much pleased with her. It was a Miss Imes.

Plainfield N.J.
April 16th /65

My Own Dear Walt

I have only time to inform you of the safe arival of your verry dear letter. It did me so much good. I did not have the pleasure of reading it untill friday 5.00 O,clock P.M. I have been visiting at New Town for the last week. Came home to find Jersey verry sick, and wanted Em. I remained home about twenty minutes, and have been with Jersey since and as she is entirely helpless, I am acting as both nurse and house-keeper. I have attempted to write you many times, but my little Walter[28] could not agree with my way of thinking. The Doctor says it will be two weeks if not longer before he can lance Jersey's absess, and then it will be some time before she must use her arm. Eugene and

---

[28]Probably Emma's small nephew, Walter Grant Runyon.

Jersey wants me to remain with them untill Jersey gets well. So Walt, my letters I'm verry much afraid will have to be like this one, tardy and short, but Walt Dear, I think of you allways. And I know you will not forget your Emma. Please write to me just when you can, and when I can I will drop you a line to let you know how I get along with my new situation. I would like to tell you how I spent last week, but time will not permit. Wait untill August next. I think as Dave does. It will not be nessary for others to go beside the four (4) mentioned, to make it pleasant for us.

Yes "You" and only you understands. Do you think you will take interest?

As to the Bonds of Matrimony I must certainly agree with you, wait for an interview. It is verry late, as you perceive I am quite nervous. Eugene is up and as Jersey is resting easier, I will bid you good night. Hoping you will not think I am cold and indiferent — for I love you Oh so dearly and pray for the time to come when I can once more clasp your hand and tell you how I have remembered and loved you while absent. Remember and love me allway[s]

as your sincerly

Emma

Oh the sad sad news — it must cause me to murmer — just when every thing was so bright. But we must all learn to kiss the evil and say "Thy will be done."[29]

M.

31 North Calvert St.
Baltimore, Md.
April 19th 1865

My Dear Emma,

Your very brief and tardy letter of the 16th inst. reached me about 8::30 A.M. yesterday. The evening previous I wrote you a brief letter, requesting an explanation for your long delay, and would have forwarded it, had not yours, arrived in the morning mail. I hope I may never have occasion to write another, such. For nearly a week, past, I

---

[29]John Wilkes Booth shot President Abraham Lincoln about ten o'clock on the night of Friday, April 14. The President died at 7:22 the next morning.

have watched each mail with much anxiety, and have been disappointed very many times. Using your quotation "Hope deferred maketh the heart sick," such was my situation until I received your last, which explains all. I doubt you not. I cannot think that you would deceive me, after expressing yourself as you have repeatedly. I place all confidence in you and trust I may never have occasion to regret it. Do not think I could accuse you of deception, no, I hold your virtues and christian principle in too high esteem to be guilty of such great injustice. I hope and trust that when this reaches you, you will be so situated that you can reply immediatly. Remember, that it is the request of one who loves you devotedly and if it is in your power, for his sake, comply. Did you receive a letter, written on or about the 5th inst.? I received a letter from Sister Mary informing me that you were quite sick, and I wrote immediatly to ascertain, if it was so, and how you were. You made no mention of it in your last. I judge it has not been received.

You stated that you had been visiting in New Town. I hope you had a very, very pleasant visit, did you not? Did you visit Uncle Joels folks while there? I presume that you found the farmers all busily engaged in preparing the ground and sowing their seed, in anticipation of a bountifull harvest. I would like to get out in the country once more for a few days. I am getting quite tired of this life. I want a change. But a few weeks more and my term of enlistment will have expired, then I am going to the country and enjoy that, for which I am longing.

Yes we have, indeed, had very bad news. In the midst of our rejoicings we were called upon to mourn the loss of our noble hearted President, by an All Wise Providence, who doeth all things for good, unto those who love him. Nearly every building is draped in mourning showing that all have lost a friend. The people are deeply affected with grief over the sad news of the murder, and the maner in which it was perpetrated. History does not record a more horrible crime. The news almost made me heart sick. I would not have been more shocked, had I received the news of the death of a near friend. I hope and pray that President Johnson[30] will mete out death to all traitors as their portion. I would like to write more upon this subject but time will not permit.

---

[30]Lincoln was succeeded by Vice President Andrew Johnson of Tennessee.

The Merchant's Exchange or Customs House in Baltimore, where Lincoln briefly lay in state as his funeral procession made its way to Illinois. (Maryland Historical Society.)

It shall be as you wish in refference to the anticipated ride in August next.

I hope that Jersey is fast improving.

I would like an interview with you, I do so dislike to write, what I would like to say. Please accept all these poor letters and remember that I am coming home soon and then I will tell you all. I must confess, I feel very stupid this evening and am quite ashamed to send this. I will try to do better next time. Please answer immediatly. I am dearest Emma,

Yours Ever,

W.

P.S. Please excuse for I have written in great haste. Walter

Plainfield. 9.30 Evening

April 23, 1865

My Own Dear Walt

You think tis a poor chance for a verry interesting letter from me. But Walt I will give you just what comes in my head, and trust to you for the rest.

I received my Missive from your own Dear self yesterday (Sabbath) about 1.30 P.M. It was like all others from you verry verry welcome. This is my first opertunity to answer it, for I'm still with Jersey. I anticipated all day yesterday the pleasure I should take writing you a verry lengthy letter and was about to commence my chat with you, by means of the pen, when Jersey requested me to answer the knock at the door, and to my surprise met Harrie and Lew who had come for me. Jennie have other company to entertain, vis. Vermont, Frank Randolph, of Newark, and Mr. Compton. We had quite a pleasant time. I come home. (I call this home) about 10.30 with a headache. I have been quite busy to day am verry tired, ought not write. But a request of "one who loves me devotedly" (but whose love cannot be greater than mine) and a willing heart responds to "answer immediatly."

I am happy to know you have such confidence in me. I trust you allways may.

Yes! Walt I received said letter of the 5th inst. and read every word with regret, not that I did not like the sentiments, and deep and as I

Postwar photograph of Emma's friend, Kizzie Potter, showing the strains of wartime life. (Courtesy, Jeannette Fitz Randolph Duryea.)

have reason to believe, heart felt sympathy, expressed therein, but instead that rumor should go so far. I was sick a few days with my Lungs enough to keep me prisoner two weeks, but not so that I allowed the Doc. called. As usual every one heard I was verry sick, but was much surprised to see me, so soon, and looking so well as they repeatedly assured me. I should not [have] informed you of my slight illness had you not received the information from Mary. I meant to have mentioned it in my last, but time was short. I [am] verry sorry it caused you any anxiety. Rest assured I'm perfectly well now. I have not felt as well in four years, as I have for the last two weeks. I wish you could be here now. This beautiful spring weather. I am feeling so verry verry well. I'm not confident enough to think it will last untill August. Oh! what anticipations I have for your return. And I shall be spared to realize them.

> "When victor shouts arise
> God hear my prayer—
> "Our Union banner free
> From treasons stain;
> And give you back to me
> In joy again."

And I suppose twill soon be floating the "Banner of the Star" triumphantly and flocks of soldiers returning to enjoy the Peace so dearly bought. I feel a stronger hatred than ever for the poor Copperheads . . . now that they have stooped so low as to murder our loved and honored and now deeply mourned President. Oh! how many verry many sad hearts it has made all over our land. But we must not murmer, for "Gods ways are just" and "The bud though bitter to the taste— How sweet will be the flower. . . . Plainfield on wednesday last present[ed] a verry diferent aspect to what was expected, for nearly all the buildings had some show of esteem for the Dec[eased] in regret at his cruel Death. There was services held in two (2) Churches 2nd Presbeterian and Me[thodist]. I went to the former. It was crow[d]ed to over flowing. The Church was draped and arranged verry nicly. The audience was addressed by three diferent Ministers. I did not like their remarks at all. I expected to hear a sermon on the Death of Mr. Lincoln Sabbath at New Market, but Eld. Rogers postponed it untill next Sabbath morning. I hope to attend, and will endeavor to remember some part of it for you, shall I? I know you would much rather hear with your own ears. I'm sure I would just as leave, "If not a little leaver." Mr. Ed Titsworth and his Bride was to meeting, and another weding couple came with Sammy Dunham[31] folks. I did not learn their names. The thought poped in my head while gazing down on them. Who next in our small congregation would step in the "halter" of Matrimony? If Harrie and Nan ever is to be one, I'll bet it will be them. I did not indulge in such thoughts long. But let them go with the fast receding storm.

By the way, Nan did not leave Uncle R's untill wednesday making quite a long visit, longer than I would stay at my intended husbands unless he was not expected to live. But Gossip does not trouble Nan. It need not me.

Yes! indeed I visited Cousin Joels and that is not all. I went to Cou's Firman and Your Aunt Sallie, "Sayers" Nichols Grandma, went with us, we come back to your home and Lew took the "Grocery," hooked his poney to it, invited Mollie and I to go to New Market with him to get

---

[31]This may have been Samuel H. Dunham, who joined the army on May 16, 1861. He was promoted to first sergeant on August 1, 1861, and was discharged from an army hospital in Alexandria on July 9, 1862.

Sayers. We did so and then all four of us went down to singing school. We had a verry livly time indeed. Sayers made Lew laugh untill he cried about a certain time when you had such funny or "queer" Cheese. I could not understand the story. I will have to ask you some time. Sayers is verry livly — no doubt he has writen to you e're this and told you what he was going to. I must close I have writen much later than I anticipated. I hope this will find you enjoying the best of health and good spirits, and that will help to while away some of your sad moments when the first of next month comes, then it will be only three more, then I shall count the days. Please write soon to one who is with much and

Everlasting Love Your most truly

M. Emma

Jennie and I call[ed] on Sallie Johnson last wednesday and she was trying to console me, telling me to be patient untill next August, especially the 12th. Jennie says she believes Dave and Sallie is going to be married then — and perhaps "Walt" and "Em." I think she will be doomed to disappointment. How you?

your Emma

Baltimore Md.

April 27th 1865

My Dear Emma

The stillness of midnight, for which Baltimore is so remarkable, reigns. Everything is perfect quiet, the tramping sounds of passers by, has ceased, the rumbling of wagons and the streetcars is hushed in silence. I am seated by my desk alone, with no one to disturb me, thinking of one whose presence would fill my heart with joy and add very much to this pleasure.

This is a rare opportunity. I seldom write you without being more or less troubled by talkative persons, of whom there are a great many connected with this office. But I am rid of them now and will endeavor to improve a few of these "golden moments" in replying to your last which I gladly received about 9::30 A.M. yesterday.

You will doubtless wonder why I choose so late an hour, to write you. Tis this, at the request of a friend. I went with him to the Theatre to see Miss Lucille Western (known all over the world as an A. No. 1

Actress) in her character of "lady Isabel" in the very affecting peice entitled "East Lynne." It was perfectly grand. The audience was brought to tears, several time[s]. I, (as hard hearted as I am) could not suppress them. This Theatre is leased by Mr. Ford, the owner of the one in which our lament[ed] President was murdered.[32] It was heavily draped and Miss Western wore a large badge of mourning. It was opened last night for the first time since the assassination. I have attended three different Theatres this week. You will probbably think that I am indulging too freely in theatrical pleasures. I do, and shall not go again for a long time. I wish that you could have seen "East Lynne" played. I know that you would like it. But enough of such trash.

A telegram, received here this morning, from the War Dept. announces the arrival at that place of the body of J. Wilkes Booth and his accomplice, Harrold. Our beloved President is at last avenged. You have, doubtless, ere this read the particulars concerning the capture.[33]

You stated that you were still with Jersey. How is she? I hope that she is fast improving. How is Gene?

Was it the Singing school at Oak Tree that you attended, with Lew? I was not aware that they continued so late in the season.

I will tell you all concerning the "queer cheese" when I have an opportunity. I also have something else to tell you, when you tell me that which you were holding back until I told you about the substitutes.

I have not yet received a letter from Sayres. I am looking for one daily.

Is Vermont attending school yet, or has he gone back to the farm? And so you think that matters are ripening with Nan and Harrie, do you? I wish them "Gods speed."

I have been up quite late every night this week and I can assure you that my eye-lids are growing heavy. I intended to write you a long and good letter, tonight, but I find I have failed. I feel too dull to write. You will excuse me this time will you not? Please accept and be prompt in replying.

> Dearest Emma remember me as,
> Yours until Death, Walter

---

[32]Ford's Theater in Baltimore was owned by John T. Ford, who also owned Ford's Theater in Washington, the scene of Lincoln's assassination.

[33]John Wilkes Booth and Davy Herrold, an accomplice in the Lincoln assassination plot, had been captured the previous morning at the farm of Richard H. Garrett in Virginia. Herrold had surrendered but Booth, who refused capture, had been fatally shot.

Plainfield Union Co. N.J.
April 30th 1865

Dear Walt

You just turn your head towards the "west" when you go to "our house." When you get as far as the corner of fifth and New sts. look up at the last window, on the west end, just over the front door, and you will spy the place where Em wrote the last letter to you while in her twentieth year. For here am I: the bed close to the window, pen in my lap and scribbling to _ _ _ Its just about the time I love to go riding (4.30). It is a splendid day, or has been, it having rained "right smart" all last evening, but clearing of[f] during the night. It has been splendid weather since. I do enjoy this spring so much. I'm so verry verry well. I have only one drawback to hinder me from being completly happy. I need scarcly hint what that is for you. I've told you many times how I miss you. But our lives being spared another spring will find us in diferent circumstances. Do you not wish for it?

Yesterday when on our way to Church Mr. I. D. Titsworth asked to ride with us and siting on my lap — (Don't be jealous it was't Jud) of course the subject turned to the never failing topic "War." Mr. I. D. said "I guess our boys will be home before their term expires," giving me a pinch to solicit a reply. My answer was — "I thought he would be mistaken." What is your opinion?

Eld Rogers preached from second Samuel 3rd Chap. 19th verse[34] an exelent discourse. He caused the tears to flow, of deep sorrow, at our "Nation's loss and hearts to burn with indignation at the Base deed." I shall never forget that sermon, the Church was heavily draped. The Choir sang peices appropriate and you could have heard a pin drop, between the interlude it was so perfectly sad and silent. There was not a dry eye in the whole congregation, when we was singing the final peice, "Peacefully lay Him down to rest." It was with dificulty we could command our voices sufficient to finish the tune. I wished you could have been there.

Yes! I'm still with Jersey she is much better. But her arm is verry weak. I rocked little Walter to sleep give him a hug and a kiss for you,

---

[34]"Abner also spoke to Benjamin; and then Abner went to tell David at Hebron all that Israel and the whole house of Benjamin thought good to do."

put him in his cradle, and have now for a little while been trying to interest my Walt. Perhaps you would like me to serve you with some of the same that I gave "Walty Dant" as Maggie calls him, just say so if you will, and I will save some. This morning I was playing with him and said "Walt, kiss me." Gene, who is full of mischief said, "I must ask 'Uncle Walter' he would give me all I wanted." How are you Uncle? I get teased more than ever since I have been here. I wish you could hear half Gene says about my housekeeping. I'm afraid you would be discouraged "But Perseverence is allways rewarded with success." Gene thinks he has given me a few lessons, and that I'm improving. They live verry happily together. I often now imagin my self married and settled down. I have grown old so fast for the last week. I hear little Walt crying verry hard. I must hasten down so "Au revior" for a little while.

10 Oclock P.M.

Dearest Walter

I have been compelled to lay this aside much longer than I antici-pated. I had just finished setting tea for Gene, Jersey and myself, and was going home a moment when as I steped out the gate a buggy come down the street and stoped at our gate. Lew helped Arelia alight and then come to meet me. They stayed at my home to tea after supper. We Lew and Rele, Ollie and your Em was just starting to make a call on Aunt Em, when we met Vermont and Jennie coming in. Harrie had brought them up home. He was going down to see Nan. Mont was going to stay all night. Mont, and Jen, went with us. We had a verry pleasant time. Lew and Rele have gone home after droping me at Jersey's door. Ollie has gone to bed. Vermont and Jennie I've no doubt are enjoy[ing] the "Sofa" Oh! _ _ _ that tomorrow was the first of August. But brighter days are coming. They was all going to give me a good "sound trouncing." But all forgot it, once I'm favored.

Let me tell you something. Last thursday night, I was verry wakfull it was impossible for me to get asleep. My mind was disturbed. Between the hours of twelve and one, I lay thinking of the Past, Present, and Future, and of course you was mingled with them. Little did I dream you was writing to me at that late hour. And now as to the Theatre — you could not have suited me better than have had me beside you, while witnessing the play of "East Lynne." I never was interested in any piece as the above, although I did not have the pleasure of finishing the story. You'll remember it and tell me, won't you?

Yes! the singing school was at Oak Tree. They do not hold it so late in the spring but several evening[s] was omited and that evening that I spoke of was the last for this term. Next winter I suppose they will have it just the same. I hope so.

Vermont is attending school. He says he will not come back to the farm. I believe he is going in a bank this summer.

Yes! I do think things are progressing with Harrie and Nan. But Harrie still persists in saying he will win the Oysters.

I meant to have writen you a verry short and somewhat cooler letter than usual, to pay you for the last two or three brief notes from Balto. But my better feelings have gained the day and my heart has dictated. You may look for a short one next time.

I received a Waverly last week, for which kind favor, please receive my thanks.

Now as that I was to tell you, perhaps you will laugh. I reckon I did although I did not feel much like it at the time. You have perhaps a slight recollection of the last evening you was at our house before your return to Baltimore and that it was quite late when you left (not 4 oclock). From some notion that I can not account for I did not go through Ma's room into the one I slept in generaly, but instead, jumped in Ollies bed (he being away at the time) and was soon in the land of dreams, which were sad with farewells. I do not remember anything untill about Eleven O clock A.M. when Ma awoke me, and asked me, had Walter gone! I told her yes! And was wide awake and then she told me how Pa had frightened them. He was going hunting and must have got up just after I went to bed, and wishing to call some one to get him some breakfast, he looked in Jen's and my room, and not seeing me he thought he would see if you had "stayed all night" and went to the little room where you slept, and found that bed undisturbed he went down stairs thinking perhaps I had concluded to spend the night there on the Sofa. But nary a sign of Em yet. He began to be frightened and when he had reached the lower rooms, in vain, he went up to Ma and waking her, told her Emma was gone he could not find her. Ma was scared, she said and asked had he looked in Ollies room. Yes he had looked and found Walter, but could not find Em. Ma said it must be me, but Pa said no! It was Walt his head lay in plain sight. His Cap hung over the post. They looked from Garret to Cellar, Ma wanting to look in Ollies room, but Pa said not disturb you. It would only frighten you. Perhaps they would look out doors thinking perhaps I had taken to walking in my sleep again. Ma now was thouroly alarmed and determined to awaken "Walter" and ask him if Em started to bed the same time he did. Coming to the bedside she stooped over and brushed my hair from off my forhead, and discovered the lost me. Oh what a grand mistake. Ollie and Jennie thought it to good to be lost, and Pa will never hear the last of it. I often laugh when I think of it.

It is getting late and I must stop this scribbling. I see Jennie R., Ed's sister has got a beau at this late hour. They have bought the house right on the opisite corner. Uncle Theodore has moved where we used to live down second street and we will have a chance to visit the old front room and sit in the "Cool window" if we wish to. I must stop.

Please write soon, and a good long letter to.

yours devotedly
Emma Randolph

Plainfield Union Co. N.J.
May 8th /65

Dear Walter

Tis with regret that I write you under so late a date, in answer to your last verry precious missive which I received friday, 6.30. Believe me it was verry interesting and quite good length. But you allready know I love to get long letters. I intended to have writen to you last evening but we had company and when they left my head pained me so that I was forced to go to bed and delay my "Chat" untill to night. Do not expect anything interesting, for my head has not improved much if any. I think bathing with cold water would tend verry much towards lessening the pain, if I had the right one to administer the remedy.

I have changed my mind in reference to a cool letter, you do not merit it, but fear this will be brief. Yes dear I understand. I shall expect a number of "make up's" when you return to Jersey (or Emma).

Gracie's birth is the same day you was wounded. I thought of you often on that day, my thoughts wher pleasant ones to what they were 1 year ago. Then I feared you would lose the use of your arm — or have to have it amputated, but Providence ruled it otherwise, surly "his way[s] are just." No pardon is nesseray for surly though painfull it interested me — in fact, you never write anything but what is interesting to me. So please write just what you think when "Chating" with me . . ! Will you?

Last friday evening Pa was enquiring for Emma and said (when I did come in from a walk with Jennie) it reminded him of the morning when he was looking for me. I asked him what he would have thought had he not found me. "I should thought you had eloped" and added he should keep his eye on us when you come home. By the way that reminds me of an expression Pa made to Jennie yesterday. "Jen" I think "Vermont" is getting interested. He has been here 4 nights out of seven 7, most as bad as Walter. Jennie looked over at me and said "Oh no. Walt was here every night but only for a week." Pa said "well that is diferent — with Walter he did not have the chance every week to come see Em when Mont can come every week." Pa asked me what I thought if things did not look serious. I wanted verry much to ask him if he thought we looked serious. Now I'll bet you could not guess who are engaged. I will not keep you in suspense. Tis Mont and Jennie. You are surprised I'll bet. Are you not? How do you imagen you will like him for a brother-in-law? Jennie informed me of the fact the 1st May, the question being settled the previous Eve. I asked her if she had informed him of our engagement. No and did not intend to, although I might tell Walt. If I chose to, and I most certainly did. The party concerned and you and I are all that know of it, and are all that are to know of it at present if you please. Mont came last wednesday from Newark and returned next morning. But more of them some other time.

Yes! the 1st of May is Em's birthday and I remember you're to be home next aniversary. But I do not feel verry much afraid. I'm a considerable heavier, consequently, a little stronger and you to remember 12th of August comes before next May, and you will have to beg pretty hard. But I must close this uninteresting scribbling, for I have been interrupted several times and it is now quite late. Please answer soon if you consider this worthy of an answer. Hoping you are having sweet dreams, I will bid you "Good night." Continue to love me and know you are dearly loved in return by

your own true Em

N.B. Look out for number two. I received a "Waverly" to night. Receive the thanks of your intended Mate

I wish they would send you home next week. I so long to see you, have you with me. I miss the clasp of your hand and the accompaniment oh so much.

Em

Baltimore, Md.
May 10th 1865

Dear Emma

In your last, which I received this A.M. you requested that I answer soon, if I considered it worthy of an answer. Although tardy and brief, I deem it worthy an answer and wish to indicate it by replying as early as I can. Please never again doubt the worthiness of your letters, when I consider them unworthy, I will inform you of the fact and cease to answer them, until then, do not say unworthy again. If you think yours unworthy, I think I have abundant reason to think mine so also, for I am quite sure that yours are more interesting than mine.

This is perhaps the last letter that I will write you in this office. All the men connected with this office, belonging to the Veteran Reserve Corps have this day received orders to report to their respective companies. I expect an order very soon. There are various reports concerning the object of these orders, some say it is for the purpose of discharging us, others that it is for the purpose of consolidating the companies or reorganization. I think the latter more probbable than the former. Time will decide it.

The mustering out of men in Hospitals, in pursuance to an order recently issued, is going on briskly. Ten (10) additional mustering officers have been detailed and ere long the Hospitals in this Dept. will be well drained of their inmates. We are very busy indeed, here, this being the chief mustering office in this Dept.

I am not a little surprised to learn that Jennie and Mont are engaged. I thought that Mont was paying his addresses to Miss Ayres of New Market and little expected to hear the above. What was the cause of the sudden change? In a previous letter, you stated that Lew and Aurelia were out riding togather, does he wait on her now? How long has Jennie known of our engagement? I informed Lew of the fact when he was here. Does either your father of mother know of it? Mine do not.

Tell Jennie that I will be happy to congratulate her upon the new relation, with Vermont, which she has promised to assume at some future time and sincerely hope that the promise may never be regreted by either.

I am aware that the 12th of Aug. comes before the 1st of May. And will have you remember that I will then be a just "returned warrior" fresh from the army.

I regret to learn that you are troubled with headache. You have spoken of late, of your being so very well, that I was hoping your headache had left you entirely. I hope you are feeling better now. Do you wear your hair short now as you did when I was home on furlough? Are you still with Jersey, if so how is she? How are Sallie and Dave?

I am quite well but I feel very dull tonight. I cannot write as much as I wish, on that account. I know you will excuse me for this brief and uninteresting letter as I am very tired.

Please write immediately and remember me as ever loving you, and

Yours, forever
W.G. Dunn

Plainfield Union Co. N.J.
May 14th 1865

Dear Walter

After having spent the evening at Aunt Grace's home with my new Cousin Mrs. L. A. Dunn, and several other Cou's, and a soldier bearing the somewhat romantic name Frank High (Jennie and I like him verry much for a new acquaintance) I have seated myself to write you a short Letter, in answer to you[r] last kind missive, which came to hand in due time, and the contents greedily devoured and with a good relish. My head is so full of the nonsense of the evening, I do not know where to commence. Jennie poor sister is the first object that attracts my attention. There she lies sleeping in the same place where you did when you verry sleeplily said, "Emma what do you want"? Jen is verry troubled inasmuch as Vermont graduated, friday evening, and has determined to start for St. Louis the first of June, with the intention of remaining two (2) years or more. I tell her tis not so bad as going to the war. The change is not sudden. Mont has wanted to come see Jennie for over a year, but she would not let him. I'm sorry that he is going. He thinks business prospects are better. I hope he will get along well. Jennie has known of our engagement ever since I was so complaining. Are you sorry[?] I'm glad Lew is not ignorant of the fact. I mistrusted he knew of it. My Parents do not know of it, but Ma jokes me about you, and I think she is of the opinion we are engaged and look forward to a Union next winter. How many will be disappointed. That reminds me of an other couple I have learned are engaged namly a Mr. Miller a widower and Louise Jo[h]nson. I jumped when I heard it. Its the truth, for I heard it from a right source. Does not that make you feel astonished? Jennie and I called to see Louise and Sallie last wednesday evening. Sallie was not home — she was at the store, where she is clerk. I've been thinking verry strongly of going at the mil[i]ners trade, this summer, but it seems to be an impossibility to get fathers consent. One more of the miliners is to leave next fall, and wants me to buy her out, and I think it is the best, and has the best run of custom[er]s of any in Plainfield. What do you think of it? Do you think it advisable or are you opposed to my gaining the name of Miliner before I change it to something els[e] [illegible][?] Please tell me in your candid opinion on the above subject, and your wishes. Please do not look over this subject in your next. Lew has been calling on Cousin Aurelia, and taking her out, over a month. Sabbath Evening they went down to Clarks then back to Granfathers. Harrie came to bring Mont up as he has parted with his horse and buggy. Harrie took me out riding a short distance — he said I must not tell you.

I'm at home, Jersey having recovered sufficient to spare Em. Little "Wally Dant" is growing finly and of course is sweet as any of the big boys. I love him dearly. I have a verry severe headache it not having left me in nearly two weeks, but live in hopes of losing it soon. I have not had my hair trimed but once since you was home, and that was when I wished to have those "grining" vignetts taken. It is now well just verry unmanageable. If you are inclined to laugh at my "queer looks" as Mont calls it, when I put my hair in a net, I shall be tempted to have it cut off. It grows quite fast however. Riley Potter is the only one of the soldiers that has returned to New Market. I shall look for the rest — you included every sabbath untill I see you. I had thought they would not muster out our New Market soldiers untill next August. Have you heard of any? I am verry anxious to know how you are, where you are, and what you're about to do — come home or stay at Balto. — untill the 30th of August. I have been at a stand wether to write to you, not knowing wether you was still at the Office. But as I received no "further orders" I have determined to, as you probaly know. I realy am ashamed to send it. As I shall not have another chance I will trust to your kindness to look over all mistakes. If you was here I would kiss you but as it is impossible, I can only hope you are having swet dreams and love me still as,

Yours Truly
E. Randolph

31 N. Calvert St.
Baltimore, Md.
May 18, 1865

Dear Emma,

You will perceive by the above that I am still at No. 31 in the office of the Comsy. of Musters 8th Army Corps. When I last wrote you, I little expected to remain here, but I have been happily disappointed. I was daily expecting an order to join my company, until yesterday morning when it came. As soon as Major Wharton saw the order, for me to "report to my company without delay," he told me not to go until this morning and he would see what he could do toward retaining me as he could not dispence with [my] services. He went, immediately, to Department Head Quarters, and had the order revoked. He will keep me as long as I am in the service. I never served under an officer that I liked as well as I do him, he is more like a father than an officer, to me.

I received your last on Tuesday morning, although brief, it was very interesting. I fear, that this will be very brief. I have but little time.

Vermont has graduated and is about to go West, is he? I little thought of his leaving home. I suppose Harrie will remain at home or on the farm, will he not? What disposition will be made of Calvin? Does he glance at Jule Dunham occasionally?

I am not in favor of your going in the milinery. It is too confining, for one reason. I think it is necessary for you[r] health, for you to lead a more active life, however do as you think best. You asked my opinion, which I have given in a few words. I hope you will not be influenced by me, if my wishes conflict with yours.

I do not expect to be mustered out until my term of service

expires, which is the 1st of August next. I little care whether I am discharged or not. I am quite certain that I can never be contented at home again. I little know where next Christmas will find me.

We are very busy. I must very reluctantly close this, and go to work. I hope you will not think me cool, by this short letter. I am anxiously awaiting an interview. Please accept and write me a long letter and believe me Dearest Emma, to be yours in much love W. G. Dunn

This is stolen time—

I am quite much suprised to hear of Louisa Johnson being engaged to a widower. I suppose that it is all right. No I am not sorry that Jennie has known of our engagement. If it is agreeable to you, I wish you would inform your Mother, some time when she is joking about us, and you can tell whether she will approve or disapprove of it. I do not wish you to ask her consent to our union, by no means. Do as you deem proper, concerning the above.

Lovingly Yours
W. G. Dunn

Duty calls, I must obey. —W.

P.S. I hope I may have time to write more next time.

One who loves you very dearly

I wish that you could see the beautiful boquet that I had presented me yesterday morning.

Plainfield Union Co. N.J.
May 24th /65

My Dear Walt

Tis sunday evening 10 Oclock and this is my first oppertunity to reply to your verry interesting, but rather short Letter which I received Yesterday after my having been to New Market to Church. I your most obedient _____ drove down, Pa not feeling able to attend. Eld. Rogers preached an exelent discourse from Romans 12th Ch. 4th verse.[35] Mr. Allen, a young minister, who is visiting the first day people is to preach next Sabbath morning for us. Eld Rogers will be at the meeting. He is

---

[35]"For as in one body we have many members, and all the members do not have the same function, so we, though many, are one body in Christ, . . ."

quite good looking, unmarried an exquisite singer, think I shall "set my Cap" for him. He glanced at me two or three times. Is not that encouraging?

Lib came home with us, by the way your father drove in the Church yard just ahead of me. Lew came to our assistance — instanter — just in time to prevent Mr. Vars from officiating. I wished you had been there. I understand Cousin Joanne expected Walter home this week. But the hope quite easily raised was doomed to be blighted when I received my letter. You may tell Major Wharton for me, I think he is verry kind, will you? Ask him if he would not like to engage you all of this year! Oh! If ever I wanted to go anywhere it is to be at Washington wednesday next.[36] It would be a verry great pleasure. But I will [willingly] remain at home to welcome those of our little band who remain to tell of the lost. I suppose they will return the last of this week. I guess there is some few who can feel perfectly contented at home. I believe I shall get jealous. If you tell me so again, and then another cause the "unknown donor" of those "Beautiful Floral" presents, she had just better look out.

I received a Letter from Cousin Jont recently. He is well, and in good spirits. He says he has got bravly over "[illegible] on the brain."

Vermont starts for St. Louis the first of June. Harrie is to remain at home. Calvin and Ike G. called on Cousins Nan and Jule, one week ago to night.

Mother and I were alone this after noon and she made an effort to drive away the sober look on my face. Then I told her we was engaged. Ma said she had supposed so. I asked her how long she had had that impression. "Not long" was her answer. Ma spoke verry approvingly of it, adding, "she had hoped to have 'Walter' for a son-in-law." A few words as to long courtships and the subject was dismissed. You will please excuse me from granting your request. I can not write much to night, if I do not feel like it, nor will I promise better next time. I know

---

[36]It is unknown to what Emma referred. The Grand Review of the armies in Washington began on May 23, as the full Army of the Potomac marched in review from the Capitol to the White House. The following day, William Tecumseh Sherman's western army marched the same route, both armies cheered by tens of thousands of spectators.

I should fail, so wishing you "Good Night" and pleasant dreams I will close this uninteresting letter and subscribe myself

as Ever yours
Emma R.

N.B. Ensley Gardner and Aleck Thorn are downstairs with Jennie and Lib. I guess they are enjoying themselves by the sound of things. Em's, Aleck Lib and I had a game of cards the first I have played in a long time. Cheating seemed to predominate. Aleck Thorn enjoyed a good laugh over 5 minutes more. He said he thought we had "close communion" that night. I am of the same opinion. I understand Cousin Susie D. is to be married next winter. Tom is coming home next week to stay three days, joy be with them. But this is not stoping so to use borrowed language "Vivi Pale"

M.E.R.

Office. 31 N. Calvert St.
Baltimore, Md.
May 25th 1865

Dear Em

Although I am feeling quite tired and dull, I will make an effort to write you a few lines, at least. I received your last brief favor duly and gladly. I think that neither of us has occasion to complain of the other writing short letters, for both those I write and those I receive, of late, have been very short. I am sorry that I am often compelled to abreviate my letters for lack of time and other reasons. I like to receive lengthy and interesting letters, such as you have been in the habit of writing, and have no doubt, you like to receive such, full as well and I regret that I cannot comply with your wishes. I hope you will consider my situation (which I have described to you), pardon me for my seeming coolness and indifference, and continue to write when and as much as you can. You understand me do you not?

I did not go to Washington to witness the "grand review" as I expected. On Monday and Tuesday, the trains arriving and leaving the city were flooded with passengers, en route for the capital. I never before saw so many people passing through this City. The clerk at the Fountain Hotel said that there had not been a larger arrival there, before for several years. I did not fancy going in such a large crowd, and as I have seen several splendid reviews, I concluded to stay in Baltimore, and avoid a tiresome trip. A large part of the Army is to march to Baltimore and take the cars here for the destinations of the different states troops. There will be a grand time when the troops reach here. I shall hunt up the 11th N.J. and go home with it, if possible. I should like very much to be mustered out when the Regiment is, but I fear that it is impossible. I presume that some of the New Market boys will soon be at home. Major Wharton told me this evening that he would go to Head Quarters tomorrow morning and try again to secure my extra pay and commutation. I told him I would prefer a discharge. After telling me, I could not be spared at present and learning my reasons for wishing a discharge, he said he would do all that he could for me. He is very influential, still I place but little confidence in a favorable result. Do not look for me home before August next, if you should, I fear that you will be disappointed. If I am so fortunate as to be mustered out before my term expires, I will inform you of the fact, until then, do not look for me.

I will never tell you again that I cannot be contented at home. I will try and make myself as well contented as I can. I anticipate much pleasure in your society and were it not for you, I doubt whether I would ever go home again to live. I am anticipating some very pleasant chats and _____ with you when I return. You need give yourself no uneasiness about the donors of my "floral presents." I have often wished that I might preserve them and give them to you. I appreciate the kindness of the donors, only. Tuesday evening while eating my supper, a colored servant brought me another beautifull boquet, the compliments of "Jennie." When I return home I will tell you who she is. I received an invitation this morning from "Jennie" to join a party in a visit to Druid Hill Park this evening, but declined, preferring to write to you.

I am happy to learn that your mother speaks approvingly of our anticipated union. I have no reason to doubt but mine would speak the same. I think my parents regard us as engaged. I hope for the willing consent to our marriage and the blessing of each of our parents.

I have a copy of the Waverly, which I will mail tomorrow. Several of the boys have read it, and you will please excuse me for allowing it to be soiled.

We are very busy now, mustering out men by the wholesalle. Our last Tri-monthly report is nearly three yards long, which will give you some idea of our business.

Judging from your last two letters, I fear that you are growing cold toward me. Have I said or done anything to cause it, if I have, I beg your pardon. I would like an interview now, for about an hour, that I might fully express my feelings upon the above subject. A little over two (2) months and then I trust we will understand each other better.

Tis growing late, and I will bid you good night and retire. Pleasant and sweet be your dreams.

Remember me as loving you dearly and devotedly. Yours until death,

Walter

8.30 Evening
Plainfield Union Co. N.J.
May 28th 1865

Dear Walter

Now for a chat in answer to the verry interesting and verry dear letter from you, which I received yesterday (Sabbath) about 3.30 P.M. And I hope this will not seem cool, for believe me, Walt, I do not intend to have you think I'm growing cold and indiferent toward you. Please tell me how you got that impression, will you? Oh! If I could only see you, I think you would change you opinion (but I would like a longer time than "one hour"). Nevertheless I understand, and you need not be surprised if you get three (3) sheets instead of one this time.

I did not think you would go to Washington to witness the grand review. But the reason was a rush of business. I did not suppose you would stay at Balto. if you could possible be spared to go. I understood that it was impossible to get anywhere, or anything at the Capital. The sight must have been grand. How I should like to be at Baltimore and see them have a grand time. I sincerely hope you can come home with the remnant of the "Bloody Eleventh." But I will try and not look for you. I should not like to be disapointed. I should think Major Wharton, if he used his influence as well to get you [a] discharge as he did to secure your services during the remainder of your time, might succeed. I shall like him some considerable better than I do now.

Walt, I do not understand why it is that you do not wish to live at your home. I know it would seem verry diferent the verry quiet life you would have there, to the scenes and changes of the last four years. Your anticipations of pleasant Chats and sweet ———— cannot be more than mine. There is not a night passes by but I dream of you, and thank you for your wishes, for they are Pleasant and sweet. Last night I dreamed we were sitting on the Sofa and you was verry sober. I had offended you I thought, you sit on the Sofa in your favorite position, and you was looking down at me. I began to repent of my fault. (I do not know what it was) you looked so sad. I said "Walt, Kiss me." But you would not, and I turned my head away, when I thought you changed your mind and was about granting that which I believe I never asked before (sleeping or waking) when my cheek came in contact — Gracie's hand. I awoke and found it all a dream.

I'm not uneasy about the "floral presents" or the donors. Walt, I was only jesting, on the contary, I am pleased that you have friends who so kindly remember you. I should like verry much to see some of them, and hope you will be favored with one that you can bring home with you. I shall be impatient to hear about "Jennie," that reminds me of "our" Jennie as Harrie calls sis. Yesterday Vermont went to Newark and then came out here in the early train. Harrie came up in the Grocery, took supper here, and then went down to see his Nancy. Was to come back and get Mont, but it rained. Harrie remained at Grandfathers, and then came after Mont this morning. Jennie is feeling better than she did for Mont has given up the idea of going to St. Louis. Ma said it reminded her of the time when Walter Dunn was home to see Jennie go through the room after 3 Oclock. I wish you was here to night but brighter days are coming, and we shall soon kind providence permiting, welcome you home again. I hope you will have to send from New Market [to] Balto. for this letter, it having passed you on the way.

One year ago today Mont brought me home and they carried me up the stairs and layed me on the bed here in this favorite room, and about this time (10) all of the family stood around me, (Ma told me to day) watching to see if I should recognize them for they thought I would not live untill morning. It has been a verry [illegible] day for me, another year has gone, my Heavenly Father seen fit to raise me from that bed of sickness and spared my life, and now I can say what I never said before, that I'm perfectly well. I am verry thankfull.

Last thursday evening Mr. Jesse Dayton and Mollie called, but learning that I was not home would not come in. About ten, we had serenaders, who seemed determined to see Em. I went out and talked quite a little while to Lew, Real and Cousin Nan. Cousin Aurelia tried to make me think you was in town but I thought I knew better. I felt that I should have seen you before that time. It was stormy yesterday, but we went to Church, and heard Mr. Allen preach an exelent discourse. I like him verry much. Next thursday is to be fast day, there is to be services at New Market. I want to go guess I shall. Next Sabbath is communion up here. Lew and "Cousin Aurelia" are intending to come home with us after meeting. Will you come to[o]? I should like to have you to verry much.

This after noon we just at evening Jane R. and sister Susie Thorn and her brother Jimmie called down to see us. We had a verry pleasant time.

Ollie has been out to Church and just came in. I guess she would not let him stay. I presume you have been to Church this evening. Alva Moffatt came and wanted me to go. But I prefered remaining at home and write you. But now I must stop this scribling for I believe I have nothing more to write at present. So I will bid you good night, and pleasant dreams is the wish of one who hopes soon to have the pleasure of seeing you. I am and ever shall be, your own True and ever

loving Emma
Write soon

Baltimore, Md.
June 1st 1865

Dear Emma

Although I feel quite tired and dull, still I will not let this opportunity pass unimproved. You may think it strange that I feel fatigued on a day of fasting, which all places of business are supposed to be closed and business suspended, such should have been, but oweing to the unusual rush here at present, it was not. All outward appearances indicated a "closed shop" but within, we were as busy as usual, a large part of the day.

I received your last, as usual, duly and gladly. It was very interesting and please accept my thanks for two sheets. I looked for the third but could not see it. I only wish that I could write you one as long and interesting. But you will take the "will for the deed" will you not, until time grants us an interview?

As yet, there is no order that will muster me out of service, nor do I think there will be one very soon. I am not very anxious to be discharged, yet I will accept one as soon as it is offered. I have not the least doubt but I will serve my full term of enlistment, which is now less than two months more. Do not expect me home before August. I will tell you then when I am held to service.

I presume the "New Market boys" will soon return home, if they have not already, for without doubt the 11th Regt. will be coming the first to be mustered out, of the Jersey troops. Large numbers of Pennsylvanians are passing through this City daily, on their way home.

I am very happy indeed to learn that you are enjoying such perfect health. I hope, and earnestly pray that it m[a]y be lasting. You cannot imagine, dearest Emma, how much anxiety I feel for your welfare. I have prayed that you might be restored to perfect health and I trust that my prayers have been answered. I am glad that you are so thankfull, and so fully appreciate the kindness of an All Wise Providence. Health is a blessing to be prised, and may you long be the possessor of it, is the prayer of a "devoted lover."

I am sorry that I cannot write you more this time. I know that you will excuse me for sending this brief letter. I am in usual health. Dearest Emma, I think of you often and am longing for the expiration of my term of enlistment, when we can and will enjoy "close communion" once more.

Fondly Yours
W.G. Dunn

Write immediately.
P.S. I will mail you the last number of the "Waverly" tomorrow.

Plainfield Union Co. N.J.
June 3rd 1865

"Darling" Walt

Once more I have seated myself to write to you. I'm very "sad Em" they tell me to night, and I feel like laying my head on your shoulder and let the pent up feelings find vent in tears. You know there is times when the heart aches for a loving word and sweet caress. And to night

I have missed you Oh! so much. I feel verry sorry indeed that you have no hopes of a discharge for I have looked for the missive bearing the welcome news of your return. "But the longest day will have an end" and I shall endeavor to put aside vain regrets knowing you would come if you could. And now shall I tell you why I feel so gloomy and sad? Tis this, I made a "crowd," causing a cousin to feel hard toward me. I imagin I hear you say "that is not telling you much." I will explain. Today was "communion" at the Plainfield Church. I attended an[d] expected Mont Harrie Lew Real Nan and Lib to come home with us, some of them having told me three weeks ago that they was coming home with Jen and I to day. But they all changed their minds but Nan, she came. We came home, and after dinner Nan Jennie and Em went down to the Evergreen Semitary. We walked around for a long time viewing the resting places of the dead, and as usual it made me feel verry sad, although I enjoy it, allways. I think it does me good. We had a verry pleasant time. Coming home we found all the persons mentioned above at our house with the addition of Little Dave waiting patiently for our return. Dave soon left and the rest of them jumped in their buggies and went up to Laign's to get his four seat buggy, which they soon returned with Lew's and Harries ponies for a team. They had told our Nan that Calvin was coming to take her out riding. She did not believe it, she had "heard it to often" but come Cal did. I did not know but we should have to get a search warrent to find Nan. Can you imagen how I made a "crowd," bear with me a little longer and I will tell you. After they prevailed on Ollie to go, I was the only "Odd" one, and finding I was not to have Lib's company, I thought I would have an uninterupted "Chat" with you. But they all set in that I should go. But not wishing to make a third, I positivly refused. I plead headache. It would make my head better, a ride in the cool air, such a splendid moonlight evening, and all Mont was getting angry, taking my words spoken in a jesting tone for earnest. (I most certainly meant them as such) and I believe I should held out "obstanate" — had not Ma came and joined with them, and reluctantly I donned equipments and as Harrie had said I should ride on the seat with him and Nan, I was put there and although Nan had been as pleasant as a [M]ay morning all the afternoon her manner changed immediatly and I would have given considerable to have been at home before we got out of sight of the house. We went up to the valley about three miles from here, where Nellie and Sarah Davis lives their father haveing rented the public house. There we were heartly welcomed. They used every means to entertain us. They all seemed to enjoy themselves but Cousin Nan and I. She was provoked that I come and so was I, they had a nice boat and a good rower. It was a splendid night and if you had only been home, but it's past. I shall not intrude again. I'm home once more having arrived 10.15. I felt as though I could not sleep and would write to you. Now my head pains me severly, my heart ache feels better, and I will wait untill to morrow to finish this. I hope you are having "sweet" dreams. "Good Night" I [am] verry weary but love you just as dearly.

Mate

"Second Edition"
Sunday Evening 10.15

Dear Walter

Now I'm going to finish this Letter to you. I have read over what I wrote last evening, and come to the conclusion that I had better destroy it. I fear if I should that this would be short, and I know you do not like such ones, consequently I will send it.

Today has been verry warm indeed. But not as warm as "Fast day"[37] not by any means. The evening before Jersey and myself was up town shoping when I received an order to "report at once at head quarters," as there was two gentlemen from Newark there wishing to see me. The order was not "revoked" and upon my arival I had the pleasure of seeing Sayers Nichols and a friend of his Mr. Ed Andruss. They came out to hold fast day with us. We all Jennie Ed Cousin Sayers and myself went out walking and seeing the reflector up at the Cream Garden or Lake House we went in and much to our surprise found it illuminated rebuilt — pointed and hung with evergreen. We quickly occupied the veranda overlooking the water, where we could enjoy the cool and refreshing breeze the soft silvery moon beams and hear the frogs holler and eat Ice cream the same time Jennie said and we had a verry pleasant time indeed they were all so livly. It was splendid (the evening I mean). Coming home Sayers and I got astray and we was talking of

---

[37]Possibly a reference to June 1, which had been a day of humiliation and prayer in honor of Abraham Lincoln.

the war as it has been and we did not notice [that?] E J was "minus."
We enjoyed a much more serious talk than we should have done, had
they been with us. After engaging our Company to go to New Market
the next morning, they went to Hattie's and stayed all night. It was
verry warm fast day. They could not get a conveyance to go to New
Market so we went in the 9.20 train, we walked over to "Lover's retreat"
met Cousin Aurelia, went [to] Church and how surprised the folks
were to see Sayers there and with me. After meeting went home with
"Aunt Anne" and took dinner. I went to the funeral of Mr. Dunham
intending to stay and hear part of the service and come up on the 4
Oclock train. But there was so many friends that the Church was filled,
and fearing we would make disturbance, we withdrew immediatly after
the friends were seated. By the time we reached home Em had a
headache. We rested a short time and then Pa's load, come from the
funeral, and they wanted to go to the "graveyard." We started not
thinking the dark heavy clouds would visit us for sometime as they lay
exact east, but we had no more than reached the "Seminary" [illeg-
ible] when the rain drops come pattering down quite to[o] fast for our
relish. We caught shelter in a new barn and what a shower we had. The
funeral prosesion drew up under the cover of the trees, what few could
of them, and remained during the storm of "Thunder and Lightning"
wind, rain, and hail. It was awfully grand those black threating clouds
in the east, the sun shining causing the rain drops to sparkle as they
fell and reflecting the various hues of the rainbow from glittering hail
stones and that long funeral prosesion (70 wagons). The splendid
lightning, the heavy thunder. It seem[ed] to portray the country as it is
at the present time. Do you not think so? On one side the deepest
gloom and sorrow, and on the other light and sunshine. We [came]
home with out seeing the burial. Pa had gathered six quarts of the
finest strawberries we have seen this season, and set Em to steming and
Sayers would assist me. I fixed him so that he resembled a butcher and
he was real handy. Oh! How he wished you would step in and catch us
"Snuffing strawberries" as Aunt Nancy calls it. We had just finished
supper, when Mont and Harrie come and then Lew. Cousin Nan and
Real come. After a while we all got seated on the "Piazze" and had a
good old fashioned sing. when Lew come it found us, Mont Jennie,
and I all alone but nary a sweet heart with me. Mont gave me a "hug
and kiss" for "Walt," he said. I told him it did verry well, but I believe I

should prefer the genuine. Then I made my escape, els[e] I do not know what my head might have suffered. Don't you think I spent "fast day"? I had not the slightest idea of writing so much. I have writen just as I should have talked to only [you?], perhaps we should have had more "interludes." I do not think I had better write any more to night. Please write soon and if possible write me a long letter. I will not say good long letter for yours are allways good. Now "Au revior" I hope for only a short time and then we being reunited will have sweet "communion." Tis the wish of your loving

Emma

P.S. To night Ensley Gardener come down and wanted Jennie and I to go up and get some Cream. It is verry warm, and we went, but had the pleasure of finding no cream, they having sold out. We had some strawberries and "Soda" and quite a pleasant walk, and enjoyed a good laugh about old times, especialy 5 minutes more and 4 miles to walk. How often I think and hear about that night. I received thanks for the "position" that was new to some of them. Those two holding "communion" near the front door. Can you remember?

I see Sallie wednesday evening, and had quite a chat with her. She said she could rejoice with me. I asked her what for. Why, the 11th is coming home and we can have that ride before the 12th of August. I told her you was not coming. At first she thought I was joking. But I told her you would not be home until August, and she said she was sorry, and I wanted to know if I was not. I won't give you my answer, perhaps you can guess it. I told Sallie I guessed "Walt" did not want to come home untill his term expired. I'm not near finished what I intended writing you. I wish I had taken another sheet, then you would not have looked in vain for the third. I met Eld Rogers in to Ernie Albertys friday after meeting and during our chat he asked if I heard anything about the reception to be given the New Market boys when they returned. I said I had heard somthing about one. Then he asked me which I thought they would have and wether they would like a Public or Private greeting. I told him "both." Mrs. Alberty allowed the Domince could not get ahead of me. Then he was verry kind to inform me who and when they was expected home. Telling me he was sorry but he thought "Walter Dunn" would not be home untill his time is out. They seemed to enjoy teasing me. I did not mind it. Now I'm

going to stop. Aren't you glad? Once more "Good night"
"Truly Yours" "Mate"

N.B. Now I guess you think I will not have anything to write about next time. Verry unfortunately it has happened that this letter has been delayed and can not go out to day. So I will make it still a little longer. This morning who should walk in the door without knocking but Cousin Susie D. and her intended husband Mr. Tom Harris. They seemed as happy as larks and Sue was as wild as ever, "only a little more so." They was to go to New York this after noon and then take quite a tour but not a wedding tour. They was laughing about going to the Dominices. Sue said that she was afraid Tom would back out, and was all the time hurrying him. Sue said she was verry anxious to get married. Tom silenced her on that subject by saying earnstly "Oh! Susie I wish you meant that." He wants to be married soon but Susie does not want to. I think they will take the "fatal leap" this winter. Write soon, and you will greatly oblige your "intended Mate."

> Office of the A. A. Provost Marshal General for Maryland and
> Delaware
> Baltimore, June 11th 1865

My Very Dear Emma

Do not think me growing cold, or that I have forgotten you by my tardiness. This is not my first attempt to answer your last, but I shall endeavor to succeed this time. I received your kind favor of the 3rd inst. in due time, and intended to answer immediately, but time would not permit. I hope you will pardon me for my delay, knowing that it could not be avoided.

Tis Sunday evening. I have not been to church today, nor was I last Sunday evening as you supposed. Just a week ago this evening, you wrote me the most interesting letter that I have received since I came in the service. I wish that you could have seen me open it, and how eagerly I read it. I am sure it would convince you of my great anxiety to receive and read your very dear and ever welcomed letters, and being fully convinced of that, I am sure you will always write me such long and interesting ones as your last one was. I feel myself incompetent to write you one, as interesting, in return, but wherein I fail now. I will make good when I return from the war. which time is not far distant.

I have learned from good authority that the 11th and 12th Regts. N.J. Infty. Vols. are now in the state awaiting their muster-out of service. I was not aware when they passed through the city or I would have seen them. I suppose the New Market boys are at home, are they not? Please inform me who of them are at home and when they arrived. We are very busy mustering-out Maryland troops as this is the Chief Mustering Office for this state. At present, I have no hopes of being discharged [from] the service until my term of enlistment expires. I might get discharged, should I urge the matter but I think that useless as my term has so nearly expired. A few weeks more will entitle me to a discharge by reason of expiration of term of service, which I would prefer, to any other.

I hope you have driven away those sad feelings concerning your ride on the 3rd inst. I do not consider it any intrusion, as you went at the earnest request of all. Do not think of it or allow yourself to harbor such sad feelings.

Tis warm weather, here, now. I wish that you was here, we would go after some cream and I will bet that we would not get disappointed for there is an abundance of it in this City.

You stated in your last that Vermont had concluded not to go to St. Louis, where does he expect to go into business? Do you think that he and Jennie will get married next Winter? I suppose that Dave and Sallie will be one before another Spring do you not think so?

I wish that I was by your side on the sofa this evening. I think I would enjoy it better than this. But that time will soon roll around, less than two months now. Keep that ride in view. I dislike to send this because it is so far from repaying you for your long and interesting letters. Although I often fail to express, what I desire, you must not think me cold or indifferent, for dearest Emma, I love you devotedly and shall ever remain yours in life. Please accept and write me as soon as you can.

Your future companion
Walter

P.S. Please excuse this official paper as I happen to have no other.

W.

Postwar photogaph of A. Judson
Titsworth, who joined the navy in
the last year of the war after his
brother had been wounded.
(Courtesy, Jeannette Fitz
Randolph Duryea.)

"Sabbath Evening" 10 O. clock
Plainfield N.J.
June 17, 1865

Dearest Walt

Perhaps you are thinking this delay is to "retaliate." But when you have perused this missive, you will think diferently.

I received your last letter on wednesday evening quite unexpectedly as it is an unusual thing for me to receive them at that time. I was disapointed and glad both. For I certainly thought I had a long letter and I thought you must surly be coming home, and had been waiting to know where you would come. I imagined it was a good long missive because it appeared quite "fleshy." Now Walt! Do you think you can ever make up to me what you think you come short of in your letters? I feel verry much afraid of it. (If I do not care what I say).

Well Walter "Dear" would you like to know what has caused me to write under so late a date? T'will be quite a tale but I will think it a pleasure if it interests you. When I received it I was deep in the unpleasant business of assisting in getting up a Straw Berry and Cream Festaval to benifit the Choir by raising money to get an instrument of music — as we are without any at present — said Festaval to be held Thursday evening June 15th in the Seminary at New Market. I was verry busy indeed. Thursday morning Pa took us girls down to the scene of action. I had a verry agreeable ride from the "Sem" [Seminary] to Mr. Martin Dunn's to get "Box" to trim the lamps with "Mr. Par's" in a "box" wagon, and one of the settees for a seat, that was the begining of the sport, the committee feeling inclined to laugh at us. "Cousin Ellis" took me in to his home to dinner and we had a verry pleasant time. I have been delayed several times and as it is verry late I will lay this aside untill tomorrow.

Dearest Walt I'm ever yours. Emma

I wish we could have the privelege of enjoying ourselves as Jen and Mont might out on the front stoop but as usual they have been spatting.

Sunday Evening

Dear Verry Dear Walt

I'm permitted once again to hold communion with you by means of the pen. Last year this time I little expected to see another spring on Earth. But from some wise plan I'm still living and enjoying the best of health, while the mesenger of Death still pass[es] us by and has chosen another loved one from those who has been called to mourn before over the inanimate form of a sweet little blossom just buding into life, little Sarah. Now it was Adelia, one who it could be truthfully said was a lovely girl in every respect, Charlie Randolphs sister, she was buried last friday afternoon week. Eld Rogers preached an exelent discourse from the words, "O Grave where is thy victory." Jen Lew and Dave came home with us after the funeral and took supper with us. The first time Dave has been here to tea since last Election day. Do you remember?

Now for the festaval — we commenced selling about seven O.clock. we did not realize as much as anticipated the course as our's was the seventh (7) festaval held on that evening within 20 miles, and then we lost money on straw berries having more than we could dispose of at the price we gave for them. Pa auctioned the things of[f], all but the Straw berries and Cream, the latter was in 8 quart pans allready hulled. They had sport off two pans full. Pa struck them off to young men, and they did not know what to do with them, Mr's French and Gardner being the lucky one's. I had a pan presented to me to preserve, and as I could not come home untill verry late I concluded to remain over night not caring to change my attire after the tiresome duties of the evening and not wishing to ride home dressed in white, for it had grown quite cool. Jennie and I went to Reals and I did not get home untill last evening. I must tell you how I come.

Our folks not coming [to] Church I went home with Lib and Nan, Mont going to Little Daves. We got home to Mothers. Lew was there. After dinner we all of us young folks went over to see States, he was asleep but Cal soon woke him up. He was home alone and we had a verry pleasant time. When they Harrie and Lew was fixing to come home or rather to start, Cal asked me how we was going. I spoke and said Lew was going to take Nan and I was going with Harrie. Nan did not say anything and I supposed the[y] took as I meant it in fun. But when ready to go to the buggies Lew spoke to Nan saying "Nan, Em says you're to go with me, so come along and let Harrie and Em ride togather." She agreed to and you would laughed to have seen Mrs. Randolph and Lib laugh. I enjoyed it hugly. We stoped at New Market and I supposed Nan would ride with us when Real went with Lew but she would not. Every one who met and knew us laughed and shook their heads as much as to say I had no business there. We all parted good friend[s] and consider it a good joke. Nan said she would "retaliate" when "Walt" come home. If so I shall not enjoy it as much as she did seemingly.

This afternoon I met with quite an accident. I was just steping out on the back stoop with my hands full and down I fell bringing the large cream pot on to the stone which "shivered its timbers" and brought my head against the door casing which was not the softest pillow imaginable. I've been lying down ever since, and after answering your questions I will close this uninteresting missive for my head aches as it has not before for many a long day.

Yes! some of the New Market boys are home. Able, Tom, Frank, Mart, and Isaac R. has come for good I believe. If I understood aright they are all looking well, but Tom he is verry dejected and low spirited — not natural at all. Kizzie Potter was telling us that "he seems like some one laboring under some heavy greif." I called on Mr. and Mrs. Rogers friday afternoon. He said that "he did not like to see one of his flock so unhappy." He added that "Tom was silent as to the cause but he look verry much as though he was broken hearted." Vermont has not desided what he will do. I do not think they will be married next winter. I think they are foolish if they do. But of course they know best what suits them. Jennie is going down to New Market in the six P.M. train next thursday and Mont is coming up to meet her he tells her he is lonsome, she must come down and see them. He is verry affectionate indeed, and if Jennie was not so fond of teasing him, they would not have so many spats. Did I ever tease you? Lew and Harrie enjoyed a hearty laugh over the "Old fashioned way" and Lew declared he had shaved his moustache off so that he could "kiss the fastest."

I most certainly think Dave and Sallie will be one before another spring and I think it is best. When Dave comes up Sabbath evening he has to wait untill eleven before Sallie leaves the store. We seen him last evening walking around waiting patiently, and to night he come up again. Oh how many happy hearts there is to night, and how many aching ones. August is coming then my heart-ache will be cured. Now "good night" and sweet be your dreams. Write soon to one who is ever yours with much and abiding Love.

Emma R.

Baltimore Md.
June 26th 1865

Dear Emma

Your last was as usual, duly received. I trust you will excuse me for not answering before as I have been very busy. I expect to be mustered out tomorrow and will, if possible, start for home in the evening. Should nothing happen, I will call at your house on Wednesday evening and answer your last letter verbally, which I prefer to this way.

Do not be disappointed if I fail to fulfill the above promise, as there is many a slip between the cup and the lip.

Farewell Dearest Emma until Wednesday night.

Yours Fondly,
Walter

Baltimore Md.
July 5, 1865

Dear Emma

I wrote you, some time since, that I expected to be discharged, and being so confident of it, I promised to call at your house one week ago to-night if nothing happened. Although I have met with no accident I am still in Baltimore, which you will perceive by the above. I would have written before, and informed you of the fact but it was not decided whether I would be mustered out or not, it only being postponed for a time. I have expected it every day until now. I have almost given it up entirely. My term of enlistment expires in a very short time and it is immaterial to me whether I am discharged now or not, yet I will accept it whenever it is offered, which may be tomorrow. I will tell you all when I return home, if it be sooner or later. I hope you will not think me growing cool by my long delay as I did not wish to write until I could give you some positive information concerning my muster-out, which I am still unable to do.

How did you enjoy yourself on the "Fourth"? I anticipated a very pleasant time in Plainfield but was disappointed. However I enjoyed myself quite well. I spent a large part of the day in Druid Hill Park which was visited by thousands. There was a very large and fine display of fireworks just a few steps from here. They were grand. I wished myself home several times, but knowing that to be impossible I tried to content and enjoy myself as well as I could under the circumstances.

My friend, Mr. Stevens was mustered out last week and expects to start for his home in N.J. tomorrow night.

The weather is very warm indeed. I am anxious to get out of the City. I prefer the country by all means, in the summer.

I know of nothing to write that will interest you, and for that reason you will please excuse me for being so brief.

I am very anxious to hear from you and hope you will write me immediately.

I am, dearest Emma
Yours in Love,
W.G. Dunn

P.S. Write immediately for the sake of one who loves you very dearly.

W.

Plainfield N.J.
July 9, 1865

My Dear Walter

After waiting and looking for you daily since I received your missive informing me of your expecting to be with me the same evening that I received it. You may know how verry verry much I'm disapointed, but I will tell you of that when you come which I hope will be before August. I do not know how to give it up. I've looked for you this afternoon thinking perhaps you would come as you did last fall, but "nary a come." I delayed writing untill it was to late to look for you, and just told Mont and Jennie my intention to write a Letter when who should drive up but Cousin Ellis. We all went out riding, got home quarter of eleven. Ell has gone home, Vermont and Jen are down stairs, enjoying themselves I'll bet, and poor me well I'm scribling to "you who loves me dearly." I feel inclined to lay my pen aside for I know I can not interest you, but for your sake I'll finish, though short it must be.

This week has been the longest week I have ever seen. One week ago to night Mr. Moffatt Jennie and myself left our house 10 minutes past 6, went to your house made quite a call and arrived home 9.15. One of our neighbor girls was to be married at 9, but Mr. Moffatt was an own Cousin, they waited for us. We had a verry pleasant time, took the Dominice just six minutes and a half to tie them. It can almost make me wish I was married.

I was disapointed on the Fourth of July that I cannot say I enjoyed myself muchly. One reason — I was tired out, for Jersey had been verry sick and as usual Em must go. I was completly tired out. Jersey is better so that I left her yesterday morning, having been with them two weeks.

Mollie expected to come up yesterday and spend the week with us, but Lew said she did not feel well enough. I feel verry sorry for her. I can sympathize with her, truly. I hope and trust she will soon get better. Vermont also is doctoring for the "Depspepsia."

I must close now, so "good night" and a "kiss" and may your dreams be sweet. Do not imagen I'm cool or that I think any less of you. No! Never. The same deep and abiding Love remains and ever will in the Heart of your own

Emma

(Please write me when you expect to come.)

View of Baltimore from Federal Hill in 1865. (Maryland Historical Society.)

Epilogue

Private Walter G. Dunn was honorably discharged from the army in July 1865. He returned home to New Market, presumably alone and with little celebration, but he probably shed any disappointment at not being welcomed with his old regiment once he spoke with his former comrades.

McAllister's "boys" had indeed become the "Bloody Eleventh," hardened veterans who had fought in every major eastern battle from Chancellorsville to the end. The 11th New Jersey had mustered in three years earlier with a strength of about a thousand, the normal complement of a Civil War regiment, and in the course of the war nearly eight hundred replacements had served under their colors. Yet disease and heavy fighting had all but wiped them out. Fewer than three hundred were left as they began their journey homeward at Appomattox. They marched through Richmond, past the capitol and notorious Libby Prison, moved on to Fredericksburg, and from there marched on to Washington, where they took part in the Grand Review. Then they boarded boxcars for home. In Baltimore they waited for hours in the stifling heat. At two in the morning of June 8, they arrived in Philadelphia, detrained beneath a banner proclaiming "The City of Brotherly Love Welcomes with Hearty Cheer the Returning Braves," and took a hearty breakfast. They boarded the train a few hours later, sat through another delay, and at 9 AM arrived in Trenton to a lukewarm welcome. After listening to speeches by the governor, whom they occasionally booed, and General McAllister, whom they tolerated, they marched to Camp Bayard to await pay and mustering out, only to sit in the sun for another week. Finally, two hundred of them marched to the capitol to learn the cause of the delay. On June 15 they were finally paid and discharged, their disgust with the government of New Jersey doubtless unchanged.[1]

---

[1] Marbaker, *Eleventh New Jersey Volunteers,* 304–15.

Once Walter was home and near Emma, all hesitation about marriage vanished. On September 19, 1865, they were married at the Seventh Day Baptist Church in New Market. (Dave Randolph and Sallie Johnson married there the same day, though which couple married first and thereby lost "the oysters" is unknown.) Quite possibly they moved in with Emma's parents in Plainfield. What Walter chose for an occupation is unknown.

The suffering caused by war does not end when the guns cease firing. Men wracked by disease and wounds continued to die, and for years to come pharmacies across the nation churned out millions of morphine tablets to ease their physical pain. In January 1866, Walter caught a cold. His condition worsened steadily, becoming the much feared illness of the lungs that had so worried Emma. As he weakened, complications from his old wound set in. After twelve weeks, on April 16, 1866, he died in Plainfield. He was twenty-three.

Soon thereafter Emma gave birth to their daughter, Mary Emma Dunn, but again there were complications, and Emma died suddenly on August 20, 1866, in her father's home in Plainfield. She was but twenty-two. Rev. L. C. Rogers delivered a funeral oration from Luke 23, chapter 28: "Daughters of Jerusalem, weep not for me, but weep for yourselves, and for your children." Mary Emma Randolph Dunn, he told the stunned and troubled mourners, had gone on to "that eternal world of joy, where now we doubt not, she has been welcomed by her Saviour, and where too she has joined the company of her dear companion, among the blood-washed throng."[2]

Less than a month later, on September 17, 1866, infant Mary Emma also died. "In this death," noted the *Seventh Day Baptist Recorder,* "the last light of the family has expired. Father, mother, and child, are now numbered with the dead. They are, we have good reason to hope, an unbroken family in the kingdom of heaven."[3] A war that had already claimed more than six hundred thousand lives, had claimed three more.

Their letters were given to Grace Randolph, Emma's youngest sister ("Gracie"), who had been born the day Walter was wounded. She later married Isaac Harris. Their son, Walter R. Harris, left the letters to Ruth Bailey, a friend of the family.

---

[2] *Seventh Day Baptist Recorder,* October 2, 1866.
[3] Ibid., SR 22:39, p. 155.

Walter Dunn's brother Lewis posed with his family in this 1894 photograph. Lewis and his wife Joanna hold their three small children, Jennie, Myrta, and Marjorie. Standing is Lewis's son, Walter G. Dunn. (Courtesy, Jeannette Fitz Randolph Duryea.)

The Families of Mary Emma Randolph

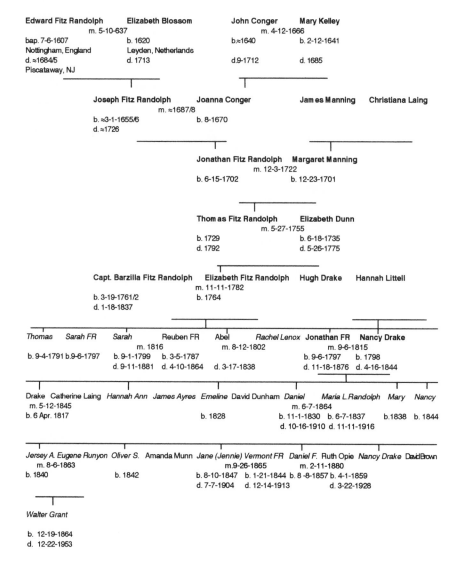

Edward Fitz Randolph — Elizabeth Blossom
m. 5-10-637
bap. 7-6-1607 — b. 1620
Nottingham, England — Leyden, Netherlands
d. ≈1684/5 — d. 1713
Piscataway, NJ

John Conger — Mary Kelley
m. 4-12-1666
b.≈1640 — b. 2-12-1641
d.9-1712 — d. 1685

Joseph Fitz Randolph — Joanna Conger
m. ≈1687/8
b. ≈3-1-1655/6 — b. 8-1670
d. ≈1726

James Manning — Christiana Laing

Jonathan Fitz Randolph — Margaret Manning
m. 12-3-1722
b. 6-15-1702 — b. 12-23-1701

Thomas Fitz Randolph — Elizabeth Dunn
m. 5-27-1755
b. 1729 — b. 6-18-1735
d. 1792 — d. 5-26-1775

Capt. Barzilla Fitz Randolph — Elizabeth Fitz Randolph — Hugh Drake — Hannah Littell
m. 11-11-1782
b. 3-19-1761/2 — b. 1764
d. 1-18-1837

Thomas — *Sarah FR* — *Sarah* — *Reuben FR* — *Abel* — *Rachel Lenox* — *Jonathan FR* — *Nancy Drake*
m. 1816 — m. 8-12-1802 — m. 9-6-1815
b. 9-4-1791 — b.9-6-1797 — b. 9-1-1799 — b. 3-5-1787 — — — b. 9-6-1797 — b. 1798
d. 9-11-1881 — d. 4-10-1864 — d. 3-17-1838 — d. 11-18-1876 — d. 4-16-1844

Drake — *Catherine Laing* — *Hannah Ann* — *James Ayres* — *Emeline* — *David Dunham* — *Daniel* — *Maria L.Randolph* — *Mary* — *Nancy*
m. 5-12-1845 — m. 6-7-1864
b. 6 Apr. 1817 — — — b. 1828 — — b. 11-1-1830 — b. 6-7-1837 — b.1838 — b. 1844
d. 10-16-1910 — d. 11-11-1916

Jersey A. Eugene Runyon — *Oliver S.* — *Amanda Munn* — *Jane (Jennie) Vermont FR* — *Daniel F.* — *Ruth Opie* — *Nancy Drake* — *DavidBrown*
m. 8-6-1863 — m.9-26-1865 — m. 2-11-1880
b. 1840 — b. 1842 — b. 8-10-1847 — b. 1-21-1844 — b. 8 -8-1857 — b. 4-1-1859
d. 7-7-1904 — d. 12-14-1913 — d. 3-22-1928

Walter Grant

b. 12-19-1864
d. 12-22-1953

Note: Names mentioned in the letters are in italic. Fitz Randolph abbreviated as **FR**.

Source: Judith A. Bailey

and Walter G. Dunn

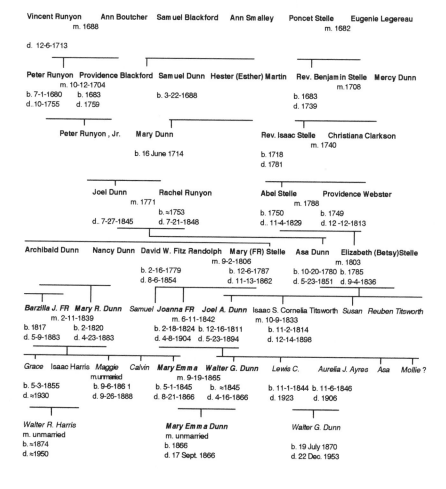

Vincent Runyon   Ann Boutcher   Samuel Blackford   Ann Smalley   Poncet Stelle   Eugenie Legereau
      m. 1688   m. 1682

d. 12-6-1713

Peter Runyon   Providence Blackford   Samuel Dunn   Hester (Esther) Martin   Rev. Benjamin Stelle   Mercy Dunn
      m. 10-12-1704   m.1708
b. 7-1-1680   b. 1683   b. 3-22-1688   b. 1683
d..10-1755   d. 1759   d. 1739

Peter Runyon , Jr.   Mary Dunn   Rev. Isaac Stelle   Christiana Clarkson
                                                 m. 1740
                b. 16 June 1714   b. 1718
                                           d. 1781

Joel Dunn   Rachel Runyon   Abel Stelle   Providence Webster
         m. 1771   m. 1788
             b. ≈1753   b. 1750   b. 1749
    d.. 7-27-1845   d. 7-21-1848   d.. 11-4-1829   d. 12 -12-1813

Archibald Dunn   Nancy Dunn   David W. Fitz Randolph   Mary (FR) Stelle   Asa Dunn   Elizabeth (Betsy)Stelle
                                        m. 9-2-1806   m. 1803
                        b. 2-16-1779   b. 12-6-1787   b. 10-20-1780   b. 1785
                        d. 8-6-1854   d. 11-13-1862   d. 5-23-1851   d. 9-4-1836

Barzilla J. FR   *Mary R. Dunn*   Samuel   *Joanna FR*   *Joel A. Dunn*   Isaac S.   Cornelia Titsworth   *Susan*   *Reuben Titsworth*
   m. 2-11-1839   m. 6-11-1842   m. 10-9-1833
b. 1817   b. 2-1820   b. 2-18-1824   b. 12-16-1811   b. 11-2-1814
d. 5-9-1883   d. 4-23-1883   d. 4-8-1904   d. 5-23-1894   d. 12-14-1898

Grace   Isaac Harris   *Maggie*   *Calvin*   *Mary Emma*   *Walter G. Dunn*   *Lewis C.*   *Aurelia J. Ayres*   *Asa*   *Mollie ?*
                 m.unmarried   m. 9-19-1865
b. 5-3-1855   b. 9-6-186 1   b. 5-1-1845   b. ≈1845   b. 11-1-1844   b. 11-6-1846
d. ≈1930   d. 9-26-1888   d. 8-21-1866   d. 4-16-1866   d. 1923   d. 1906

Walter R. Harris   *Mary Emma Dunn*   *Walter G. Dunn*
m. unmarried   m. unmarried
b. ≈1874   b. 1866   b. 19 July 1870
d. ≈1950   d. 17 Sept. 1866   d. 22 Dec. 1953

Index

ABOUT THE EDITORS

Judith Ann Bailey teaches school and writes from
Centreville, Virginia. Robert I. Cottom is editor of the
Maryland Historical Magazine and co-author of *Maryland
in the Civil War: A House Divided,* published by the
Maryland Historical Society.

Cover and page design by Gerard A. Valerio
Bookmark Studio, Annapolis, Maryland

Composed in ITC New Baskerville by
Publishing Concepts, Baltimore

Printed and bound by Thomson-Shore, Inc.
Dexter, Michigan